Western Canada

Past and Present

Western Canada

Past and Present

Edited by Anthony W. Rasporich

University of Calgary

McClelland and Stewart West

ISBN 0-7712-1005-1

McClelland and Stewart West Limited
Calgary, Alberta

The publisher wishes to acknowledge with thanks the assistance of
Thomas Nelson & Sons (Canada) Ltd. for permission to reproduce
"Map of the Northwest in 1885, from D.G.G. Kerr, ed., *A Historical
Atlas of Canada*.

Cover Photo – Glenbow-Alberta Institute

Printed and bound in Canada

CONTENTS

PREFACE

The Western Canadian Studies Conference was held for its sixth successive year at the University of Calgary in March of 1974. While sponsored
by the Department of History, it has remained an interdisciplinary forum
where scholars of all disciplines and laymen gather to exchange views on
western development. Recent public interest, perhaps sparked by the
energy debate and by the renewal of western regional protest, served to
attract a greater number of participants than ever to the conference.
The quality of comment and dialogue apparent at the various sessions
demonstrates the continuing feasibility of topical conferences where the
generalist and specialist may interract. Without the continued interest of
the university and granting agencies, the conference would not of course
have been sustained this long, and thanks are due to the University of
Calgary and its marvellously efficient conference office, to the Canada
Council for its sustained support, particularly in the area of travel support to visiting scholars, and to the Department of Youth Culture and
Recreation of the Province of Alberta which sponsored the banquet.

Concerning the publication of the papers collected here, I would like
to thank McClelland and Stewart West for their interest in this book,
and to the helpful comments and advice of its editor, Mr. David Scollard.
To Miss Jenny Radsma of the Department of History, who typed the
manuscript; and to Miss M. Medwid of the Department of Geography,
who prepared the charts and maps, I extend my sincere appreciation.
Lastly, acknowledgements are due to the Glenbow Archives for the photograph of Big Bear used to illustrate Rudy Wiebe's article.

Anthony W. Rasporich
Calgary, December 1974

INTRODUCTION

The papers collected in this volume represent some of the most recent scholarship on selected aspects of Western Canadian development. Where possible, the contributors have cast a wide net to encompass the broader features of social life, economic growth and intellectual development. While the essays cannot pretend to offer a definitive or total picture of Western Canada's history or contemporary society, they do offer some important insights and analysis into selected aspects of a complex region. The papers are divided roughly into six sub-themes: farm life and prairie sociology; early western cities; railway expansion and coal as factors of economic growth; Hutterite communal societies; traders, missionaries and Indians; and Western Canadian literature.

The first two papers treat the broad theme of rural society on the prairies, and the peculiar character of its social evolution and its political institutions. The co-authors of the first article, John W. Bennett and Seena B. Kohl, teach anthropology respectively at Washington University and Webster College, both of St. Louis, Missouri. Dr. Bennett is perhaps the foremost commentator on prairie society today, having written two important books on the region, *Northern Plainsmen: Adaptive Strategy and Agrarian Life*, and *The Hutterian Brethren*. Dr. Kohl, his co-author, has been involved in field research on the southwestern area of Saskatchewan for the past ten years and has a book in progress on rural agricultural families in that region. Their paper deals with the complex of responses which the succeeding generations of pioneers and their descendants showed towards homesteading and farming on the prairies. Challenging directly the assumptions of the frontier school of rugged individualism, they stress the collective and adaptive responses of farmers to changing economic circumstances from frontier farm to modern agri-industry.

The companion piece on rural society in the prairies explores the single theme of collective social organizations among Saskatchewan farmers in the twentieth century. Its author, Dr. Donald E. Willmott of the Department of Sociology at Glendon College, York University, has had extensive field experience as a research officer with the Centre for

Community Studies at the University of Saskatchewan, and has published various articles on the social life, political organizations, and local government of Saskatchewan farmers. Much as the first essay challenges the notion of frontier individualism, this one also demonstrates the complex network of collective social systems and formal organizations which permeate the farm community.

An urban dimension of early western Canada is provided by way of contrast in the next two papers. The first, by H.C. Klassen of the History Department at University of Calgary, examines the social life of frontier Calgary, a small ranching city in the far West. Professor Klassen has painstakingly gathered most of the available oral reminiscences of early pioneers in the city, and blended this oral history with traditional elements of the written record (newspapers, diaries, and letterbooks) to give us an insight into the urban past before 1914. The Calgary of his account also runs counter to the frontier image of an egalitarian cow-town. Purse-proud and status conscious, the civic elite was separated by a wide social gulf from the common labourer and skilled craftsman. Equally, British and central-Canadian traditions counted heavily in such a stratified metropolitan society, from Edwardian fashions and Victorian literary tastes to profound veneration of the Empire.

Another prominent theme of western-Canadian urban history is developed in the essay by Elizabeth Arthur on inter-urban rivalry between Port Arthur and Fort William. Metropolitan competition is not a new phenomenon peculiar only to the West, since it reaches far back to the business competition between Paris and London, and in central Canada, between Montreal and Toronto. But nowhere was civic rivalry and boomerism articulated and advertised so well as in Canada's westward movement at *fin de siècle*. Dr. Arthur, who has taught history at Lakehead University for the past ten years, has elaborated upon the historical sources of the irrational rivalry which divided The Landing (Port Arthur) from The Plot (Fort William) in her book *The Thunder Bay District, 1821-92*. In this essay she explores generally the economic and political sources of antagonism which created two hostile camps across the McIntyre River. It was a story bred of the railway age, which pitted new towns and cities against one another across the West – Selkirk and Winnipeg, Moose Jaw and Regina, Calgary and Edmonton, Vancouver and New Westminster. And for those who managed to survive, and some did not, the struggle carried into all spheres of civic life – into health, education, and sports, as well as industry and commerce.

The source of much of the urban competition in western Canada is the subject of T.D. Regehr's essay on the Canadian Northern and its two irrepressible promoters, Mackenzie and Mann. As agents of a second national policy engineered by Sir Wilfrid Laurier, Mackenzie and Mann buoyantly symbolized the decade prior to World War I; in their bankrupt demise during the war they equally symbolized the national insolvency they had helped create. The Canadian Northern had indeed done much to create a second and "larger Canada" by saving certain communities like Port Arthur from extinction, and establishing others like Prince Albert and Saskatoon in undeveloped northern parkland. Professor Regehr, who teaches history at the University of Saskatchewan, has written a number of articles on railway and business history, and has recently completed a full-length study of the Canadian Northern.

A related theme on the subject of economic development of western Canada is Alberta's coal industry. Professor A.A. den Otter of Memorial University in Newfoundland explores the reasons for the rise of the industry, and its close connection with the transcontinental railways; and describes the rapid demise of coal following the appearance of diesel power and the widespread domestic and industrial use of oil and natural gas after World War II. A current and lively subject of debate, the revival of the coal industry is a much-talked-of energy alternative to rapidly dwindling oil supplies. The peculiar historical problems faced by Alberta coal in gaining access to an impenetrable central-Canadian domestic market also offer instructive reading in any future federal-provincial debate over a national energy policy.

The following three papers deal with a social subject somewhat more distant from capital development and material progress. The Hutterites' attempt to remain a separate denominational counterculture in an integrated western economy and society is explored in a past and present perspective. The first paper, by Dr. Karl Peter of the Sociology Department at Simon Fraser University, carefully explores the historical evolution of the Hutterite communal ideology and its dialectical contradiction with the family ideal pursued by Mennonite and Amish sects. It concludes by examining the amalgamated communal-family ideology which has been worked out over the past one hundred years, and its potential for survival in a largely alien world. Following upon this, J.W. Bennett, distinguished author of many publications on the Hutterites, delineates the marked changes which recent technology has wrought upon Hutterite material culture and social organization. Further, he sees a rapid political and social integration occurring within the sect, which in fact constitutes a good reason for outsiders to emulate the collective agriculture which the Hutterites have perfected. The editor has also included a third paper on the Hutterites, which became available after the conference was held in March. This essay, by Robert MacDonald, a doctoral candidate in the Faculty of Education at University of Calgary, is the result of two years field experience among the Hutterites in southern Alberta. It explores historically the repeated assaults upon the sect's educational isolation by rural pressure groups from World War I to the present.

The tension between rapid economic adaptation and the spiritual resistance of minority cultures is the subject of the next pair of papers on western Indians. While the first paper on Ojibwa and Cree society is set geographically in what is now Northern and Northwestern Ontario, its historical setting in the eighteenth century makes the native experience there indistinguishable from the woodland tribes of western and northern Canada. Dr. Charles Bishop, an anthropologist at Oswego College, New York, who recently completed *The Northern Ojibwa and the Fur Trade*, reflects here on the socio-cultural effects of the fur trade on Indian society. Ecologically, the effects upon tribal migration and conflict were as profound as they were upon the wildlife ecology which the fur trade had altered.

As a contrast, the second paper on native studies, by Jacqueline Gresko, selects a level at which white man's policies were far less effective. Professor Gresko, who teaches history at Douglas College in New Westminster, shows the fallacies of the utopian educational schemes which were implemented by missionaries and Indian agents on the Qu'Appelle reserve in the late nineteenth century. Their failure to displace traditional Indian dances by alien white rites illustrates graphically the persistence of native spiritual beliefs, despite drastic economic and social changes occurring both on and off the reserves.

Professor Rudy Wiebe's paper, as one of the final pair on Western Canadian literature, reveals the dilemma of the novelist *cum* historian. In his discussion of the literary and historical reconstruction of *The Temptations of Big Bear*, Wiebe carefully explores the limits of the biographer's imagination and the historical evidence he must deal with. Philosophically his method of rethinking Big Bear's thoughts comes close to the historical idealism of R.G. Collingwood's *Idea of History*. And the biographical result perhaps comes closer to this historical ideal than most biographies by practising historians.

The last paper, by Dr. Sandra Djwa of Simon Fraser University, is a deeply penetrating insight into the prevalence of Biblical theme and archetype in the western novel. Using Sinclair Ross's *As For Me and My House* as its centrepiece, she examines the harsh Old Testament world of the western prairie that is compounded by the social philistinism and puritan self-doubt apparent in the novel. Then, turning to Margaret Laurence, Professor Djwa explores the theme of Israelistism in *The Stone Angel* and *A Jest of God*, and uncovers the moving force which Biblical metaphor imparts to these novels.

A last and thoroughly delightful talk, which does not appear in this collection of papers, is the banquet address to the conference delivered by the eminent prairie novelist W.O. Mitchell. This was an oratorical masterpiece which focussed on the theme of the "Usable and the Unusable Past" in Western Canada. Mitchell reflected at some length upon those imported traditions which did not suit the West and withered quickly on the prairies – from cricket clubs and tennis courts to the outmoded class structures of the old world. On the other hand, as an example of a culturally useful tradition, he singled out the hired hand as an often-neglected hero in the social history of the prairies. Jack-of-all-trades, helpmate, and homely philosopher, the hired hand did more to shape the physical and mental landscape of western Canada than the legion of politicians and officials who adorn our trophy room of the western past.

The broad theme of past and present thus gives a rough unity and dialectic to the essays presented in this collection. The tension between inherited traditions of the past and the constantly changing economic and social forces in the present is the central dynamic of western Canadian history – indeed of all history. The absence of one or the other of these elements would result in a distortion of time and space, which are essential in balanced proportion, not only to history, but to social science and to literature as well.

One

CHARACTEROLOGICAL, STRATEGIC, AND INSTITUTIONAL INTERPRETATIONS OF PRAIRIE SETTLEMENT

John W. Bennett and Seena B. Kohl

Individualism as Characterology

George F.G. Stanley writes

The history of the Canadian West from the earliest days of which we have knowledge by written word or oral tradition, has been one of survival and adaptation to environment. Hence my suggestion that the characteristic spirit of the Westerner is that of independence, self-reliance, willingness to strike out on a new path.

A surviving Saskatchewan homesteader told us,

The data on which this chapter is based was obtained during a decade of research in southwestern Saskatchewan, in a continuing effort known as Saskatchewan Cultural Ecology Research Program. We collected data on strategic behaviour and general social and economic development over a period beginning in the 1880's, with the initial ranching settlement. We sampled the 1960-70 population of our region of five thousand square miles by selecting one hundred and seventy families operating agricultural enterprises, and another thirty-odd families living in small towns. We also interviewed a sample of thirty-one homestead pioneers, including both ranchers and farmers. By 1972, over half of these pioneers were deceased. District history books, compiled for the Saskatchewan Jubilee, were also of great help in pioneer reminiscence, and we have

*If there'd been a bridge across the ocean, we would have walked home!
But there was no bridge and no money, so we stuck it out. What else
could we do?*

These quotations illustrate two views of the settlement process, one academic, the other native. The first defines the settler in terms of certain
desirable character traits; the second in terms of hardship and sheer
survival.

While the academic view of the frontier experience has consistently
emphasized the spirit of individualism, there have nevertheless been
periodic challenges, like that of M.C. Boatright, who writes

*. . . why is the myth of frontier individualism so generally accepted? As
I have implied, the myth springs in part from the social and economic
predilections of historians. It springs in part also from the multiordinal
nature of the word "individualism."*[2]

We shall return to the issue of the "multiordinal nature of the word
'individualism' ", but first let us continue with Boatright's remarks:

*The pioneer seems to have been less disposed than others to inquire into
the private life of his associates, or to interfere in quarrels which he regarded as purely personal; he attached less importance to adventitious
circumstances of birth and wealth; he was more tolerant of eccentricities
of character; and he was more often called upon to exercise individual
judgment and initiative. He was perhaps more self-reliant. But all this is
not to say that he was individualistic in the sense that he eschewed
collective action or advocated unrestricted individual opportunity to exploit the national resources or make money by other means.*

If "individualism", then, does not mean an absence of co-operation
and affiliation, it can mean a degree of self-reliance imposed by the
simple shortage of resources on the frontier. This element of self-reliance
is usually exemplified by reference to specific tasks, like the repair of a

---

quoted from some of them in this paper. We made detailed studies of all
families – their history, their economic experiences, and the general social and
physical environments surrounding them. We also talked with people who
migrated from the region in order to obtain data on the circumstances of this
process. Our conclusions, in preliminary form, were put into a book, *Northern
Plainsmen* (Bennett, 1969), and a more recent summary.[1] We are at present
working on a final monograph on the adaptive behaviour of the farm-ranch
population; a detailed study of the topic is summarized in this paper. Data
from our study used in this paper are illustrative of general points – they are
not scientific proof of formal conclusions.

saddle from materials at hand – an experience, which as Boatright points out, can lead to a certain contempt for the affiliative necessities:

Here is the typical non sequitur: the daughter of a frontiersman writes in her diary: "Father's saddle wore out, so he made a new one out of cypress and rawhide." Now the ability to make a usable saddle, however crude, is an evidence of resourcefulness. Resourcefulness means self-reliance, which implies scorn for collective action and exaltation of individual initiative.

Professor Stanley's characterization of the pioneer emphasizes "survival and adaptation to environment" and suggests that the means for survival were based upon a "spirit of independence, self-reliance and willingness to strike out on a new path."* But adapting also means, especially in the harsh conditions of a cool, semi-arid, and undercapitalized and undertechnologized frontier, a matter of bending, cooperating, getting along with your neighbour because you need help, of waiting patiently for resources to materialize, and suppressing desires for a better life. Of course the individual often had to depend on himself. However, the emphasis on individualism neglects the quality of *flexibility* – to be able to do what is necessary in order to survive – which can include passive conformity and dependence upon others as well as innovation.

Now to return to the "multiordinal nature" of individualism. Certainly in general usage we assign distinctive or unique qualities to those we consider "individualistic". *Webster's International* (1963 edition) notes this usage in terms of "individuality". Obviously there is more to the term, particularly as it has been used in describing the Western pioneer. Webster defines it further as "the ethical doctrine or principle that the interests of the individual himself are or ought to be paramount in determination of conduct."

---

*Professor Stanley's characterization of the Prairie Personality[3] is also discussed by sociologist M.L. Lautt who writes:

The plains of Canada, as the last frontier, are generally thought to have produced a people who exhibit pragmatism (from the harsh realities of rural life), individualism (economic and otherwise), optimism, devotion to hard work, courage in the face of a challenge, and a confidence in the existence of the principle of equality of opportunity.[4]

Lautt cites the familiar mixture of characterological labels which seem at least partly contradictory and which do not offer an explanation of how people cope with changing conditions. A pragmatist is not one who always has "confidence in the principle of equality of opportunity" – on the contrary, he may respond to a bargain land market by doing his best to do his neighbor out of every acre he can – the struggle could be, for the pragmatic Prairie settler, a survival of the fittest, not the equal. But even here he had to be careful, because if he was too rapacious, he would lose the support of his neighbors.[5]

Although independence, initiative, and self-reliance have been emphasized as characteristic of the pioneer, other concepts are associated with the term "individualism". Among others, there is the notion of romantic adventurism, as typically portrayed by the lone frontiersman in the Western film. This characterization concerns the drifter without permanent social ties. Certainly among the early settlement population of southwest Saskatchewan such characterological types were present. However, they left the region soon after their arrival, and they were not part of the settlement process in the sense of the establishment of community.

All of these characterizations include images of admirable feats (the settlement of the frontier), as well as descriptions of behavior observed by both participants and non-participants. While these attributes were not shared by all settlers, they were qualities shared by a sufficient number to make the list a familiar one. Therefore the qualities existed, and are useful as a general description of pioneer behavior. However, as analytical devices they leave much to be desired.

As behavioral analysts, we prefer a study of strategies to characterology. It is not so much a matter of traits, of what people *were* or *are*, but how they responded to conditions, and especially how they changed their strategies when conditions changed. Whether the Prairies forged a character or a personality is something we do not wish to speculate about; we believe that this approach can be taken no further than descriptive literature. Tribal men, penned up in their little isolated exotic communities, may have produced a true cultural character, but Prairie people were not and are not tribalists. They are moderns, like us, and like us they have had to cope with a series of changing resource parameters through the seventy years or so of settlement. There are, in short, Prairie personalities, just as there are urban personalities.

One must first distinguish between the people who left the Prairies after attempting settlement, and those who stayed. We believe that often these two are confused – the experts on Prairie life and history are sometimes Prairie people whose families left the Plains after the attempt to make a home and a business failed,[6] or was simply not sufficiently promising. There is a tendency for such persons to confuse their own gumption, or the courage of their parents, with the behavior of the people who stayed – many of whom were either too broke to leave, or who had the requisite patience, or even lack of pressing ambition, to try to come through.

Second, as we hinted at the beginning, it is necessary to distinguish between the traits or characteristics *imputed* to people, from those provided by the people themselves. We never heard our Saskatchewan friends use such phrases as "optimism", "courage", and "individualism" – these are labels attached by outsiders, or people who may once have been insiders, but whose subsequent experiences have assisted in reformulating their conception of the Prairie character.* As a matter of fact, our protocols are remarkably consistent with the actual histories of adaptive strategies in western Saskatchewan – the survivors see their own behavior in terms precisely coordinate with the nature of their coping styles. To call a Prairie settler "courageous" would be viewed as silly and literary, an affectation, since so many of them stayed not out of courage but rather because of the lack of a better alternative.[7] And for a Prairie survivor to call himself "individualistic" would be considered by many to be arrogant, in the light of his dependence on his neighbors.

The Nature of Strategic Choice

People get through life by bringing resources to bear on what they consider to be their needs and objectives. Humans are generally "rational", which does not mean that they always make sense, but simply that they usually try to relate means to ends – to think ahead and adjust their present behavior to future outcomes or needs. People in a position of privation are probably required to relate means to ends more accurately than others living in less constrained environments, or with greater opportunities, especially when they have generalized middle-class aspirations – as did most of the Prairie settlers.

Moreover, time does not stand still: a frontier becomes a settlement; camps become ranches; homesteads become farms; subsistence undertakings become economic enterprises; a pioneer becomes an entrepreneurial operator; a homesteader becomes an urbanite. These are tangible ends which are consequences of human decisions and choice-making; activities which are based on goals and perceived alternatives.

The following set of terms, therefore, are important in our approach: *goals, strategies, choices, alternatives,* and *decisions*. A strategy is any course of action designed to get you to the desired goals. A choice is made as to the specific tactics, methods, or resources required to make up this course of action; alternatives refer to the number of choices available. Selection among choices, of course, constitutes decisions.

The sociological, anthropological, and historical literature is replete with studies of the migration of rural peoples. However, they are most

---

*The second-generation respondents in the 1960's phase of our research were asked to indicate agreement or disagreement with a long list of reasons why the pioneers came West and settled in southwestern Saskatchewan. The largest percentages of agreement were found on: "wanted free land" (93%); "wanted freedom to do as they wished" (79%); "wanted a better place to raise a family" (76%); "didn't know what they were getting into" (64%). In other words, one out of the four highest has an ideological-individualistic implication; one is historical accident; and two are purely acquisitive or practical.

often studies in their *new* setting; for example, the successes of rural people migrating to different rural settings with greater opportunity, or the failures of rural people migrating to cities in search of a better life.[8] For our part, we considered it important to emphasize the question: who *stayed* – and what conditions led to the decision and ability to stick it out? After all, the development of Prairie settlement and its particular configuration of means and ends is a result of the choices and decisions of those who remained. (Of course, one must take into account the opportunities made possible by the abandonment of homesteads in significant numbers.)

However, both groups of individuals, those who stayed and those who left, offer the same basic explanation: "there was nothing else we could do." The same explanation is also used to explain decisions to return after leaving and staying away for various periods.* The idea of "nothing else" is the way alternatives were perceived, and it is here that character, personality, or culture are expressed in human choices.

Southwestern Saskatchewan is now, by and large, in the "third generation of control",** which means that the majority of enterprise operators are of an age which makes them equivalent to grandsons of the founders of these enterprises. (As a matter of fact, the majority of enterprises in the 5,000 square mile area around the town we call "Jasper" are in the hands of actual sons or grandsons, although this high rate of succession has been diminishing.)***

---

*A majority of the Saskatchewan farm operators in our study had work experience elsewhere. Well over half had both farm and non-farm experience, and only a fourth had never left the region.

**This does not always mean that everyone operating enterprises at any one date was of the same generation, since enterprises were established at different times (although one of our advantages in studying southwestern Saskatchewan was the relative homogeneity of settlement – most of the ranchers came between 1880-1906 and most of the farmers between 1906-15 – both rather brief periods, and rather close together). Nor does it mean that the "generations" always mean *kinship* generations (although here again the coincidence is quite high). "Generation in control of enterprise" means whether or not the man running the place was the first one to do so (squatted or homesteaded it); a man of an age to be the son of this man; or one who is of an age to be the son of the son. That is, whether he was in the direct kinship line, or simply had bought the enterprise later, is not the decisive factor: what is important is his generational status in the region.

***In one of the intensively studied, heavily homesteaded prototypic townships, the number of surviving enterprises operated by original homesteader, son, or grandson, or new owner, were as follows: original homesteader, 6; son of the original homesteader, 14; grandson of homesteader, 4; new owner, 3; homestead abandoned or sold with land being acquired by other homesteader, 53. This township was homesteaded during the period 1909-11. Where the homesteading took place earlier, as in ranching districts, there are more grandsons operating than sons.

We have, then, three generations to deal with – that is, three generations whose goals, choices, available alternatives, and decisions need to be studied. Each of these generations forged its strategies in a different cultural and historical context, and each was required to make decisions about different things in order to survive, or to permit continuity of the family and/or the enterprise.[9] Briefly: for the pioneers – the first generation – the main issue was settlement itself: how to find good land, build buildings, and obtain tools, and whether or not to stick it out and try to build something permanent. For the second generation, the task of building an enterprise continued, but much more important, the problem soon became one of *protecting* and *maintaining* what existed during the periods of drought and economic depression. For the third, and contemporary generation, the big issue is not maintenance, but development: how to make the enterprise more secure, bigger, more productive – and also, how to protect and enhance the level of consumption of the family.

Let us look at these three generations in more detail.

The First Generation

The homesteader was concerned mainly with the meaning of the homestead itself. For some, it was equivalent to settlement – was made within a particular historical and adaptive context which permitted leaving and starting again somewhere else; that is, the context permitted migration, and as history has demonstrated, this was an option which a major portion of homesteaders in the Prairies eventually chose.[10] For those who remained, other considerations were vital: all were in debt, but some degree of choice existed as to the amount of debt the individual wished to shoulder. Similarly, everyone had the legal option of pre-emption, but choices could be made concerning the accumulation of land: how much, and how soon after homesteading.

In one of the prototypic heavily homesteaded townships we studied in southwestern Saskatchewan, we found that in 1915, four years after the initial homestead date, forty-eight homesteaders had assumed their preemption, and twenty-nine had not. The choices at that time were made based on views of the future, or as one homesteader wrote in a district history book,

How was this district going to turn out? ... Some settlers got "cold feet," sold their belongings and moved out. Others came in and took up their deserted land and stayed with it. ... Others proved up their homesteads but abandoned their pre-emptions. I did that myself, as I doubted if it was worth paying $4.00 per acre for it.

These choices were also based upon views of "enough" and perceptions of "need". For some, a quarter section of land was an enormous grant; for others with greater resources (and perhaps vision), it was not. In fact, we find that nearly all those who chose to pre-empt their second quarter either were already married when they homesteaded or married soon after.[11]

Practically every homesteader had a practiced skill in addition to farming (or at least he had personal labour power which he could sell), and he could choose just how much of this to use in order to accumulate cash. There were important needs for service which those with special skills were able to supply to their neighbours.

One of the homesteaders writes in a district history,

Combining homestead duties with other activities the professions gave help and comfort to the community. Dr. X.F. Offerman, a chiropractor . . . homesteaded a few miles west . . . Charlie Tinsley was a lawyer, Dr. Russel a dentist. . . . Trades were well represented, the carpenters perhaps being in the majority . . . Bert Manning, a builder, who could build a home with all the plumbing and wire it for electricity even to making the cement blocks. George Hendrikson and Martin Ademark were bricklayers and built all our chimneys. John Bakken, the plasterer. Frank Robertson and Al Golpin, our painters. W.A. Olmstead, our first undertaker, was also one of our first settlers.

In addition, with a saleable skill, a decision to go elsewhere to earn money could be made, which probably a majority of homesteaders in western Saskatchewan did during the early years.

One pioneer records,

Now it was mid-August, 1910, and I and others set out for the harvest fields further east in order to make our grub-stake for the winter. . . .

and another writes:

By fall, cash was getting scarce. The men decided to go to Gull Lake for threshing; I went along with them with the hayrack. I got a job in a cook car cooking for thirty men. Mother was left with the children for seven weeks.

We find that there are particular patterns of choices which characterize the families who stayed. For instance, in the first generation a young bachelor often quickly married a young woman, thereby creating a link to a second household which provided social as well as economic support and aid. The first generation also had to be able to diversify and find other resources to exploit (for example, to practise blacksmithing as well as farming). Another pattern was displayed by those who were willing to utilize the labour of their children and kin while they went off for the winter months to earn cash, or who were able to place kinsmen in situations which would bring cash into the homestead. People who made these strategic choices were usually those who persisted and built the homestead into an enterprise.

The Second Generation

The second generation – the offspring of the homestead pioneer, or else those persons who themselves arrived late – was faced with a different set of decisions and a different cultural context. This generation experienced recurrent economic depression and drought, and had to choose between succession or migration – between the hope of continuity and the risky promise of a better chance elsewhere. When succession and continuity were chosen, financial need forced many out of Saskatchewan, at least for a period of time.

The large-scale migration away from southwestern Saskatchewan and the widespread abandonment of land had consequences for those who remained by enabling them to add to their land holdings. To acquire land in this period implies determination and what the local people called "holding on" in order to maintain oneself. Included in this attitude is an awareness of the available alternatives: migration out of the region, or else the self-denial of luxuries or indeed of anything other than bare necessities.* For this generation the issue of government assistance and the acceptance of governmental agricultural programs becomes important.

The Third Generation

The third or contemporary generation is in one sense a product of a long line of men and women who learned to "do with less". Those

---

*The Royal Commission on Agriculture and Rural Life *Report No. 10* handily sums up the level of living among Saskatchewan agriculturalists in 1950. They note:

> Saskatchewan was the lowest of the provinces (not considering Newfoundland) for four of the items – electricity, piped-in water supply, mechanical refrigerators, and flush toilets. . . . Perhaps Saskatchewan's most noticeable deficiency in comparison to farm homes elsewhere, even in the other prairie provinces, was in connection with electricity and the distribution of conveniences made possible by electricity.[12]

In 1961, nearly all western Saskatchewan households had electricity, although not all had indoor plumbing. By 1971 the house without indoor plumbing was a rarity, and consumption wants are concerned with dishwashers, wall-to-wall carpeting, or travel and personal luxuries.

members of the previous generation who wanted more than the resources could provide are long departed. However, the present generation also lives within its own distinctive cultural context. It too faces major choices involving decisions of succession or migration, but for those who choose to remain, their goal – unlike their fathers' – is development, not simple maintenance of a *status quo*. This is so because the third generation not only has higher consumption standards, but is aware that sheer survival in a high-cost economy requires higher productivity. The contemporary entrepreneur is faced with the necessity of deciding how much to spend on the domestic establishment and on the farm, and whether to favour family consumption or go for machinery and land purchases.*

From Strategies to Institutions

The generations have commonality and continuity in certain features of strategic behavior; we fix on pragmatism or flexibility as the most prominent pattern of behavior among our Saskatchewan survivors, and we prefer this to statements declaring that the Prairie settler had a certain type of personality.

But we have seen that the generations differ in terms of the particular kinds of coping strategies demanded of the settlers by changing conditions. The first generation had to establish an enterprise in a wilderness; the second had to maintain it under conditions of climatic and economic disaster; the third had to develop it to a "modern" level of efficiency and productivity. These differing demands, or goals, required different kinds of behavior.

The goals were also related to, and produced, a series of differing institutions and organizations, and it is these we wish to describe as the concluding section of this chapter.

The first institutions of importance are *private property* and *individual entrepreneurship*. These institutions were brought to the Plains by the settlers from the East, and reinforced by a multitude of regulations and arrangements imposed on the frontier by the outside world: the land survey; the homesteading system; the railroad land sales; the economic market for agricultural products; the taxation system. All of these and others were based on the concept of independent, freeholding entre-

---

*This, of course, refers to the post-"take-over" period in the life cycle of the family. During the take-over period the son is responsible, even under the most generous succession agreements, for providing income for the parental household as well as his own. During this time, deferment of consumption is an expected deprivation. The comments in the body of the article are set in the context of the development cycle of the enterprise, whereas the problems at take-over are best seen in the context of the life cycle of the family.

preneurs, and on the whole, but with compromises and modifications to be discussed in a moment, this is exactly what emerged. We believe that the emphasis on individualism and innovativeness which runs through the historical literature is in part a translation into characterological terms of these pervading institutions of private property and entrepreneurship. People who are expected by the outside to "make it on their own" and to "own their own place", especially in an environment of constraint, are going to have to display qualities of independence and stability, or they will not survive. As we all know, only a fraction of them did survive, in the sense of sticking with the original homestead. But it turns out that their survival was due as much to their patience and their flexibility as to their independence. Or rather, that the *institutional* demands for independence, thrust on them by circumstances and the nation, required them to take adaptive postures of great variety.

We therefore have a starting point for a study of evolving institutions: a system of private property and entrepreneurship, interacting with a highly specialized physical environment and a constrained economic environment. Institutions developing out of this confrontation then will reflect special characteristics of both – a series of compromises. Such institutions may function at purely local or microsocial levels, or they may concern the larger interactions of the settlers with the national-level institutions of politics and the economy.[13] Moreover, the institutions will evolve as conditions change, which means that they may be related chronologically to the generations.

Certain institutions were particularly important for survival on the Prairies. The first of these is *mutual aid*: the practice of "neighbouring", of extending help locally where help was needed. Neighbouring appeared on the frontier simultaneously with settlement. In a sense it is the converse of "individualism", since no-one could survive alone, without resources, in a harsh land. Mutual aid has become the major symbol of the past; the nostalgic evidence of the finest side of the human personality, it is recited in countless ways in every local newspaper on the Plains,* and is recreated carefully when circumstances permit, and with full publicity. There has been, and is, far more emphasis on helping people than on rugged individualism in the local literature about the "old days", and there is no sign of a letup. Even more, there is a definite

---

*A recent example comes from the Maple Creek News, January 23, 1974, where on the front page directly under a news story of a house fire there is the following:

> The Maple Creek Kinsmen Club, with support from the Ken Club, was quick to bring into play the old-time spirit of helping neighbors, or those to whom misfortune has struck, when they had an executive meeting and decided to sponsor a dine-and-dance in aid of Mr. and Mrs. Alvin Lightfoot and family, whose home was destroyed by fire last week.

fear that the present is becoming *too* individualistic, as farms and ranches grow in size and become affluent and self-sufficient, and hence do not require mutual aid. The falling-away of neighbourliness is seen as a *loss*; too much "individualism" is seen as evidence of decline of the true Prairie spirit.

If mutual aid was the first generation's informal response to the need to survive, *co-operation* was the first and second generations' formal response. As an institution, it transcended the locality, or the natural community, and included organizations extending far beyond, and resources far in excess of those the community could bring to bear on mutual aid. Its emergence was a collective strategic response to the pressures and constraints imposed on the Prairie producer by the organizations of the national and international market: the grain companies, the railroads, the banks. In short it was a response to exploitation, or rather, to the inadequacies of individual entrepreneurship in the face of exploitation by outsiders.* It was probably based on mutual aid and the presence of neighbourliness in the minds of the settlers, and its growing symbolic value must have reinforced the urge to combine and collectivize significant portions of their economic activity. Hence organized co-operation was local mutual aid projected onto the national scene; an adaptive response of locals to their institutional position in the nation.

Just as mutual aid was the other side of the private property/entrepreneur coin, so was co-operation a compromise with the individual producer's "right" to dispose of his own resources, and to produce in any manner he saw fit. In co-operation, the producer yielded these rights in part, by authorizing the government to operate community pastures and irrigation programs, by accepting a standard price on his grain, by pooling his cash and buying power in consumer co-ops and credit unions, by pooling his land in grazing cooperatives. Collective ownership; collective use; collective management: steadily moving through the Prairies, especially the drier parts of Saskatchewan and Alberta, for the past forty years.

And between the second and third generations, and out of co-

---

*In southwestern Saskatchewan, the farmers combined not only against outside institutions, in their support of the Wheat Pool and the farmers' political movements, but also against some of their own neighbours: the ranchers. Farmer groups in the southwestern section of the Province actively led the movement to establish community pastures and grazing co-operatives by removing portions of leased grazing land from rancher control. However, both farmers and ranchers worked to establish community irrigation systems and other resource-sharing measures of the PFRA. Actually the farmers in the southwest often were less supportive of the CCF than farmers in other parts of the province, due largely to an identification of co-operatives with the Liberal Party. However, as noted, they were vigorous proponents of collective-use resource management.

operative institutions – or perhaps along with them (the history is complex and it is not our purpose to recount it) – emerged *populist politics and government*. Mistakenly called "socialism" in one of its most significant manifestations, the early CCF, it was in essence the classic political expression of compromise between the institutions of private property and the survival needs for co-operation and collectivization.[14] This compromise protects the basic property rights, but permits mobilization for an attack on the exploiters, and in union there is strength, politically as well as economically. The CCF and other similar organizations of the Great Plains in both Canada and the U.S. were outstanding successes, while collective leadership and union were important as a means of protecting property rights, but tended to wane when these rights were secure or when prosperity was achieved. And these organizations were successful when they socialized (or collectivized) basic services like electric power or medical care, but they failed whenever they attempted to move into the sphere of currently profitable entrepreneurship, as in the famous attempts of the CCF and the NDP to develop pooled marketing for cattle and hogs. (Both attempts were opposed by the producers who felt they were getting fair prices from private companies.) Moreover, any suggestion that a left-populist government might move toward the socialization of land ownership has been met with resistance. But the mechanism here is not ideological: the owners and producers resist these reforms only so long as they obtain income satisfaction with present institutional arrangements protecting private property. A series of economic disasters in the livestock field, for example, would in all likelihood lead directly to a clamor from the producers for a marketing system. And so it goes; pragmatism remains the key strategy.

All these institutions have one very clear and very simple objective: to reduce the risks of production in a specialized and constrained environment. Their ideological component, as we have suggested, was actually minimal. The settlers of the prairies, whether they were derived from the "Scotch" Ontario communities described by John K. Galbraith (1964), or whether they were the Ukrainians described by Vera Lysenko (1947), were practical, frugal people faced with the task of establishing a farming enterprise as well as a social community. Of course there was a more mobile and perhaps truly individualistic element – the early ranchers – but these were small in number, and the ranchers who stayed ultimately fitted into the same strategic and institutional mold we have described. They too wanted to reduce risks, and they too formed co-operative round-ups; and in later days, they too would no doubt accept marketing boards if private systems of marketing of cattle should collapse. These are survival necessities; ideology is their trimming, but not their guide.

Finally, these strategies and institutions are essentially those of members of modern society, and are not the behavior of romantic ruralites or unsophisticated countrymen. Except perhaps for a brief period of isolation on the frontier, one could never describe these settlers as hicks; they have always been, in essential ways, cosmopolites, heterogeneous in personal cultural background and tradition, open to pragmatic persuasion, aware of the nation around them, and fully capable of comprehending the organizations that have tried to exploit them. There is, in fact, no significant difference in the strategies of the Saskatchewan farmer and the rising urban businessman; they are both part of the same larger world, and it is time we saw them in this modern light.

Two

THE FORMAL ORGANIZATIONS OF SASKATCHEWAN FARMERS, 1900-65

Donald E. Willmott

We are told by the most respected sociological authorities and the most ardent journalists that formal organizations and voluntary associations are urban phenomena. The story goes that the simple life of farm folk requires no more than the family, the church, and the rural neighbourhood to provide for their practical and emotional needs. But when migrants begin to congregate in cities, their loneliness and uprootedness drives them into groups formally organized to serve their special needs. Bureaucracy proliferates, the family and church disintegrate, and the alienated urbanite finds solace in voluntary associations.

This is not the place to analyze the urban episodes of this mythology. What I wish to do here is to carry forward the de-mystification of the rural story – a task first undertaken from a sociological perspective by Lipset in his book *Agrarian Socialism*. A corrected view of the role of formal organizations in rural life will not only contribute toward a better understanding of voluntary associations in general, but will better illuminate the history and social structure of the Canadian prairies.

Material for this chapter is drawn primarily from a number of studies and surveys carried out by the Centre for Community Studies at the University of Saskatchewan about ten years ago. Since the work of the Centre was confined to the Province of Saskatchewan, I am uncertain to what extent one might generalize to the region as a whole. For example, differences in the size and functions of local governments, and in the strength of the various political parties, might well make some of my interpretations invalid for Alberta or Manitoba. Saskatchewan may in fact have the highest saturation of rural organizations of any region in the world.

Lipset reported this to be the case in the mid-forties.[1] Twenty years later, it was equally true. In spite of efforts toward local government reform, there are over three hundred Rural Municipalities in the province, averaging only about one-fifth the size of counties in Ontario or Alberta. In 1962, we studied one of these, Fertile Belt RM, which will serve well to demonstrate the extent of formal organization in the Saskatchewan countryside. Here the RM Council assisted in handling the finances of twenty-eight Snow Plow Clubs; it also collected dues for the Saskatchewan Farmers Union, fees for seven different farmer-run telephone companies giving service within its borders, and taxes for thirty-seven School Districts (each with its own three-person board). Within this same rural municipality there were numerous other organizations, such as a Fish and Game League, three open-country churches, several 4-H and Homemaker Clubs, a consumer co-operative, and various sports and social groups – not counting the dozens of organizations in village and town.

In 1960 and 1961, the Centre for Community Studies conducted surveys both in the Rural Municipality of Biggar, which is twice the average size of a Saskatchewan RM, and in the town of Biggar. Although school amalgamation had reduced the number of School Boards from thirty-three to seven, there were seventy-six rural-based organizations in the RM, with a combined membership of roughly twelve hundred. The latter figure includes only the board members of the telephone companies and co-operatives, and the committee members of the Wheat Pool. If we were to include all telephone subscribers and co-operative and pool members (most of whom do not even attend the annual meetings), the total for all rural organizations would be slightly above two thousand members. To these may be added about eleven hundred memberships which country residents hold in town associations – as estimated by leaders of the latter, in replying to interview questions about the members of their own groups. This makes a total of three thousand one hundred memberships. There were about one thousand adult rural residents in this area in 1961. After eliminating from consideration about one hundred youth memberships, we find that the average number of memberships per adult was about 3.0. This figure may be compared with the results of our 1961 interview survey, which showed an average of 4.4 memberships for men and 2.2 for women in rural areas. The corresponding figures for the town of Biggar were 2.4 for men and 1.6 for women. If we leave out of account those organizations, such as the co-operatives and the Wheat Pool, which have only one membership meeting per year (and that poorly attended), no significant difference remains between average number of memberships in town and country.

It is impossible to compare with any precision the organizational participation rates for different areas, because researchers use different methods and different definitions. Nevertheless, it may be worth reporting that among the studies I have so far discovered – reporting on eleven separate rural and urban areas in the United States – the proportion of the adult population who claim membership in voluntary associations ranges from forty percent to sixty-five percent. In the town of Biggar it is seventy percent for women and eighty-four percent for men, while in the countryside it is seventy-six percent for women and ninety-eight percent for men.

The 76 rural organizations in the Biggar RM in 1960 were found to have about 210 offices. Among the leaders interviewed in our survey, about one-half held one office, one-third two offices, and one-sixth held three or more. Allowing for the fact that the interviewed leaders were more active than average, we estimate that from 150 to 170 persons were holding the 210 offices in rural organizations. As there were about one thousand adults in the area, it may be seen that one out of every six or seven was taking part in the leadership of these local organizations.

This finding corresponds closely to Lipset's report that in the mid-1940's at least fifteen percent of the farmers of Saskatchewan held community posts to which they had been elected by their neighbours. Lipset went on to say:

This proportion of formal community leaders to total population is much larger than has been attained in any urban area. It is probably also greater than that found in other rural areas, for Saskatchewan has the largest co-operative movement on the continent and more local governmental units than any other American rural state.[2]

One interpretation of this situation might be that prairie farmers have become an integral part of the Canadian urban-industrial society, whereas originally they did not depend upon formal associations. This would accord with the popular ideal-type concepts of *Gesellschaft* and *Gemeinschaft*. The German sociologist Tönnies, who proposed these terms, claimed that urban-industrial communities are characterized by bureaucracies and voluntary associations, whereas rural communities, with their family ties and neighbouring, do not need such formal organizations.

Certainly there was much about pioneer life on the prairies which suggests a *Gemeinschaft* type of community. For example, there was no formal organization behind the barn-raising bees, the co-operative threshing crews, and the earliest picnics, parties, and dances. In each rural neighbourhood, everyone knew everyone and informal mutual aid thrived.

But this was not the whole picture. What I want to emphasize here is that formal organizations were as integral and indispensable a part of rural life in pioneer times as they are today. (By the term "formal organizations" I refer to organized groups which have an official name, regular or publicized meetings, and traditional or written regulations specifying the terms of officership and membership.)

Let us consider, then, the nature and extent of these early formal organizations. In the first place, certain groups of settlers arrived on the prairies in already-established religious organizations. The Doukhobors and Hutterites will suffice as examples. J.W. Bennett tells us that Hutterite communities have a complex structure which is virtually identical everywhere and dates back to the sixteenth century.[3]

Other ethnic communities established communal or community organizations soon after their arrival. For example, Swedish homesteaders in the Stockholm area of Fertile Belt RM set up a "Scandinavian Colony Club" in 1889, less than three years after the coming of the first settler. This club succeeded in getting the Territorial Government to build an "immigrant house" as a temporary residence for newcomers. Hungarian settlers in the same area built their colonies around Catholic churches, which soon developed Altar Societies, youth clubs, and other groups.

Protestants were less likely to start with church organization. Nevertheless, this sometimes did happen, as in the case of the Pinwherry community near Biggar, which had its origins in a sod church built in 1908 by homesteaders from the Maritimes, Scotland, Ontario, and Iowa. Although affiliated with the Congregational Church until 1925 and with the United Church of Canada thereafter, it was a community church which attracted virtually all the Protestants of the district. Such churches, unlike those of the Catholics, were much like other voluntary associations in that they were governed by elected boards of laymen. They often conducted services and their entire Sunday School programs without the aid of their itinerant ministers. And they, too, soon developed associated organizations, such as Ladies' Aid, Epworth League, Christian Endeavour, and C.G.I.T. Referring to the period before the establishment of local government in the area, a local history of the RM of Cory reports:

The three churches in pre-Cory were rallying points for community activities which in summer consisted mainly of picnics and in winter, concerts, socials, and projects of the various interest groups. The picnics demanded diversified but almost total participation, keeping everybody busy like a colony of ants when their ant hill has been disturbed.[4]

In many districts, School Boards were the first organizations to be established. As soon as an area was settled densely enough for ten to twenty of its children to walk to some central point where a school could be built, the parents got together and formed a School Board. Thereafter, three Trustees had to be elected every year at an annual meeting of local residents.

Since the schools were very often the only suitable place for community meetings, the School Boards presided not only over the education of children but also over community affairs. The schoolhouse was the meeting place for all kinds of organized activities: concerts, plays, sports of various kinds, dances, political rallies and meetings of special-interest groups. In the Tweedyside School District near Biggar, for example, the school became the centre of activities for six organizations: the Ladies' Grain Growers, the Baseball Club, the Dramatic Society, the Ladies' Softball Club, the Study Club, and the Carpet Bowling Club. Similarly, Burnet found that schools and their boards were "a vital integrating force in community affairs" in the Hanna area of Alberta.[5]

Local government units were usually set up later than School Boards. Under enabling legislation of the Territorial Government, fifty-seven Statute Labour and Fire Districts were established in the Saskatchewan area between 1890 and 1896.[6] These had two functions: the construction of roads and the ploughing of fireguards. Both were carried out by compulsory labour of local residents. Ratepayers, through annual meetings, were given almost complete control over the work to be done and the means of doing it. They were subsidized by the Territorial Government, but could not borrow money.

In 1897 the Territorial Government reorganized the settled area under its jurisdiction into 438 Local Improvement Districts. These LID's were run in "town meeting" style – annual meetings of ratepayers levied taxes, determined what work should be done, and elected an overseer to supervise it. Assessed taxes could be commuted to day labour, and most ratepayers chose this alternative. Thus early budgets were small. Expenditures of one of the Fertile Belt LID's were $21.50 in 1899 – sixteen dollars for the overseer, five dollars for the returning officer, and fifty cents for stationery and stamps. Ratepayers gave 106 days of labour on roads and bridges, and 30 days on fireguards.

These early LID's were one township in extent – that is, only six miles square, or about twice the size of the School Districts. The territorial Government soon concluded that they were too small. Against considerable local opposition, a new Local Improvement Ordinance was passed in 1904. The LID's were reorganized into units of from three to six times the size. In the Fertile Belt area, the four one-township LID's were combined and two more added to them. The new ordinance introduced representative government into the LID's. Instead of making policy decisions, the annual ratepayers meetings in each township elected councillors. The new LID Councils chose their own chairmen and conducted the business of the area in regular meetings. Revenue was divided among them, and each councillor became, in effect, an independent overseer of public works in his own division.

Much the same structure was maintained in the nine-township Rural Municipalities which succeeded the LID's between 1909 and 1912. Since that time the boundaries and structure of these three-hundred-odd RM's have remained virtually the same, but their autonomy has been undermined by Provincial financing and control in most areas. Thus we see local government evolving from very small units, involving collective labour and a high degree of citizen participation, to medium-sized units in which citizens have little to do but to vote and to dicker with their divisional councillors.

Churches, School Boards, and local governments were the first formal organizations in most pioneer areas. But there were many others. In the Monarch District north of Biggar, a Literary Society held monthly meetings for debates, book reviews, and the publication of a "newspaper" only a year after the arrival of the first settlers. In the following year, 1909, a Ladies' Aid Society was established. The Monarch School District was organized in 1910, and a local branch of the United Grain Growers in 1911. Later, Monarch farmers played a leading part in forming the North Biggar branch of the Saskatchewan Wheat Pool. During the depression years, the Monarch Lodge of the United Farmers of Canada was especially active. Its monthly meetings, held in the homes of members, included much sociability and fun, as well as discussion and action on political and economic problems. The same was true of the local branch of the CCF youth movement, the CCYM. For virtually all of the young people of the district, regardless of the politics of their parents, it served as a focal point not only for study and discussion, but for recreation as well.

As McCrorie has shown, prairie farmers have been involved in a social movement of agrarian unrest, protest, and political and economic action throughout this century.[7] The movement has been more or less continuous, though with dramatic upswings and downswings of participation and organization. A succession of associations – farm interest groups, co-operatives of various kinds, and political parties – have come forward as specific vehicles of the farm movement at different times. There is no need to recount the history of these organizations. But I wish to illustrate two points here: that even in the early years of settlement these groups were ubiquitous, and that they served many different functions.

In response to the deteriorating economic position of farmers vis-a-vis the railways, the grain companies, and the eastern manufacturers, the Territorial Grain Growers' Association was established in 1901. With several early victories to its credit, the organization grew rapidly, setting up branches throughout the province. By 1916, it had 1,300 locals and a membership comprising about 27 percent of all farmers in Saskatchewan.

The Grain Growers' was organized as a farm pressure group, and history usually identifies it by this primary function. It is important to recognize, however, that the association had many functions. The following excerpt from a local history will serve to illustrate this point:

The contribution of the S.G.G.A. Branches to their local communities cannot be over emphasized since they did their best to be all things to all men, and women and children too. Lady Grain Growers were among the first non-church women's organizations, and not only did the Branches encourage junior farmers but their buying co-ops often acted as purchasing agents for school Boards and sometimes undertook school maintenance projects as well. . . . Sponsorship of the annual picnic was the best-known social achievement of a Cory Grain Growers' local.[8]

Hence we see that at the local level the early prairie farmer political action groups also provided sociability, recreation, economic co-operation, community improvement, and mutual aid. This has been more or less true of all farm organizations right up to present times. Earlier we saw the multi-purpose communal nature of the United Farmers of Canada and the CCF youth movement during the Depression years. In an interview in 1961, a leader of a Farmers Union local in the Biggar area stated that monthly "social evenings" were the most important activity of the group. He pointed out that these meetings were held in members' homes rather than in their own Union Hall.

*   *   *   *   *

Thus far I have tried to establish the point that far from being unique to urban life in Canada, formal organizations have been central to the community life of prairie farmers from pioneer times to the present. Indeed, I have suggested that there are higher rates of membership and leadership in organizations in rural Saskatchewan than in any city in Canada. We turn now to consider various explanations of why this is so. Lipset says:

Repeated challenges and crises forced the western farmers to create many more community institutions (especially co-operatives and pressure groups) than are necessary in a more stable area.[9]

The "challenges" elaborated by Lipset are mostly economic. He argues that prairie wheat farmers constitute a single class with common economic interests which bring them into conflict with local townsmen, the railways, the grain companies, and Eastern commercial and manufacturing interests. Their only recourse, then, is to organize among themselves, with no reliance on the middle-class businessmen and professionals who tend to monopolize leadership in urban voluntary associations and politics.

A similar explanation was offered by T.C. Douglas in the Foreword to a 1956 book on consumer co-operation:

Visitors to our province often ask why the co-operative movement is so much stronger in Saskatchewan than in other provinces of Canada. The answer is to be found in economic necessity. . . . Under the pressure of sheer necessity our people have turned to co-operatives as offering the best means of survival in a highly monopolistic economy.[10]

The author of the book introduced by Douglas was the prairie journalist J.F.C. Wright. He too undertakes an explanation of the unique development of co-operative organization in Saskatchewan. Five of his reasons are economic, paralleling Lipset's. The sixth is that prairie farmers had to solve unique problems of isolation – which he elaborates in this way:

Living on isolated farmsteads, prairie settlers gained early recognition of their interdependence. Unorganized, or more correctly, unincorporated, neighborly co-operation was spontaneous. . . . Neighbors were helped to do what they couldn't do alone – digging a well, raising a barn, harvesting in the time of the steam-driven threshing outfits requiring crews of twenty men. Like all co-operation, it emerged from physical circumstances and need combined with the better side of human relations plus group know-how in a combination of the ideal and the practical.[11]

This quotation actually includes several kinds of explanation, but let us concentrate on the ecological one first. The widely scattered settlement pattern, the consequent thinness of population density, and the long distances to major urban centres created problems which could not be solved by the single-farm family or the profit-seeking business enterprise. Some of these problems were practical: farm tasks which required the work of many people; the building of roads and schools; the ploughing of fire-protection belts; the extermination of gophers and other pests; the setting-up of telephone systems; the clearing of snow from the roads.

Other problems, however, were more personal and social, as suggested in the following excerpts from an account of the isolation and loneliness of early settlers in the Alberta area studied by Burnet:

. . . Isolation was a severe hardship. The first settlers found it difficult to travel to and from . . . the nearest railway towns, by horse or by oxen for supplies. They sometimes got lost in winter storms or blizzards. They suffered grievously from loneliness, which seems peculiarly acute in prairie lands where the absence of neighbours can be verified at a glance.

The women were more isolated than the men, who in the course of their work met their neighbours. The women spent their lives within tiny shacks, engaged in ceaseless heavy toil. They could not get skilled medical aid in childbirth. Frequently, when the men were busy with harvest or a round-up, they were completely alone for days. . . . The hardships of frontier isolation were severe enough to lead to great efforts at contact.[12]

In his book *Northern Plainsmen*, a community study of a locality in southwest Saskatchewan, Bennett also suggests the connection between isolation and organization:

The physical isolation of a sparsely-populated countryside is the key to many Jasper cultural patterns. Communication and social contact usually need to be planned; they do not emerge spontaneously when neighbors are miles apart and the urban habit of visiting across the lawn is impossible.[13]

In the rural areas, then, people had to depend upon organized activities to provide opportunities for sociability and recreation. As we have seen, any formal organization could become a means to these ends: a school, a "literary society", a farm pressure group, or a church. The following excerpts from a local history will illustrate the latter:

The immigrants from Hungary had been living in villages before coming to this country. It was very difficult for them at the start to live on scattered farms. But this change was made comparatively easy under the circumstances, as the inhabitants on farms were connected by many common ties. . . .

What appealed most was the cultural and spiritual atmosphere, the congenial environment where they could associate with people of the same origin, mother-tongue, and religion. . . . This was definitely assured when a church had been built. . . .

The whole colony seemed to be practically one family.[14]

The widely scattered settlement pattern, combined with great distances and poor means of transportation between major centres, also made it impossible for the decision-making and service functions of government to be concentrated in the Territorial, or, after 1905, the Provincial Government. The organization of essential public services, and decisions about these, can be carried out for large numbers of people by single governmental units where population density is high, as in cities, or where communications and transportation are well developed, as in modernized rural areas. But these conditions were lacking for the early settlers. They could get very little aid or direction from central government.

Nor could they depend upon an established elite, as in many long-settled areas of the world. The dominant class of merchants and professional men in prairie villages and towns had different and sometimes conflicting interests compared to those of farmers.[15] Furthermore, as a newly arrived middle class, often with farm backgrounds, these merchants, lawyers, and doctors had no tradition of *noblesse oblige*. Hence prairie settlers had to operate their own school and local government system.

We have thus far dealt only with the economic and ecological reasons for the high degree of organizational participation of prairie farmers. Let us not overlook culture. For in all this mutual aid and joint activity, a supportive value system was bound to emerge. The nostalgic accounts which old-timers give to pioneer times make it clear that mutual aid and co-operation were not merely for convenience or necessity alone: they involved an ideology which grew out of, and in turn reinforced, the loyalty and solidarity which the early farmers developed among themselves. The following excerpt (which includes a quotation from Chester I. Barnard) from Burnet's *Next-Year Country* will illustrate this point:

On the informal level there was a wealth of activity – visiting, bees, plays, concerts, dances, picnics, and charivaris. Gatherings, which people sometimes endured great hardship to attend, lasted a long time and were very hilarious. They created the possibility among the dry-belt farmers "of accepting a common purpose, of communicating, and of attaining a state of mind under which there is a willingness to co-operate." Out of them grew formal structures, which in turn strengthened the informal relations.[16]

In describing the "Northern plainsmen" of southwest Saskatchewan, Bennett also makes the connection between the emergent culture and organizational participation, in such passages as the following:

These co-operative strategies, required to establish farming in a difficult environment during a period of rising agricultural costs, prepared Saskatchewan farmers for collective action against the railroads and grain elevator companies at a later date. . . . The co-operative habits were reinforced also by a number of farmer leaders who had been trained in the English co-operative movement and Fabian socialist doctrines.[17]

There is no doubt that imported values, not only from England but from Scandinavia, did influence the ideology of prairie farmers, particularly through the charismatic leadership of such men as Partridge, Crerar, and Douglas, and many local agitators. But we must remember that whereas these men saw collective action in society-wide terms, the co-operative values of farmers were rooted in the local community. Thus their mutual-aid ideology could sustain and support group action and organization in face-to-face situations, but did not automatically dispose them to participate in movements of regional or national scope.

Incidentally, this point appears to be a significant addition to the thesis that the CCF in Saskatchewan should be seen as a populist rather than a socialist movement. The co-op grain elevator with its local committee, the nearby Farmers Union Hall with its varied activities, the monthly meetings of the CCYM – these manifestations of the wider movement had a mutually reinforcing relationship with the mutual-aid ideology of farmers. But socialist plans for the reorganization of industry and society in co-operation with distant groups, such as organized labour, had no precedents in the early grass-roots culture of the prairies. Similarly, the limited scope of the cultural roots of the co-operative principle must be taken as a significant part of the explanation for the strong opposition to amalgamation of schools, co-ops, credit unions, and churches; and to the reorganization of local government into larger units.

We may now summarize the foregoing section by listing the factors which have contributed to the high degree of involvement of prairie farmers in formal organizations:

1. common economic interests of farmers;
2. ecological conditions which required collective labour;
3. ecological conditions which encouraged organized recreation and sociability;
4. ecological conditions which required small units of local government;
5. emergent cultural values which encouraged collective action at the local level.

*   *   *   *   *

The factors listed above, which have been suggested or hinted at by other authors, have been brought together here as a basis for assessing past and future trends in the role of formal organizations among prairie farmers. Let us consider their implications, one by one.

Economic interest as a basis for participation provides a major explanation for the rise and decline of the various organizations which have emerged as the concrete expression of the farm movement. But because farmers have been more or less continually disadvantaged, and because the political economy of Canada shows no signs of reversing this condition, we may expect that economic interest will continue to constitute a pressure toward organizational activity. Economic and occupational goals accounted for the existence of thirty-nine of the seventy-six organizations in the rural areas of the RM of Biggar in 1960.[18]

With regard to our second point, the revolution in farm and construction technology which has occurred since pioneer times has virtually eliminated the need for collective labour. The single-farm family and its employees can now accomplish almost all of those tasks which brought groups of neighbours together for mutual aid in the past. Thus one very important basis for organized activity has been removed.

The situation with regard to recreation and sociability is more complicated. To a considerable degree the communal needs in this area have been reduced by radio, television, and increasingly easy access to the various kinds of commercial recreation available in towns and cities. The sense of isolation and loneliness has been greatly reduced. In addition, the penetration of urban culture into the countryside has diversified the leisure-time interests of farm families, so that many of these can no longer be provided for in the local neighbourhood. Rural depopulation and the centralization of schools and churches has caused many local organizations to collapse or fade away. The consequent decline in neighbourhood activity has meant that the local neighbourhoods themselves have tended to wither or disappear as centres of social life.

According to students of rural social life in the United States, the same trends occurred even earlier in that country. For example, Kolb and Wiledon reported as early as 1927 that in place of the declining country neighbourhoods, villages (up to populations of several thousands) had become the centres of rural social and organizational life.[19]

The picture is not that simple in the areas studied by the Centre for Community Studies. For example, a few predominantly farm organizations meet in Biggar itself, and some town groups attract rural members. But only a small part of the organizational life of the countryside can be said to have shifted to Biggar. The trend may well continue as roads and means of transportation improve, as more country people develop common leisure-time interests with city folk, and as the rural adult population includes more and more graduates of the central high school in Biggar.

On the other hand, there are certain obstacles which make integration of town and country social and organizational life very difficult, if not impossible, at present. These obstacles include such practical problems as time, expense, and baby-sitting; economic and political cleavages (as dramatized in open conflict between town and country during the Medicare crisis in 1962); differences between town and country "ways of life"; and difficulties of co-operation and sociability with strangers of different backgrounds.[20]

Therefore it cannot be assumed that the sociable and recreational needs of farm families will soon be met primarily in the larger centres. An example from the Monarch district will illustrate continuing social organization in parts of the open countryside. In 1960, a recently established Curling Club was sponsoring an annual picnic, a baseball tournament, a winter banquet, and a children's Christmas party, in addition to the regular curling bonspiel. Most residents who did not curl were nevertheless members of the Curling Club, as a matter of "community spirit" and neighbourly co-operation.

Turning now to the question of local government, the relevant ecological, technological, and social conditions have changed markedly. With advancing technology, improved communications, and rising demands for services, one by one the various functions of local government have been organized or reorganized on a district or regional level by the Provincial Government. The local School Boards have disappeared as larger school units were created. Hospitals, public health, social welfare, agricultural services, and even roads and highways are now largely planned and directed by district or regional units. The tiny Rural Municipalities have been reduced virtually to overseers of back roads and tax- and fee-collection agencies. A widespread preference for small-scale local government, on the one hand, and the special interests of local councillors and the opposition party on the other, combined to prevent reorganization into larger municipalities or counties in 1961-62. Nevertheless, it seems only a matter of time until the present Rural Municipalities are completely replaced by larger units. Another element in the strength of local organization will have disappeared.

With regard to the fifth reason for intensive organizational involvement – that is, the grass-roots co-operative ideology – we have seen in the foregoing discussion the steady decline or disappearance of some of the conditions which gave rise to the commitment to mutual-aid values. Collective labour and involvement in local government are now so infrequent as to have lost their communal significance. Since 1930, rural depopulation has brought about the amalgamation of schools, churches, co-operatives, and branches of interest groups, almost eliminating organized activity in these fields from the rural neighbourhood.

When surviving pioneers contrast the "community spirit" and co-operation of the early years with the "apathy" and individualism of today, they are no doubt exaggerating. Yet it is plausible to believe that a significant ideological change away from communal values has been taking place, because many of the ecological and social conditions which underlay those values have disappeared.

*   *   *   *   *

This examination of the factors which encourage participation in formal organizations among prairie farmers has shown that some remain while others have disappeared. The needs for economic solutions, for the maintenance or improvement of community facilities, for recreation, and for sociability have remained, though with fluctuations. On the other hand, conditions requiring collective labour and small-scale local government have largely disappeared, and co-operative values have been considerably undermined.

The changing conditions we have described have killed many rural organizations. Others, such as Snow Plow Clubs, have newly emerged in response to new conditions. Still others, such as the co-operatives, have modified their structure and functions. It is clear that the small, close-knit, country neighbourhood of the past is disappearing. But the over-all picture of rural life is one of transformation rather than decline. The recurring dynamic of the farm movement and the continuing quest for sociability and local improvement seem likely to involve farm people in an active social and organizational life for years to come.

This life will be different from that of the past. Present trends suggest that it will be based more upon special interests, and less upon neighbourly sociability. Organizations will be fewer, larger, and more often centred in villages and towns. They will involve more contact with strangers. Better-qualified leaders and more professional assistance will probably be available, but member participation may be less frequent and less significant. Co-operation will be less ideological and more utilitarian. Organization will be more centralized, more formalized, more impersonal, and perhaps more efficient.

Three

LIFE IN FRONTIER CALGARY

Henry C. Klassen

This chapter deals with the cultural and social life that Anglo-Calgarians had created for themselves by the opening of the twentieth century. Particular attention is given to certain key aspects of their lives – the homes in which they lived, their literary interests, and their entertainment world, although even these aspects are not depicted in all their fullness. The purpose is to indicate the importance of homes, books, and amusements in Calgary society in its formative period from 1875 to 1902, and explore the extent to which they illustrate the social structure of the city.

Calgary citizens generally estimated an individual's place in the social scale in terms of his economic status. By the turn of the century a somewhat stratified society had developed consisting of a small group of wealthy men, a growing class of moderately prosperous families, and a large class of relatively low-paid people. This chapter is a general outline of these social classes. While it is not a full-scale analysis – research was based primarily upon interviews and findings in local newspapers – it may serve as a preliminary report on the structure of Calgary society as it was over seventy years ago.

* * * * *

Calgary in 1902 was a very young city, less than thirty years old.[1] It was then a small centre of six thousand people. Built in the valley of the Bow and the Elbow rivers far away from the major concentrations of population, it was still a frontier city, not particularly wild but somewhat crude and unfinished. Over the previous two decades, however, CPR trains and covered wagons had brought numerous individuals who were determined to civilize their new surroundings.

The cultural life of the fledgling city was predominantly English Canadian and British in character. About eighty per cent of its residents had come from Ontario, the Maritime provinces, and the British Isles. Besides bringing with them their skills and a little capital in order to make a living, they brought to the raw western community their traditions, cultural and religious values, and tastes in entertainment. Although the eastern Canadian and British newcomers had much in common in their cultural backgrounds, early Calgary was in a sense an experiment in blending the cultures of Maritime and Ontario settlers with the cultures of English, Irish and Scottish immigrants. Despite squabbles and rivalries among them, by and large they lived in peace and gave Calgary a distinctly British Canadian flavour. Among the non-Anglo-Canadian newcomers were a number of Americans and a few French Canadians, Germans, Scandinavians, Chinese, Jews, and Italians. The latter groups added their own interesting lifestyles to the community, but lacked the numerical strength to make a strong impact upon the social and cultural scene.

Outside inspiration for the predominantly Anglo-Canadian way of life in Calgary constantly came from the older provinces of Canada and the mother country. The arrival of a letter from back home was usually considered an event, and no-one waited for it more anxiously than the lonely young housewife who was pining away for mother and old friends. Not infrequently, relatives and hometown acquaintances were the guests of Calgary families. So important were the visits of these guests to the life of the community that they were often noted in the pages of the local press. Those Calgarians who could afford it took lengthy vacations in the East and the United Kingdom that undoubtedly stimulated a renewed zeal to duplicate in Calgary the cultures from which they themselves had originally sprung. Merchants making business trips to cities like Toronto, Montreal, and London came back with the latest fashions, proudly displaying them in their stores on Eighth Avenue. The traditions of older English Canadian and British societies were also imported through newspapers, for in Calgary homes one could find recent issues of the London *Illustrated News*, the St. John *Telegraph*, the Montreal *Star*, and the Toronto *Weekly Globe*.

*   *   *   *   *

One of the most significant features of the Anglo-Canadian culture was the home, and Calgarians began the process of refining their community by building dwelling places that provided more than basic shelter. As Calgary grew from a Mounted Police post to a town in the 1880's, and then to a city in the 1890's, the contrast between the homes of the well-to-do citizens and those of small-income families became increasingly more apparent. Calgary possessed an open and fluid society in which opportunities existed for advancement, but not everyone acquired wealth, property, and domestic comforts at the same rate and to the same degree. Class distinctions quickly arose in the frontier society, and those who lived in the more comfortable houses soon began calling themselves the better class of people. Even within this group the dwelling houses varied considerably in terms of cost, size, and conveniences. They ranged all the way from compact cottages to the more spacious two-storey houses and the impressive sandstone mansions.

Men took different routes to become owners of homes from which they could derive satisfaction for a good number of years. Some newcomers of the 1880's started in tents or log shacks and ended up in respectable frame houses before a decade had passed. Others found temporary quarters in rooming and boarding houses until they could move into their own newly built homes. Sometimes a man of means would come to Calgary ahead of his family, live in one of the best hotels while his house was being constructed, and then take pleasure in sending for his wife and children and providing them with a fully completed and nicely furnished home. Single men with money would do the same for their sweethearts whom they had earlier left behind in Britain or eastern Canada. Such men usually had as much pride in their new city as in their new homes, but sometimes they had difficulty in convincing their wives that Calgary was a city. In the late 1890's one wife, after her long journey from England, got off the train at the centrally located railway station and greeted her husband with the words, "My dear, where is the town?"

Citizens with enough capital to satisfy their hankering for a fine home belonged to a small but heterogeneous group that included the bigger merchants, lawyers, hotel proprietors, doctors, bankers, Mounted Police officers, journalists, real-estate agents, building contractors, and ranchers; as well as the owners of industrial enterprises like the Calgary Planing Mills, the Eau Claire Lumber Company, and the Calgary Brewing and Malting Company. Profits were made in all of these ventures, but in many cases the money needed to establish and maintain a good residence came from real-estate speculation. The rapid expansion of Calgary in the mid- and late 1880's had led to a scramble for land. Small fortunes were made between 1886 and 1888, when the value of choice property in the business district shot upward from $500 a lot to $2,500.[2] This steep climb in land prices had a marked effect upon the structure of

Calgary society, for it gave the town its first moneyed class, and widened the gap between the prosperous and the low-income people. By the end of that decade most of the well-to-do had assets valued between $2,000 and $10,000, a few were worth over $15,000, and one man had accumulated property worth over $30,000.

Before 1902 no exclusive neighbourhood had been set aside for the homes of the more affluent citizens, though the houses of many of the moderately prosperous residents were located on Fourth, Fifth, and Sixth Avenues near the centre of the city between Fourth Street West and Sixth Street East. Several magnificent homes already stood on Twelfth and Thirteenth Avenues south of the railway. A few beautiful residences could be seen east of the Elbow River, as well as beyond the city limits north of the Bow River and in Rouleauville south of the city.

The wealthiest Calgarians had very large establishments costing up to $20,000. They resided in three-storey stone homes with dining rooms, wide circular stairways, carpeted floors, libraries, at least half a dozen bedrooms, and often wine cellars and billiard rooms, all of which were finished throughout in British Columbia cedar or Ontario oak. Such houses usually had full basements and enormous coal furnaces, and were equipped with two or three bathrooms, hot and cold running water, and electric lights. The grounds, spreading over as many as twelve city lots, were usually covered with flower gardens, green lawns, shrubs, and trees, and were enclosed with handsome stone fences. A solid two-storey stable, standing at a suitable distance from the house, would contain stalls for horses and ponies, a carriage room, and living quarters for the coachman. From time to time the owners of these establishments displayed their wealth, status and luxury by inviting the elite of Calgary and district to parties in their fashionable drawing rooms. Photographs of the more impressive dwellings were included in a pamphlet on Calgary published in 1900, that showed that the civilization being created in the western wilderness could almost compare in refinement to the urban East.[3] The mansions, like other Calgary homes, looked out on plank sidewalks, dusty unpaved streets and sometimes a stray cow, but they still gave the youthful city a sense of accomplishment.

The respectable-looking homes of the moderately prosperous class were likewise a source of civic pride, and photographs of over eighty of these houses appeared in the same Calgary pamphlet. Typical of this category of homes was the two-storey frame dwelling with a veranda; stone and brick houses and attractive one-storey cottages were also popular. Costing from $1,500 to $5,000, these homes offered the basic comforts on a modest scale. A dwelling with a parlour, wall-papered dining and living rooms with bay windows and lace curtains, three or four bedrooms, and one bathroom could give considerable pleasure to its occupants. The owners furnished their homes in a variety of ways, but elegant dining- and living-room furniture and a piano were usually looked upon as essentials. Such homes were kept warm with a furnace or coal stove, and like the large stone mansions many had sewers, running water, electric lighting, and sometimes a telephone. Signs of the rural character of Calgary were clearly visible in the back-yards and barns, in which many families kept not only horses but also one or two cows and some chickens. The grounds were nevertheless remarkably tidy in appearance. Carefully laid out, and surrounded with neat, white-painted picket fences, they were often filled with spruce trees, Manitoba maples, lilac bushes, and lovely flower and vegetable gardens. It was the treeless town-site that had made life almost unbearable for the early women in the community. Trees and gardens represented civilization, and the editor of the Calgary *Herald* argued that if more homeowners would beautify their grounds, fewer outsiders would regard Calgary as a "wild west prairie town."[4]

Although prosperous men's wives were often capable cooks and house-keepers, the families as such could not get along easily without servants. Maids, Chinese houseboys, and coachmen were viewed as status symbols, and were also expected to lighten the domestic burdens of the family. While only a few homes could afford a coachman, by the beginning of the twentieth century a growing number of families employed household servants. Both single and married British-born female do-mestics were in particular demand, but there never seemed to be enough of them to go around. Because there was still an acute shortage of women in the Prairie West, the high society of Calgary was faced with the problem of a rapid turnover of maids. Single girls who had barely been trained in household duties and had just begun to settle into the life of a domestic servant would leave to marry unattached city men or bachelor farmers. Not even wages of between $15 and $30 a month, which was well over double what their counterparts in Ontario were receiving, would hold them for very long if a better life was beckoning.[5] In consequence, more employers began to employ Chinese servants, who also were in short supply. Paid $25 a month, a Chinese houseboy was quick to give courteous service, and generally worked hard. Employers of houseboys as a rule had little difficulty in training them in the ways of servanthood.

In spite of the fact that maids were generally entirely competent and gave excellent service, the matter of training female domestics some-times presented problems to employers. Learning to clean the house, cook, serve meals, and look after the children was not all that was required of a maid. Employers who themselves had been raised in homes with servants tried to transplant old traditions to their Calgary households, and expected their maids to be familiar with and practise common social courtesies. For example, they wanted their maids to dress in becoming uniforms, aprons, and caps. They taught them how to receive invited guests and how to turn away unwanted visitors. Above all, a maid was expected to observe the social boundaries between herself and the members of the family. Most female domestics could be persuaded to follow these customs, but the freedom that the frontier brought to Calgary society encouraged them to adopt a more easy-going lifestyle. Some got into the habit of starting conversations with guests, and others tended to become overly friendly with older sons. Employers naturally deplored such behaviour, and the situation was complicated whenever guests and older sons took the initiative in talking to maids. At any rate, in the eyes of the employers it was more appropriate for female domestics to have friendly chats with persons like the milkman or the German laundry woman who came in one day a week from Germantown north of the Langevin Bridge to do the family washing. Although the maids resented this sort of attitude, they usually responded favourably to good treatment. And in numerous households good relations existed between employer and servant.

Within Calgary's lower-income population were the small merchants, skilled working men, ordinary labourers, and the poor. There were no well defined areas for these groups, just as there were none for the well-to-do families. Prosperous men, small wage earners, and the poor intermingled, and their homes stood on the same streets and often on the same blocks. At the same time, many of the homes of the lower-income families could be found on First, Second, and Third Avenues near the Bow River; around the Eau Claire Mills; on Seventh, Eighth, Ninth, and Tenth Avenues among the business establishments; in Germantown; and down in the Brewery Flats. But none of these areas had degenerated into slums. Low-paying jobs did not necessarily lead to wretched living conditions, and while there were always some run-down homes, these were not concentrated in one district. No section of the city had become crowded, and everywhere there were open spaces and empty lots.

Living conditions varied considerably among the families with relatively low incomes. At the top of this class were the small merchants and the skilled working men. These usually lived in modest frame cottages, though the merchants sometimes made their homes in the back or the upper storey of their shops. The income of the average skilled working-man enabled him to secure a lot for $50 to $150, and build a cottage costing between $700 and $1,500. Masons, plasterers, and bricklayers earned from $3.50 to $4.00 a day, and carpenters were paid $2.50.[6] With these wages they could support homes with a kitchen, a dirt cellar, a living room, and two or three small bedrooms. Such houses were usually heated with kitchen and living-room stoves, though many were not insulated. Nor did all the houses have electricity, running water, and sewers. Wells and outdoor privies were common features in many backyards. Most of the homes were nevertheless comfortably if not expensively furnished. If the family was musical, there would likely be a reed organ rather than a piano in the household. The families could eat fairly good meals, for most of them had vegetable gardens, cows, and a few chickens. Their well-cared-for lawns were often just as picturesque as those of the more prosperous families. Not all skilled workingmen were homeowners, however, and those who rented cottages generally showed much less interest in beautifying their grounds.

At the very bottom of the economic and social system were the unskilled labourers. Most of the men in this category were of Anglo-Canadian origins, but it also encompassed almost all the Germans and Chinese. Earning only $1.30 a day on an average, these men toiled in Calgary's industries and were employed as ditchdiggers, waiters, bartenders, and cooks. There was a great deal of diversity in the housing conditions of this group. A large number of families rented frame dwellings and paid from three to five dollars a month rent, some erected shacks for themselves, and others lived in their own small cottages built at a cost of between three hundred and six hundred dollars. Only a few households had any of the modern improvements, and most of them got along with coal-oil lamps, used or home-made furniture, a cook stove, and a pot-bellied stove in the living room. Although some of the tiny cottages had only three rooms, a kitchen, a bedroom for the parents and a living room where the children slept, they were usually clean and in a state of good repair. No matter how low their wages, many families were thrifty and produced their own milk, butter, eggs, meat and vegetables. They clearly took great pride in their independence; and the number of needy people who periodically received groceries, coal, and wood from the city's relief committee, charitable organizations, and kind neighbours remained relatively small.

*   *   *   *   *

Anglo-Canadian traditions had a strong hold upon the educational and literary life of Calgary in the 1890's. Many fathers and mothers wondered how they could educate their children in the Prairie wilderness to which they had come. To a large extent, they looked to the local schools, hoping that their sons and daughters would emerge from them as decent and literate young men and women with a love for their British Canadian heritage. Though some boys and girls in the schools resisted the emphasis on obedience, the need to build their society upon Anglo-Canadian foundations was something they all took for granted. Students of all economic and social strata were enrolled in the elementary and high school classes of the Calgary public schools, the Sacred Heart Convent, and the Lacombe Separate School. Here they could develop a sense of pride in their past by learning the stories and poems in the Ontario Readers, singing patriotic songs like "Soldiers of the Queen" and "Rule Britannia", reading English literature, participating in Shakespeare's plays, and studying the political and military history of Britain and Canada. Many students undoubtedly benefitted from their experiences in the Calgary schools, but the large, crowded, and poorly ventilated classrooms often made the learning process extremely difficult.

For the children of Calgary's prosperous families the educational opportunities were not limited to the curriculum and the somewhat primitive conditions of the city schools. A few never entered these schools, while others received only part of their education there. Wealthy parents, with or without a privileged education in eastern Canada or Britain, were anxious to give their children more than an ordinary schooling. In Calgary, private kindergarten teachers, household governesses, and tutors with degrees from Oxford or Cambridge all played a part in educating the young sons and daughters of these families. Later the children were often sent to private boarding schools. Their parents hoped that they would return well disciplined and schooled in the manners and amusements of ladies and gentlemen. Looking upon a men's boarding school as a good preparation for a professional career, fathers sent their sons to the English public schools or to Upper Canada College in Toronto, Trinity College in Port Hope, Lakefield Preparatory School near Peterborough, or St. Boniface College in Winnipeg; and then encouraged them to go into law, train for a military career in the Royal Military College in Kingston, or take up medical studies at McGill or the University of Toronto. Very few Calgary girls went to ladies' boarding schools with the intention of becoming career women. Instead, after spending several years in schools such as Bishop Strachan School in Toronto or Ontario Ladies' College in Whitby, they usually married educated men and became community leaders. Like the men who had gone away to boarding schools, they often came back with a strong liking for eastern and old-country customs, and saw to it that they were perpetuated in Calgary.

Many of these young men and women brought back with them a taste for reading, and they now joined other Calgary booklovers in reading the works of Dickens, Scott, Thackeray, Shaw, and Bulwer-Lytton. The libraries of the more well-to-do families sometimes contained magazines like the *American Field* and *Forest and Stream* for sports-minded men, and *The Ladies Home Journal* for the women. In the children's section of the library there was usually a copy of Hans Christian Andersen's *Fairy Tales*. Calgary readers also took an interest in books on Canada, especially on the Canadian West. Among the popular western titles was *Pathfinding on Plain and Prairie* by the Rev. John McDougall, whose move to the city in the late 1890's enabled Calgarians to claim him as their own author. Educated at Victoria University in Toronto,

McDougall was a product of the Ontario culture and his book was an extension of the literary traditions of eastern Canada.

Even families of very modest means could acquire small collections of books. In all ranks were persons with neither the inclination nor the time to read through a volume, but by the turn of the century the city had a large enough reading public to support both Linton Brothers' Bookstore and Mackie's Bookstore. The local newspapers were likely more important than books in the reading fare of the average Calgarian. For almost a decade during the 1880's and the 1890's newspaper readers and businessmen sustained two dailies, the Calgary *Herald* and the Calgary *Tribune*. Each had a wide appeal among the citizens, and it was the hard times of the early and mid-1890's rather than a declining interest in the local press itself that temporarily drove one of the dailies out of the field.

A considerable part of the popularity of the *Tribune* and the *Herald* rested upon their good coverage of local affairs. Along with the attention they gave to the business scene, local and territorial politics, town council meetings, and court sessions, they reported at some length on sports, picnics, skating carnivals, balls, and dances, as well as on the activities of churches, schools, friendly societies, and literary and musical groups. They also printed the speeches of visiting lecturers and the occasional book review. News of eastern Canada and foreign countries usually appeared in the form of short telegraphic reports. Space in the small four-page dailies was at a premium; in order to make them financially viable the editors had to fill the bulk of the papers with advertisements from businessmen and professional people. Readers who preferred light reading could subscribe to the weekly editions in which they could follow serialized stories like *The Gold Seekers of the Sierras* and *Carnival of Crime*. Although the local press was small-town in content and mood, the editorials made frequent reference to eastern Canada and the mother country. In arguing for the retention of corporal punishment in the Calgary schools, for instance, one of the editors pointed to the benefits resulting from the use of the rod in the great public schools of England.[7] The example of the Toronto Public Library was used to enlist support for the establishment of a similar institution in Calgary.[8]

Citizens of Calgary would have to do without a public library until 1911, but from the mid-1880's onward some always took an active interest in various literary activities. They organized the Calgary Institute of Literature, Science and History, and held regular meetings in the Presbyterian and Methodist churches.[9] At the meetings, which usually included singing and instrumental music, members read papers on subjects such as "Thackeray's *Vanity Fair*", "A Natural History and Topography of British Columbia", and "My Experiences as a Bicycle Rider in Scotland". They saw their efforts as a way of promoting the intellectual and moral well-being of the membership. Since only a few of the working-class people joined, the impact of the institute upon the community was limited. Most of the one hundred members supporting it came from well-to-do families, though individuals of all classes made use of the books and magazines in its reading room.[10] The churches, in addition to meeting the religious needs of the frontier community, strongly encouraged literary endeavour. In an era of co-operation among the religious denominations, the Knox Presbyterian Church Literary Society attracted to its meetings not only Presbyterians but also Anglicans, Methodists, Catholics, and Baptists. Large audiences filled the basement of the Knox Church when the Society held debates on "The Destiny of Canada" or "The Merits of the Canadian Senate".[11]

The literary and the wider political interests of leading citizens were fused during the 1890's in debating clubs.[12] The first of these was the Calgary Literary and Debating Society. Its meetings were open to the public, and men like F.H. Turnock, A.L. Sifton, and James Short provided the debating talent. The debate on Imperial Federation, described as an "intellectual treat" by the *Tribune*, indicated that frontier Calgary had men who were well-informed on and had given serious thought to the question of Canada's relations with the United Kingdom. The second venture, known as the Calgary Parliamentary Debating Society, was more ambitious than the first. It organized a full-fledged mock parliament in the city. The formation of this Society, in the spring of 1896, a few months prior to the Dominion election of that year, was designed to provide men with a chance to develop their debating skills and give Calgary voters an opportunity to become conversant with the political issues of the day. For the sixty members who took their seats in the mock parliament assembled in the Alexander Hall, the discussions proved to be both instructive and enjoyable, and their great interest in the proceedings was shared by the numerous men and women who packed the galleries evening after evening.

Lectures by visiting speakers provided pleasure for Calgary's literary folk.[13] Nicholas Flood Davin, the Irish-born journalist and politician of Regina, gave an assortment of readings, including Tennyson's "The Revenge" and one of his own pieces entitled "Love Making at an Irish Fair." Toronto author Goldwin Smith, who spoke to a big gathering on "Canada's Commercial Relations with the United States", pleased his attentive listeners when he commented upon their civilized way of life in the West. Cartoonist J.W. Bengough of the Toronto *Grip* entertained a large audience with his witty lecture and cartoons of local men, one of them a political sketch portraying the Conservative Wesley Orr presenting a baby called "National Policy" to Sir John A. Macdonald. Bengough's impressive performance immediately led to a marked expansion of *Grip's* circulation in Calgary. From Inverness, Scotland, came Baillie Stuart, and many Scottish Calgarians turned out to hear his address on Highland life, literature, and music. On another occasion, a small and appreciative group listened to a lecture on "Scotland and France: the Land of John Knox and the Home of Voltaire", by the Rev. John Robbins of Truro, Nova Scotia. These and other visiting speakers brought diversity to Calgary life, and helped the city to maintain contact with the larger literary world.

*   *   *   *   *

A striking feature of Calgary society in the 1880's and 1890's was that it provided most of its own entertainment. Basically, this entertainment consisted of a variety of social gatherings in homes, churches, and halls, as well as a great many outdoor activities. The isolation of the frontier community encouraged people to make friends, and every gathering was an opportunity to confirm old friendships and see new faces. Not surprisingly, the forms they used to create a society for themselves in the Prairie city closely resembled those they had known in eastern Canada and Britain. Some of their diversions were inspired by the western setting, but in the main they found enjoyment in the traditional amusements.

Many citizens were very fond of music and theatricals. A small part of this kind of entertainment came from travelling companies touring Prairie cities and towns during this period, and Calgary residents took delight in concerts presented by Madame Albani's Company of Quebec, Canadian violinist Nora Clench and her Company, and the Jubilee Singers of Nashville, Tennessee. But most of the dramatic and musical entertainment was the work of local amateurs. In the small community of those years, almost everyone with any ability in drama and music was expected to spend time and energy in the presentation of concerts, plays, and operas. The stage facilities and buildings for these performances were gradually improved, and the playgoing public enthusiastically greeted the appearance of Hull's Opera House in the early 1890's. With a large, attractive stage, the Opera House had a seating capacity for six hundred people.[14] The three tiers of upholstered seats in the gallery facing the stage were reserved for the elite, while the rest of the audience sat on chairs without cushions.

Both the upper crust and the more humble of the city attended the performances at the Opera House, though the more prosperous men and women usually dominated the audiences. Among the local amateur actors who entertained the theatre goers were Paddy Nolan, Crispin Smith, Lillian Rankin, and Mr. and Mrs. W. Roland Winter. The Calgary actors produced chiefly comedy pieces; one of their early successes was Byron's play *Our Boys*. Their presentation of Gilbert and Sullivan's comic opera *The Pirates of Penzance*, with an orchestra conducted by John J. Young, had a particularly warm reception.[15] Calgary audiences also greatly appreciated the production of other works of Gilbert and Sullivan, like *Iolanthe* and *Her Majesty's Ship Pinafore*, and the amateur players and musicians continued to rely on comedy to fill the Opera House.

Like the amateur performances in the Opera House, church concerts were often given not only to provide amusement but also to raise money for the local hospitals and the poor. The performers in church and theatre were frequently the same people, and nearly every patron of the Opera House was a supporter of a church. Collectively, however, the churches attracted larger and more mixed audiences than the theatre. The informal atmosphere of church socials and concerts tended to discourage class distinctions. Church concerts were social mixers, and the familiar folk songs and refreshments around which these gatherings were organized did much to bring together men and women of different social and economic classes.

All layers of Calgary society enjoyed card parties and dancing to fiddle music, and a great deal of this kind of entertaining was done in the homes. The more prominent members of the community had their share of dancing in their fine homes and at balls. The balls given by the Mounted Police, the firemen, St. Andrew's Society, and St. Patrick's Society were especially popular. Invitations were issued to the elite of Calgary and district, and people from Millarville, Okotoks, Midnapore, Springbank, and Chestermere, arriving in buggies, carriages and on horseback, helped to swell the attendance at these brilliant gatherings where everyone appeared in formal evening dress. Most of the local men and women walked to these dances, while the wealthiest Calgarians came in carriages. Ranchers, bank clerks, mounties, and remittance men were the favorite dancing partners of the single young ladies, who were always accompanied by chaperones. The dances usually lasted until three o'clock in the morning, giving most country folk enough time to return home shortly before – or after – daybreak.

The celebrations of the patriotic and cultural societies in Calgary were a form of entertainment which a number of ordinary people shared with individuals of higher social standing. Cultural groupings were represented in the Scottish St. Andrew's Society, the English St. George's Society, and the Irish Orange Order and St. Patrick's Society, as well as the French-Canadian St. Jean Baptiste Society. The large gatherings of the Irishmen, Scotsmen, and Englishmen, as compared to the small handful of citizens who met to keep alive the French Canadian traditions, drew attention to the preponderant Anglo-Saxon civilization of the city. While the entertainment provided by these societies included concerts and balls, a significant aspect of their annual celebrations was the dinner. Like the St. Andrew's dinner, where Scotsmen sat down to eat haggis while the strains of the bagpipes filled the banquet hall, the dinners of the other societies featured dishes and music reflecting their cultural traditions. Members of the English, Scottish, and Irish societies saw their activities as a way of strengthening the bond between Canada and Britain, and they often attributed their achievements as Canadians to the qualities they had inherited from their forbears and to their warm affection for the races from which they came.

Within the Anglo-Canadian society of Calgary, the banquet meetings of these societies were by no means expressions of narrow culturalism. There was an almost universal feeling among Calgarians of English, Scottish, and Irish descent that old country animosities had no place in the Prairie city. It was customary especially for the members of the St. Andrew's, St. George's, and St. Patrick's societies to attend each other's banquets. Their main desire was to have a good time. Even the Catholic and Protestant Irishmen began to participate together in the St. Patrick's Day festivities. Orangemen still had their parades and demonstrations on July 12, but they were generally quiet and orderly affairs. Illustrative of the liberal spirit that prevailed among Anglo-Canadians was the St. Patrick's Day program held in the Royal Opera House in 1888.[16] Present along with the Roman Catholic fathers were the Anglican, Presbyterian, and Methodist clergymen. The group providing the musical entertainment was comprised of one Catholic and eight Protestants. The audience was half Protestant and half Catholic, and the financial purpose of the gathering was to raise money for the building of a Roman Catholic church in the city. There were always some members in each of the patriotic groups who were irritated by the zealous activities of the others, but seldom were these feelings translated into hostile actions.

The social advantages of belonging to the friendly benefit societies appealed to many men, and every class from a caretaker to a medical doctor was represented in organizations like the Masons, Oddfellows, Foresters, and the Sons of England Benevolent Society. For the men who joined these societies, the amusements they offered were no less important than the benefits they provided in the event of sickness or death. At their fortnightly or monthly meetings they made friends, played cards, and drank beer. In those days it was not uncommon for men from the country to travel long distances on horseback to take part in these convivial gatherings. Storytelling was one of their favourite pastimes, and many an evening was spent in telling and listening to yarns that had their origins in western experiences. Banquets, concerts, dancing, and church parades all helped to brighten the social life of these societies. One of the most enjoyable occasions for the more well-to-do members of the Sons of England was their traditional paper chase, the hunting party in which the horsemen were joined by lady riders on beautifully groomed horses in a run covering about twenty miles in the country to search for the scraps of paper scattered along the trail by other members of the party.

Most Calgarians of the 1880's and 1890's frowned upon Sunday sports and agreed that organized sport should be restricted to week days. But until the early 1890's, when the merchants finally decided to close their shops at six o'clock every evening Monday through Friday rather than follow their old custom of keeping them open until eight or ten o'clock, there was not very much time for outdoor recreation during the week.[17] Once the early closing time was adopted, the leisure hours available for sports were significantly increased.

Although the sports activities of the various social ranks overlapped, polo and horse racing were largely the amusements of the prosperous citizens. The well bred horses seen on the Calgary polo grounds and race tracks usually belonged to members of the Ranchmen's Club and other wealthy citizens, as well as the Mounted Police. The range of people covered by the city's cricket, football, and curling clubs was considerably wider. With annual membership fees varying from $3 to $5, these clubs included both the high-income citizens and the rather low-paid book-keepers and bank clerks. Various classes of men also went out to the countryside around Calgary, fishing in Bragg Creek and the Bow River, and hunting prairie chickens, ducks, and pheasants. A number of leading families had tennis courts, and there they often played games with their city and country friends. Bicycle riding was a popular amusement of the more well-to-do families during the 1890's. Costing anywhere between $50 and $90, a bicycle was also within the reach of the average skilled workingman but usually beyond the means of the ordinary labourer.[18] The kinds of games a person played were not governed solely by his financial status. It was natural for Englishmen and Upper Canada College graduates to enjoy cricket, and for Scotsmen to prefer curling. Yet natural inclinations and cultural preferences were frequently overshadowed by the consideration of how much a person could afford to pay for his amusements.

People of all economic strata shared the pleasures of baseball, skating, and hockey. These activities were not associated with any particular class, but one of their distinctive characteristics was that they fell within the economic scope of the less affluent citizens. Because these sports were not necessarily dependent upon a regular baseball diamond and ice rink, and because they could be enjoyed without much expense, many individuals with little money organized their outdoor recreational life around them. Adults and youngsters alike commonly played baseball on vacant lots. During the winter months such lots were flooded and used by the same people for skating and hockey games. Primitive as these makeshift playgrounds were, the players had many hours of fun on them and derived considerable physical benefit from the exercise.

The frontier setting of Calgary encouraged citizens of every class to seek relaxation in various pastimes other than organized sport. Walking in the fresh air of the open countryside was a common activity during the warm season. With almost every home in the city no farther than a half mile from the country, older and younger people spent Sunday afternoons and many a weekday evening taking long walks along the banks of the Bow and Elbow rivers and strolling over the nearby hills. For the adults these rambles provided relief from the drudgery of work, and for the children they were opportunities to snare gophers and collect wild flowers. In those days there was still no door-to-door mail delivery, and the daily trips to the post office for mail gave people a chance to gossip with their friends and neighbours. On Saturday, the day when the stores and shops were always open from early morning until midnight, the auction sale was the scene of a large gathering of citizens, many of whom had come for no other reason than to witness the interesting spectacle dominated by the imposing figure of the auctioneer. Saturday night was the great night of the week, the night when the city really came to life. In the many bars and saloons, which were filled with city and country men drinking whiskey, occasional fights sometimes led to smashed heads, but rarely were guns brought into play. Hundreds of urban and rural shoppers, most of them dressed sharply for the occasion, made their way from store to store, running up bills that would be paid at the end of the month, and, in the case of the farmers, after the crops had been harvested. Although some people complained that there was nothing to do on Sundays but attend church, meeting the Sunday evening train was an exciting experience that many customarily enjoyed. After the evening church service, numerous churchgoers as well as other citizens headed for the railway station to wait for the arrival of the train. One young Montreal teenager, arriving on one of these trains and being unaccustomed to the ways of small-town life, asked her father, who had accompanied her, to explain the presence of the big crowd. When he replied that the people had come to meet him, she at first believed him, for he was a man of high social standing and had been in the city before, but she soon discovered that most of them had come merely to amuse themselves.

*   *   *   *   *

Anglo-Canadian Calgary at the beginning of the twentieth century was a society of contrasts. Life could be very informal in a youthful Prairie city where urban and rural living blended easily. In the churches and bars and on the platform of the railway station, as well in the patriotic groups and friendly societies, citizens of all kinds mingled good-naturedly, and class lines became vague. In some respects, however, the community had become stratified. Almost everyone worked hard and put in long hours, but there was a wide disparity between the standards of living of the well-to-do class and the ordinary wage earners. People of some style and moderate wealth imitated the fashionable ways of eastern Canada and Britain, and theirs was a world of fine homes, afternoon teas, servants, the more expensive sports, and glittering ballrooms. The low-paid workers and their families lived very simply, though not without hope of gradually improving themselves. With their basic food supplies coming from the cattle and poultry they kept and the vegetables they grew, many managed to save some money and better their position. If the various people of the city were not on the same economic and social footing, citizens of all walks of life had a tremendous admiration for the British Empire. When the Calgary contingent left for the South African War early in 1900, more than three thousand people, well over half of the city's population, gathered at the C.P.R. station to bid the men farewell.[19] Like other recently transplanted societies, Anglo-Canadian Calgary was strongly attached to the mother country.

Four

INTER-URBAN RIVALRY
IN PORT ARTHUR AND
FORT WILLIAM, 1870-1907

Elizabeth Arthur

In the years in which a transcontinental railway was being planned and then built, many new communities appeared, and, not infrequently, acrimonious battle raged between them. But the rivalry of Port Arthur and Fort William in the late nineteenth century may be regarded as unique in the history of Canadian cities. Primarily, this is due to a number of circumstances in combination: the nearness of the communities to each other; their mid-continental position which left them basically alien to both east and west; and the pre-railway history in which one of them had played a significant part. Parallels might be found in the history of Minnesota, but there the contest over the location of the territorial and then the state capital allowed "chauvinism, self-interest, and exploitation of real estate,"[1] as well as conspiracies real and imagined, to emerge on a larger stage, and the comic opera to be played to a larger audience. In examining the history of the Lakehead cities, one is confronted by incomplete accounts kept by those with local interests to serve who did not have to defend their positions in any national or provincial forum: records that have not usually been scrutinized by historians; records that are fragmentary, suggestive, perhaps misleading.

One might question whether the term "urban" can appropriately be applied to the warring hamlets of the 1870's, or indeed at any time up to the incorporation of the cities in 1907. But if an urban area can be defined as the residence of non-agrarian specialists,[2] Fort William qualified in 1815. It is not surprising to find that neither community followed any classic model of development through clearly defined stages from market town to financial centre, gradually extending its influence over a hinterland; indeed, it is questionable that that model was followed by any Canadian city.[3] But, unlike the cities of southern Ontario, the struggling towns of Port Arthur and Fort William were the creation of the railway; unlike the emerging cities of the West, their region had had a prior experience that could be called urban, and the hinterland they served – instead of being agricultural – was dominated by the mining and forest industries that, like the fur trade of an earlier era, created an urban organization and what has been called a rural proletariat.[4]

The fierce rivalry between Port Arthur and Fort William that dominated so many local decisions in the last quarter of the nineteenth century was based on the conviction that the building of the transcontinental railway would indeed create a city in northwestern Ontario, but that it would not create two. There was even a time when it appeared that the whole Lakehead area would be by-passed and Nipigon would become that one city.[5] From 1875 on, however, the choice had narrowed to two locations, only a few miles separated from each other, and the inhabitants of each location were equally convinced that the loser would forfeit any hope of separate urban status.

In the 1870's, the Mackenzie government's decision to utilize water transport as much as possible meant that railway building to the west would begin at a point several miles up the Kaministikwia River, a point called West Fort William to distinguish it from the location of the Hudson's Bay Company fort farther downstream. Such a plan left the future city of Port Arthur at least seven miles from the end of steel. Out of the controversies of that time came an atmosphere of suspicion and resentment, but the battles themselves were fought over issues that were already dead or dying by 1880. Once the Canadian Pacific Railway Syndicate was formed and the route for the transcontinental line was at last decided, there was no longer any question of only one of the communities being served by rail. Also, much of the animosity directed against Fort William's vision of itself as representing gentility in the wilderness arose from two rapidly changing circumstances: the very newness and crudeness of the hamlet then called Prince Arthur's Landing, which lacked any fur trade history, and the apparent triumph of a small minority living in Fort William that exercised some influence on government decisions.[6] The will of the majority, it appeared, was being flouted. With a few exceptions (which may themselves be traced to the legacy of suspicion from the 1870's), the battles of later years raged with all disputants assuming that a direct relationship existed between the numbers living in a particular community and the influence it could command.

It was this pride in numbers that often consumed the local press; varying estimates of the population were constantly being offered and disputed. Even now, all that can be firmly established is that Fort William rose from inconsiderable numbers as late as the mid-1880's to take the lead over Port Arthur for the first time in the census of 1901. The margin of Port Arthur's superiority in earlier decades remains in doubt because of discrepancies in the census records themselves and variations in the categories used in different enumerations. For example, the 1901 returns indicate Fort William's population as 3,997 in one reference[7] and 3,633 in another,[8] while the Port Arthur figure remains constant at 3,214; in addition, the 1891 returns did not isolate Fort William from the township of Neebing of which it was still a part,[9] although the 1881 returns had made the distinction.[10] Far more important than these considerations, however, is the question of rapid increase and decline in the years between enumerations. Port Arthur claimed that its population and the number of business houses within it both doubled in 1882.[11] The town reached its maximum nineteenth century population about 1886, and that maximum was variously estimated. The number 6,000 was frequently mentioned; a more conservative publication cited 3,500;[12] but decline had set in well before the next census which reported a population of 2,698.[13] Fort William, so far eclipsed in earlier decades, could by that time pride itself upon steady growth, and ridicule a neighbour which was even then attempting to extend its boundaries at the expense of other municipalities. The Fort William *Journal* observed:[14]

One would naturally suppose that an area large enough for a population of 6,000 would suffice for one of 2,500, especially when the tendency is in the direction of a still further decrease. Such, however, is not the view taken by our Port Arthur neighbours; as the population decreases, as the value of real estate grows less, their ideas in proportion expand, and they seek, by ways that are dark and tricks that are vain, to at least extend their limits if they cannot add to their numbers.

The building boom of the preceding decade had been based upon railway construction and the expectation of continued railway development, upon the needs of rapidly expanding mining interests (Port Arthur liked to describe itself as "The Silver Gateway"), and, to some extent, upon the construction of government buildings considered appropriate for a District Capital. It was clear that the tempo of the early 1880's could not be maintained, especially when world prices for silver fell, and Thunder Bay mining operations began to close down. But when Port Arthur residents compared the prosperity of one decade with the depression of the next, they tended to concentrate upon one dramatic event as the explanation of their difficulties: the decision of the CPR to make Fort William the divisional point, the terminus for lake steamers, and the site of the larger elevators.

Given the disparity in size between the two communities in the early 1880's, it was perhaps natural that Port Arthur residents should have expected a decision in their favour, but the records of the CPR offer many references to the potential value of Fort William, especially after

Hudson's Bay Company lands were acquired there. As early as 1883, when the transcontinental railway east of the Lakehead was still under construction, William Van Horne was reporting to the CPR Board of Directors on the need for developing facilities in both communities.[15] In the same year, the engineer Henry Perley was urging the federal government to give top priority to building a breakwater at Port Arthur, at an estimated cost of $240,000, in preference to dredging the Kaministikwia River (estimated cost $370,000).[16] Van Horne noted that the CPR would prefer both enterprises to go ahead, but that if only one was to be budgeted for, they wished the river development to be undertaken first. Perley disagreed, and it was his advice that was taken at the time. A year later, Van Horne was renewing his pressure on the government to have the river dredged, and, at the same time, making plans to locate the first one-million-bushel grain elevator near Old Fort William.[17] The citizens in the prospering town of Port Arthur in the mid-1880's did not yet perceive the real threat CPR plans might pose to them. There were irritations with the railway – its choice of a location for the passenger station, its failure to maintain its right of way to the satisfaction of the town council, its view of the amount of taxes due to the corporation[18] – but there was no way of knowing that the first two of these complaints would not receive attention from the company for twenty years,[19] and the third would erupt into a local dispute that assumed legendary proportions.

The tax dispute was set out in detail for the first time by the Port Arthur Council of 1887, but the climax was not reached for another two years. An interested Fort William observer saw the delay in terms of individuals and their political affiliations:[20] the mayor in 1887 was George McDonnell, a Conservative businessman who was not anxious to precipitate a quarrel; two years later, the office was held by Thomas Gorham, a young Liberal lawyer who had formerly worked in the CPR office in Winnipeg, and thought he saw advantages in confrontation and defiance. It might also be argued that the changing economic picture in Port Arthur during the two years made the money allegedly owing from the CPR more vital to the town council and also made the mood of both councillors and electors more truculent. In any case, the tax collector was ordered to seize an engine and several railway cars until the tax bill was paid.[21] William Whyte, the CPR superintendent in Winnipeg, rushed to the scene, and an agreement was promptly reached. Port Arthur received its taxes, but not the accrued interest it had claimed; the engine and cars were released. Even as these arrangements were being made, rumours were circulating that Fort William had already been chosen as the divisional point, and that the mayor of Port Arthur had offered to cancel the entire tax bill if that decision were reversed.[22] It seems clear that there was no direct cause-and-effect relationship between the seizure of CPR property and the decision to locate the divisional point in Fort William; even the Port Arthur press at last came to that conclusion, at the same time raising the old conspiracy theory of the 1870's to account for the action: it was the evil genius of the arch-conspirator, Donald Smith, working within both the Hudson's Bay Company and the CPR, that was seeking to destroy a promising town.[23] At the time, however, the rapid sequence of dramatic events led many to deduce that there were direct links between the action of a Port Arthur town council – most of the members of which did not contest the next municipal election – and a company decision disastrous for the town. Van Horne was widely quoted as prophesying that grass would grow in the streets of Port Arthur as punishment for its effrontery – although no evidence has been found that he ever made such a statement.

But faced with the very real possibility that grass would indeed grow in its streets, Port Arthur fought back in a number of ways. Its business-men continued their investments in shipping,[24] expanded their interest in timber lands as hope for pulp and paper development glimmered after 1892,[25] and tried to attract new industries to the town.[26] Above all, they renewed their efforts to get other railways built as alternatives to the CPR. Originally, the Thunder Bay Colonization Railway scheme of the early 1880's had been launched with the idea of supplementing the east-west transport line by building a railway to provide access to the mining districts far from the CPR. By the time construction had begun, however, under the new name of the Port Arthur, Duluth, and Western (the P.D.), the identification with the interests of one Canadian town and the idea of alternate transport to another developing city and Lake Superior port were clear indeed. The Port Arthur Council made it a condition of sup-port that all P.D. shops be constructed within three-quarters of a mile of the town's main street.[27] But even before construction began, the mining communities the railway was intended to serve were themselves vanishing. The P.D. was completed to a point just beyond the American border; it provided a convenient route to isolated mines and lumber camps, but its chaotic finances and its failure to reach Duluth gave evidence that it could not be Port Arthur's salvation. The desire for an alternate route to Winnipeg was as old as the idea of an Ontario and Rainy River Railway Company, and Port Arthur enthusiastically greeted the news that Mac-kenzie and Mann were buying up railway charters, using the eighteen miles of P.D. track from Port Arthur to Stanley, and then building west to join the line from Winnipeg.[28] A triumphant banquet at the Northern Hotel honoured Mackenzie and Mann;[29] a new railway would now make Port Arthur its headquarters, construct elevators and coal docks; the mil-lion dollars the CPR was reputed to have spent on Fort William in the early 1890's[30] would now be duplicated and even surpassed.

But the triumph of 1902 was far in the future as Port Arthur contem-plated the rapid development of its rival, and some immediate and decis-ive action was necessary or else the residents of the town would continue to leave to find work elsewhere. One rather obvious idea was to re-draw

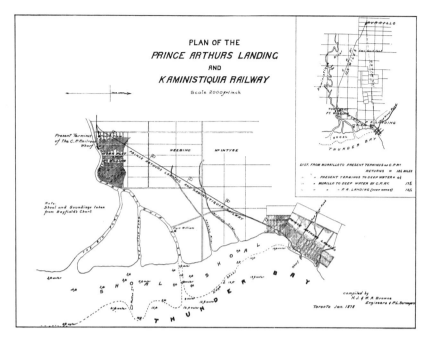

PLAN OF THE
PRINCE ARTHURS LANDING
AND
KAMINISTIQUIA RAILWAY
Scale 2000 ft/inch

Source: E. Arthur, *Thunder Bay District, 1821-92* (Champlain Society: University of Toronto Press, 1973), p. lxxxix.

Port Arthur's boundaries so that they would include all the land to the Kaministikwia River,[31] but to add the new CPR shops to the town – an early plan for amalgamation – would still have left important questions of urban transit unresolved. In any case, the plan did not succeed, merely leaving in Fort William increased resentment of amalgamation, and of Port Arthur machinations. As late as 1900, the Fort William Council refused to pay for a map of the town drawn by the Port Arthur surveyor, A.L. Russell.[32] Mr. Russell was present at the council meeting and apparently answered all questions satisfactorily, but three members of the council remained obdurate: although they could see no evidence of Port Arthur's schemes on this occasion, they remained convinced that there must be some nefarious design to rob Fort William of territory. The vote to accept the map tied 3-3, and the mayor had already voted in favour; the motion was accordingly lost. Of the three dissidents two were close relatives of the man who had led the Fort William forces in 1892, the first mayor of Fort William, John McKellar.

But it was not only the memory of an abortive annexation plan that rankled so long and left such suspicions. Port Arthur had a much more imaginative ploy: the construction of a street railway[33] linking the business and residential areas of a town already established with the new shops the CPR was building in what was then the township of Neebing. If the plan succeeded, there might never be a town of Fort William. Several miles of track with a fare of eight tickets for 25¢ applying in morning and evening rush hours[34] might provide such efficient transport for workers that they would continue to live in Port Arthur and patronize its businesses. Alarm in Fort William grew as it was perceived that enabling provincial legislation had a greater chance of being passed because a town was requesting permission to run an electric railway through a neighbouring township – a town, moreover, whose enterprising and progressive businessmen believed themselves to be riding the wave of the future.*

Fort William's response to such a challenge was immediate. First, an act for the incorporation of the town was introduced in the provincial legislature;[37] then, as an equal, the new town demanded certain regulations be imposed if the railway was to be permitted to run through Fort William. An Order-in-Council[38] stipulated that the railway had to be extended – a total of eight miles – to include West Fort William as well, and thus provide transportation for workers living there to the shops in East Fort William. The frequency of the service (so that it could not be used to the exclusive advantage of Port Arthur), the cost of the tickets, the regulations concerning the maintenance of the right-of-way through another town, and the options for joint management in the future were all written into the agreement. That Port Arthur was assured any profits arising from the enterprise in its early years was a rather grim joke in the 1890's, since the project, especially as specified in the Order-in-Council, proved very expensive, and threatened to push Port Arthur still further toward bankruptcy. Fort William, meanwhile, sought to oppose any increase in fares, and tried to make sure that every expensive requirement was meticulously carried out.[39] Eventually, the government of Ontario did intervene to the extent of sanctioning a fare increase without the consent of both councils,[40] but the Fort William Council Minutes afford plenty of evidence of the contemporary attitude there: this was a Port Arthur project, initiated with an intention hostile to Fort William, and it should be used to the full as a convenience by the people of Fort William, with Port Arthur paying pounds of flesh as a punishment for its earlier folly and assumptions of superiority. These same minutes suggest

---

*It is interesting to note that John F. Due's *The Intercity Electric Railway Industry in Canada*, which deals with so many lines built after 1887 (including lines incorporated but never built, like that from Fort Frances to Lake of the Woods[35]) makes no mention of the Port Arthur Electric Street Railway. The railway's name gave no indication that it was an inter-urban operation, and Professor Due, in 1966, through his omission, unconsciously was accepting Port Arthur's 1891 vision of itself as the city of Thunder Bay with Fort William as its bustling railway suburb.[36]

that the P.D. was also identified as an alien enterprise, while the inevitable questions of maintenance of lines, tax agreements, etc., involving the CPR were handled with far greater despatch and fewer recriminations.[41]

In an earlier decade, when Port Arthur was so evidently the leader, Fort William had begun to weave for itself a supportive mythology – of a community with links with the fur trading past, a name known on two continents, an elite made up of a very few people with specialized knowledge of a district to which settlers were beginning to pour. It was that vision that Port Arthur had found so infuriating in the years of its own rapid development. By the 1890's, the situation had altered so that Fort William relied less and less on its earlier support and appropriated to itself the picture Port Arthur had earlier presented – of rapid growth, efficient management, and a progressive citizenry. At the same time, Port Arthur, fighting for its life, came to cling to what might be called a city-on-the-hill myth. The unattractiveness of the flat lands and muskeg upon which Fort William was built became a recurring theme; one could measure the rising fortunes of Port Arthur dwellers in terms of the distance up the hill to their residences; the full effect of fine public buildings was more visible there; the views of the surrounding district were more spectacular. When the pamphlet *Port Arthur Illustrated* included photographs not only of Kakabeka Falls, presumably on neutral territory, but also of Fort William's Mount McKay and even its grain elevators, the Fort William *Journal* commented:[42] "Port Arthur is like a clipped and plucked rooster trying to steal a few peacock feathers."

Few of the buildings of which Port Arthur was proud were more than a decade old in the 1890's, but the townspeople referred repeatedly to the newness of their rival; what Neil Thompson has called "the atomistic quicksilver machinations of the frontier mind"[43] had already resulted in the conviction that Port Arthur was no longer a frontier. Possessing a number of churches, organized lodges, the first hospital in the area, and the first high school, the city on the hill could be portrayed as the centre of enlightenment and culture. Perhaps the clearest illustration of the growth of the myth and the extent to which it imposed itself upon Port Arthur citizens lies in the records of the town's Board of Health. Members of the Board based a number of their decisions upon two rather dubious assumptions: that diseases of all kinds were bred in the swamps of Fort William, and that it was possible to isolate Port Arthur from contagion. Consider, for example, the following 1892 resolutions:[44]

FIRST, *that the Electric Street Railway Car Conductors be instructed to carry no passenger or passengers who appear to them to be ailing from any contagious disease unless such person or persons hold a certificate bearing mandate from some medical practitioner known to them to the effect that they have no contagion. . . .*

SECOND, *that the Mother Superior be requested to take into the Hospital no patients outside of our Corporation except such as it is necessary to admit because of accident to them.*

More than a decade later, investigation by Professor T.A. Starkey of McGill did establish a long-suspected connection between typhoid epidemics and the Fort William water supply,[45] but the reports of provincial health officers throughout the 1890's made clear the peril in which both towns stood. Dr. Peter Bryce argued that it was inadequate medical examinations of immigrants at the port of entry that was the cause of serious problems.[46] Communicable diseases, he claimed, were only diagnosed when the transcontinental trains had reached northwestern Ontario; then the quarantine of all passengers on the train became essential; isolation tents had to be set up to cope with the crisis, and the possibility was ever present of contagion spreading to the residents of hill and flatland alike. This same report, based on a visit to Thunder Bay in the spring of 1894, made some comparisons between the two towns.[47]

Neither has a proper public water supply although Port Arthur is partially supplied by wells or by water carried in barrels. Some sewers exist in Port Arthur, and both towns have a number of good buildings. They are connected by an electric railroad. Both are in a fair sanitary condition although cleaning up had barely begun owing to the late spring. Diphtheria has been prevalent more or less in Port Arthur during the past year or so.

This last statement is borne out by the records, but the preoccupation of the Board of Health in the years 1892-94 seems to have been denial of reports of the prevalence of disease and the number of cases.[48] The obsession with numbers became as significant in this aspect of town rivalries as in the estimates of the population; in both cases one can perceive the desperate effort of a town to convince itself and others that it had a future. From the city-on-the-hill myth flowed the belief that Port Arthur possessed not only the more salubrious location but also the more enterprising inhabitants. Fort William was portrayed as the creature of a railway company, tamely submitting to monopoly – unimaginative, acquiescent, as lethargic as the water standing in its swamps.

To the outside observer at the time and to the student three-quarters of a century later the local myths have often appeared to be ludicrous; it has been the common features of Thunder Bay development that have seemed deserving of study from a distance in space or time. William Van Horne, in urging the development of a Thunder Bay harbour project including the river and the lake front of both towns, observed how similar the political and social attitudes of the neighbouring communities actually were.[49] At the same time, he was quick to exploit any advantage local friendships and enmities might provide.[50] By the late 1890's, the residents of both Port Arthur and Fort William found themselves confronted by a number of common problems. Fort William's earlier exultation over its rapid growth and Port Arthur's decline changed as its own future looked increasingly bleak. The direct result of the Dingley tariff in the United States was idle saw mills at Fort William,[51] but, as the Port Arthur press had pointed out in the 1891 federal election campaign, any victory for Liberal continentalist views and reduction of tariffs would destroy the CPR and Fort William with it.[52] However tolerant Fort William might appear to be to that railway, there was no indication that it was content to enter the twentieth century as a company town. Diversity of industry and, for that matter, diversity of transport routes were as attractive to its citizens as to those of Port Arthur. Both towns gave enthusiastic support to the idea of a second railway to Winnipeg;[53] both saw the CPR and Bell as unholy allies battling against public ownership of utilities.[54] Negotiations with American interests prepared to develop hydro-electric power at Kakebeka Falls taught the majority in both councils the advisability of some degree of co-operation,[55] although individual councillors remained suspicious.

As the optimism of the early twentieth century succeeded the depression of the 1890's, there was a new conviction that the two cities would in fact develop. If there were room for two, much of the bitterness of the preceding decade might be forgotten. In both towns, the individuals who had been involved in the controversies of the 1870's and 1880's were unlikely to be holding public office; rapid expansion brought to both towns floods of newcomers, many of them recent immigrants to Canada, for whom the rivalries of the past had little meaning. C.D. Howe's reaction to the divisions within the Lakehead area when he arrived in 1916[56] does not seem to have been markedly different from that of Van Horne thirty years before. But Howe's distaste for local "boomerism" indicates how persistent were the myths formulated to support two struggling communities in the late nineteenth century; remnants of them have survived, in prosperity and depression, in twentieth century Thunder Bay.

It has sometimes been argued that rivalry had a healthy effect in promoting the development of each city. But the quarrelling that became rancorous in critical times could hardly be regarded as a positive factor. There can be little doubt that it delayed important projects, or that it impaired the effectiveness of attempts to secure favourable legislation in Ottawa and Toronto.[57] The nearness and availability of a scapegoat frequently obscured common aims and common problems. There is some suggestion that the rivalry retarded the development of any sense of community, not only in the towns themselves, but also in their hinterland, and perhaps accentuated the pull of Winnipeg upon the area west of Thunder Bay. The shifting locations of mines and lumber camps and the scanty records of the attitudes of the "rural proletariat" makes this suggestion incapable of proof. But within the urban area at the beginning of the twentieth century there appeared increasingly a dissociation of the working class from the local myths formulated by the early residents.[58]

This dissociation in itself reveals much concerning the character of the myths and the men who created them. It was a very narrow group that preserved Fort William as a recognizable community in the 1870's and even that secured its incorporation as a town in 1892. It was a somewhat larger association of business and professional men who fought to maintain the town of Port Arthur. Whatever their numbers, these groups shared many values; they represented the elite of each community battling for the success of an enterprise in which they were and would remain the leaders. A study of the rivalry in Port Arthur and Fort William, then, provides further evidence of Professor Careless's observation that a more realistic look at western cities would dispel some of the myths concerning frontier democracy.[59] But what of that other tradition in both East and West, that geographical isolation brought with it certain pioneer virtues – an individualism and a sense of community that antedate urban development? A study of the nineteenth century Lakehead towns raises a question to which neither eastern or western urban studies have yet provided an answer: what characteristics of a society can be traced to the geographical isolation from the rest of the country of two competing urban areas?

Five

WILLIAM MACKENZIE, DONALD MANN, AND THE LARGER CANADA

T.D. Regehr

In 1904 Canadians everywhere were urged to vote for "Laurier and the Larger Canada."[1] Optimism and confidence in Canada's future abounded, but few Canadians committed themselves as strongly to the building of the larger Canada as railway promoters William Mackenzie and Donald Mann. Laurier and his government never fully endorsed the particular projects of these promoters, but the two certainly were not ignored either. The history of Mackenzie and Mann and their Canadian Northern Railway is an integral part of the attempt to build "the larger Canada." This chapter seeks to define the attitudes of these two men toward Canadian development, the nature of their own involvement, their relations with politicians, with their employees and contractors, and to suggest why their railway eventually failed.

The most notable characteristic of the two promoters was a virtually unbounded faith and confidence in the future growth, development and prosperity of Canada. To them Canada was a vast treasure-house of natural resources, and railways the indispensable prerequisite for the development and exploitation of those resources. According to Donald Mann the Canadian Northern was worth "what the soil will yield; what the mines will produce; the timber and the fisheries."[2] Every Canadian Northern official was prepared at a moment's notice to quote voluminous statistics to demonstrate the worth of those resources, and hence of their railway.

Both Mackenzie and Mann had grown up in the backwoods of Ontario and were greatly impressed by the railways which opened up their home districts. Both took contracts on local railway construction projects, and in the 1880's went west to work for the CPR. They were so impressed with the riches of the country, and particularly the fertility of the northern prairies, that in 1896 they began their own career as railway promoters and builders. Their first road was a small Manitoba branch line, but within twenty years they expanded that line into a ten-thousand-mile transcontinental railway system.

Associates of Mackenzie and Mann said they were completely saturated with the spirit of the frontier.[3] Their attitude to frontier development was very clearly expressed in a curious publication called the Canadian Northern Encyclopedia. This seven-volume encyclopedia was essentially a handbook for Canadian Northern officials and lobbyists.[4] Much of it was written by William H. Moore, an old-fashioned Liberal who was the Canadian Northern's most notorious lobbyist and the colourful subject of many a tale of wondrous events and schemes hatched in smoke-filled rooms and private railway cars.

Moore began his railway career on a moonstruck scheme to build a railway from Sudbury to James Bay. Rather typically he believed the James Bay Railway would open up one hundred million acres of choice agricultural land in the northern clay belt. The mining and lumbering prospects of the region were, of course, even more promising.[5] Moore's attitude, if not always his detailed calculations and predictions, was typical of the frontier spirit that motivated Mackenzie and Mann and many others building the larger Canada.

Mackenzie and Mann enjoyed building railways, and they very firmly believed their railways would prove successful.[6] And, contrary to false or malicious accusations by some politicians, two royal commissioners, and a number of historians, they committed their own resources to the success of those railways.[7] Detailed Canadian Northern memoranda and legal files, government audited accountants' reports, and public statements in the House of Commons by Prime Minister Borden and Finance Minister White all attested to the very large investments made by the two promoters.[8]

They did not, it is true, invest their cash directly in the Canadian Northern Railway. Instead, they chose to operate through a promotional, contracting, and financing corporation called Mackenzie, Mann and Company Limited. The entire personal credit and cash resources of the two promoters, their diverse properties, and their promotional and financial talents were placed at the disposal of this corporation, which in turn made them available to the Canadian Northern Railway. In return Mackenzie and Mann, or Mackenzie, Mann and Company Limited received virtually the entire common stock for the Canadian Northern Railway. That stock, while carrying a high par value, was really worthless unless the railway itself succeeded.[9]

When asked about the relations between the Canadian Northern and Mackenzie, Mann and Company Limited, Canadian Northern officials replied without hesitation that "the Canadian Northern got the better of it all the time."[10] They had convincing legal files and accountants' statements to support that claim. Far from enriching themselves at the expense of the railway company, Mackenzie and Mann impoverished themselves in a desperate attempt to bring the railway successfully through the difficult war years. When the Canadian Northern was nationalized in 1918 its promoters were, for all practical intents and purposes, bankrupt. Their chief creditor, the Canadian Bank of Commerce, did not actually throw them out on the street, but it left very little that these two men could leave to their heirs.[11]

Private resources have rarely been sufficient to see major Canadian developmental projects through to completion. Canadian economic development from the earliest days has been the product of joint participation by governments and private interests.[12] Monopoly protected fur-trading companies of the early days, tariffs protected industries under the National Policy, and numerous subsidized transportation ventures all reflect this partnership between governments and businessmen. Even the best of business projects initiated in the most optimistic of times seemed to falter without some government aid.

Canadian governments have, from time to time, undertaken desirable development projects themselves, but public ownership and operation of large undertakings had not, prior to 1900, been a success in Canada. Patronage, political pressures, and simply a lack of business acumen and experience combined to make government-owned-and-operated projects less than profitable. At least that was the opinion widely held by Canadian businessmen, politicians, voters, and taxpayers alike. Laurier explained it this way to one advocate of public ownership:

The government's operation of railways in this country has not been successful and, I very much fear, cannot be made successful, except under different conditions which have not yet arisen. There is at present a supreme consideration, superior to all others, against the acquisition by the Government of Canadian railways; those railways would have to compete with railways managed by keen and ambitious men whose chief preoccupation is to take traffic away from their rivals, and they are always planning and thinking over that object. For the Government to own railways of this country and to have to enter into competition with American railways would mean one thing, and that disaster, which would certainly follow in the end.[13]

The proper course of action, Laurier believed and most businessmen heartily agreed, was for the government to support and assist projects which were of general benefit to the country, but not to manage or operate such projects.

The particular forms in which Canadian governments have assisted worthy business ventures have varied. Railways have received land and cash subsidies, tax or tariff exemptions, monopoly provisions and bond guarantees. Some companies like the CPR received help in all these forms. Mackenzie and Mann relied almost entirely on bond guarantees. There were excellent reasons for this. The monopoly provisions, tax and tariff concessions, and land grants given the CPR were often condemned because it was thought they retarded settlement and economic development. Cash subsidies were politically unpopular and for some governments quite impossible. The bond guarantee, however, proved curiously seductive in times of general optimism.

A bond guarantee was simply an undertaking by the government to pay specified fixed charges if the railway could not do so. The government became a co-signer for loans obtained by the railway from the public. Such a guarantee instantaneously transformed a highly speculative bond issue which was only as good as the earning power of the railway which had issued it, into a very safe government-backed security.[14] Guaranteed bonds could be placed easily in the London market at low discounts and interest rates, thus significantly reducing capital costs. The consequent savings could then be passed on to the users of the railway in the form of lower freight rates. All of this need never cost the government or anyone else a single cent.[15] It only required a good measure of faith in the future of the country and one of its development railways to predict that a bond guarantee would provide, without any additional costs, a host of benefits. The optimistic builders of the larger Canada had found an easy way of getting something for nothing. Their opponents, moreover, could be castigated for being not only pessimistic, but downright unpatriotic.[16]

Government assistance in the form of bond guarantees for the Canadian Northern Railway became absolutely irresistible when Mackenzie and Mann agreed not only to build the needed lines and cut rates, but also to allow governments specifically to regulate and control the rates they charged.[17] This policy was strongly criticized by many in the business community, particularly because government control over Canadian Northern rates provided the government with indirect controls over the rates of their competitors as well. The CPR, for example, found that it had to match Canadian Northern rates to remain competitive on the prairies. For a time the CPR did use two rates – one for centres where Canadian Northern competition existed and another higher rate where the CPR had a monopoly. This simply led to a crazy agitation for Canadian Northern extensions to every CPR whistle stop, and soon the lower rate levels set by the Canadian Northern prevailed across the prairies.[18]

Acceptance of government control over Canadian Northern freight rates was regarded as a significant change in the relations between government and businessmen. It was not, however, a very daring or dangerous concession. Bond guarantees were different from subsidies and grants. They in effect committed the government to the success of the assisted railway. If the railway failed, the government would have to pay the guarantees which the voters had been told would cost nothing. It would therefore be well nigh suicidal for any government to force rates down to unprofitable levels on any assisted railways. This clearly was more than an ordinary partnership between businessmen and politicians, with limited liabilities on both sides. It was a marriage which committed the government to maintain the railway's economic health in good times or in bad. Few well informed businessmen believed that the controls accepted by Mackenzie and Mann would prove ruinous. They would merely prevent the railway from earning unreasonably large profits. A Grand Trunk Pacific official expressed the mood of the business community when he said the government controls would prevent the Canadian Northern from earning "very much in the way of a surplus above fixed charges which would be applicable for dividend purposes."[19] Mackenzie and Mann were evidently willing to accept what the politicians might regard as reasonable operating returns. They wanted to build a great railway system which they believed would be a great success if it earned reasonable and consistent operating profits. The bond guarantees were their insurance that rates would be set at levels ensuring such profits.

For a number of reasons, Mackenzie and Mann were the logical partners of the Laurier administration in building the Larger Canada. Their optimism, their willingness to invest in projects which would develop the country's resources, their belief that governments should assist but not operate worthy projects, and their willingness to accept unusual governmental controls over the rates they charged on the Canadian Northern Railway should have collectively qualified them for the task. But politics and personalities led the Laurier government to favour the Grand Trunk Railway when plans were formulated in 1903 for the construction of a second Canadian transcontinental railway.[20]

The personality and manner of the Canadian Northern promoters, and particularly of William Mackenzie, account in part for their difficulties with Sir Wilfrid Laurier. These men were, quite simply, not gentlemen. Mackenzie was a humourless but domineering character with an almost unbounded energy, tenacity, and enthusiasm. He loved to intimidate people, and attempted it whenever he could.[21] Often he was not overly careful about the ways and means he adopted to achieve his objectives, and those who felt aggrieved or cheated by his actions were not likely to take the matter lightly. His career is strewn with legally proper but morally dubious transactions, and it is clear that he frequently irritated Laurier by his unscrupulous and unorthodox activities.

The most persistent criticism was that the Canadian Northern promoters bargained unethically, resorting to trickery, bribery and corruption when it suited their purpose. Numerous complaints were made against the two, although many of these were were never documented by the complainants and cannot now be documented on the basis of the evidence available. Some of those who did business with the Canadian Northern nevertheless did leave records which suggest sharp, perhaps unethical, but legally proper practices.

Martin Nordegg, a coal-mining promoter and one-time partner of Mackenzie and Mann, complained that when he wanted to finalize his agreement he was referred from one party to the next. An understanding with Mackenzie drew objections and demands for further concessions from Donald Mann. Once Mann was appeased, Zebulon Lash, one of Canada's foremost corporation lawyers and the Canadian Northern's chief solicitor, found further fault with the agreement. Then, in the final wording of the agreement, the rights and privileges of Mackenzie and Mann were very carefully and specifically spelled out, but some of Nordegg's rights and privileges were left out, or stated so ambiguously that they had to be referred to the courts later.[22]

Nordegg was certainly not alone in making complaints of this nature. Officials of the Department of Railways and Canals, Members of Parliament, sub-contractors, and other businessmen all complained about sharp practices of this kind. The government-appointed commissioners of the National Transcontinental Railway became very well acquainted with the trickery of the Canadian Northern when they negotiated a running-rights agreement. The National Transcontinental lacked both a Winnipeg station and suitable trackage into the city. The Canadian Northern had good facilities but wanted a bond guarantee to expand these further. The guarantee was eventually granted, subject to the signing of an agreement whereby the National Transcontinental would be allowed trackage and the use of the new Canadian Northern-owned Union Station. The agreement was duly signed, and the National Transcontinental, which ended at Winnipeg, was allowed to bring all its traffic from the east to the new station. The agreement, however, neglected to provide for the handling of traffic from the National Transcontinental's western associate system, the Grand Trunk Pacific Railway. The Canadian Northern in due course refused east-bound Grand Trunk Pacific traffic if it was destined for the National Transcontinental. This left the National Transcontinental with virtually no eastbound traffic. Protests, complaints, and harsh words by the politicians achieved nothing. The agreement had been signed, leaving out an elementary provision, and the Canadian Northern refused to make any accommodations or changes. The National Transcontinental eventually had to build its own line into Winnipeg. It had already spent substantial sums on construction of this line when it was discovered that some of the land to be crossed by the new line was owned by another Mackenzie-and-Mann-controlled company. A bill of $2,500,000.00 was sent to the National Transcontinental as soon as its line crossed that land. The government-guaranteed bonds to aid the construction of a station in Winnipeg had, of course, been sold.[23]

A somewhat different problem confronted the federal government when, as a result of improper construction procedures in the Fraser valley, huge rock slides obstructed the salmon run. The Fisheries Department tried unsuccessfully to have the Canadian Northern remove the debris. Eventually the Department decided to do the necessary work but to bill the offending railway company. Trying to collect for departmental expenditures subsequently proved extremely difficult. Who should pay – the parent Canadian Northern Railway? the local subsidiary Canadian Northern Pacific Railway? the contracting firm of Mackenzie, Mann and Company Limited? the sub-contractors? the surveyors? or the federal Department of Railways and Canals which had approved the surveys? Ottawa bureaucrats almost went dizzy trying to deliver the bill, but with the help of Canadian Northern counsel they eventually got it across the street to the Department of Railways and Canals. That Department, in the end, deducted the amount from a federal subsidy payment due the Canadian Northern Railway.[24]

The fact that Mackenzie and Mann could appear in such a variety of corporate manifestations worried and irritated the government officials concerned with the Fraser Valley clean-up, as it irritated many others. The Canadian Northern Railway system was a menagerie of some forty different companies, a state of affairs useful in deception or delay when it suited the promoters. In part the federal Railway Act was to blame for this state of affairs. It provided that a railway company should only own assets or interest directly related to the operation of the railway. Thus if promoters thought it in their interest to own other assets, a new company was incorporated. Similarly a company with purely local interests, or a railway company hoping to obtain a provincial subsidy or bond guarantee, was almost always incorporated locally, but amalgamated with the parent company as soon as the local subsidy was collected. Sometimes additional federal subsidies or guarantees for the same mileage were then sought. The existence of separate companies was acknowledged as necessary by all concerned, but this often lead to delay, confusion, and on occasion, outright deception.

It is clear that the promoters of the Canadian Northern Railway not only resorted to rather dubious practices, but that they really enjoyed doing so. It was a situation which suited their temperament. It did not suit Sir Wilfrid Laurier and many of the other politicians and businessmen who did business with the brash and uncouth entrepreneurs from the Ontario backwoods. A widespread hostility to Canadian Northern methods accounts in part for the federal decision to use the National Transcontinental and Grand Trunk Pacific Railways as the prime instrument of federal railway policies. Unfortunately the Grand Trunk Pacific bluntly and categorically refused to match Canadian Northern concessions for lower freight rates and more branch lines in western Canada. The Canadian Northern therefore continued to receive rather grudging federal support.[25]

Laurier's decision to deal with the Grand Trunk in 1903 cast the Canadian Northern Railway in the role of a latter-day "happy hooker" of Canadian railway politics. Despite occasional spats, the CPR and the federal Conservative party were really very close. The 1903 contract tied the Grand Trunk equally closely to the Liberal party. Both parties did have important affairs with the Canadian Northern, but these were usually convenient arrangements to meet specific failings of the other two transcontinentals. Laurier expressed the true state of affairs when he wrote, "I am certainly not in love myself with Messrs. Mackenzie and Mann, but that is altogether beyond the question. The only thing in which I am interested is to have the railway built."[26] The fact was that Mackenzie and Mann were often the only ones who would build the desired developmental railways and operate them at low government-controlled rates. Liberals and Conservatives regularly came to them, usually with propositions already rejected by the CPR and the Grand Trunk.

Mackenzie and Mann had a simple political policy. They supported those who helped them, irrespective of partisan politics. They first did business with the Liberals of Manitoba, but when Premier Greenway abandoned them and started a forlorn courtship of the Northern Pacific, the Canadian Northern promoters did not find it hard to consummate a momentous agreement with the government of Rodmond Roblin, an erstwhile Liberal who had disagreed with Greenway and became Conservative Premier of Manitoba in 1900. This did not, however, disrupt their amicable relations with Clifford Sifton, nor did it preclude successful agreements with other Liberal premiers in Saskatchewan, Alberta, Nova Scotia, Ontario, and Quebec.[27] Officially, William Mackenzie was a Conservative, and Donald Mann a member of the Liberal party, but their railway was simply Canadian. And wherever politicians talked of building the Larger Canada, Mackenzie and Mann offered their services.

It was often alleged that the franchises and guarantees earned by the Canadian Northern were the result of bribery and political corruption. There is strong evidence that Mackenzie had been guilty of such practices in connection with his Toronto Street Railways scheme, but the surviving records relating to the Canadian Northern offer no convincing evidence of such wrong-doing. There were certainly campaign contributions to favoured candidates, but these were usually personal contributions from one of the promoters. Both major political parties frequently complained about lack of strong financial support from the Canadian Northern. Some of the private contributions may have been corrupt, and such corruption would not normally be recorded for posterity in the records of the company or in the private papers of the politicians. Specific charges of corruption were not successfully proved in the courts and a careful examination of all the available evidence very strongly suggests that the Canadian Northern franchises and guarantees were granted because of the needed developmental rail services offered, not merely because of bribery and corruption.[28]

Patronage also played only a minor role. Successful politicians and their friends and relatives were sometimes employed or received contracts, but they generally found that they had to give fair service for whatever salaries and bonuses they earned. Once they were employed, moreover, they, like all other Canadian Northern employees, were forbidden further political activity. It took D.B. Hanna, the railway's senior operating officer, some time to educate Manitoba politicians Rodmond Roblin and Robert Rogers, but eventually even those gentlemen learned that Canadian Northern employees were not and should not become a part of the provincial Conservative political machine.[29] For a time the Manitobans were grievously affronted, and threatened to sever all connection with the railway, but eventually they realized that the Canadian Northern was still worthy of their bond guarantees. Many years later, when Hanna was offered the presidency of the nationalized Canadian Northern Railway, he made his acceptance conditional on the continuance of the rule that employees stay out of active politics.[30] Canadian Northern employees were not coerced to vote as senior officers of the company saw fit. It could hardly be otherwise when good friends and bitter enemies of the company could be found in both political parties.

The influence and power of the Canadian Northern Railway was based primarily on the willingness and ability to build and operate railways. The voters and politicians of that time had a mad passion for railways, more railways, and yet more railways.[31] Political careers blossomed or were blighted as railway construction proceeded or was halted in various constituencies. Prairie governments in particular were always urging more construction and voting far more guarantees than even the most ambitious promoters could accommodate. Announcement of a new project in his constituency could save almost any government candidate. The announcement of enormous new railway projects just before an election usually assured the government of an overwhelming victory, no matter how bereft that government might be of ideas and talent elsewhere. The very strong and often-denounced Canadian Northern lobby in Ottawa and the provincial capitals did its best work when it simply explained the value, political and otherwise, of Canadian Northern lines, constructed and proposed, in a particular election. Several examples illustrate what happened:

CASE ONE   In 1899 T.A. Burrows, Clifford Sifton's brother-in-law and the Liberal M.L.A. for Dauphin, found himself in serious political difficulty. The election in his constituency was deferred, but in the provincial election the Liberals had gone down to a decisive defeat. The main election issue was railways. Burrow's chances of re-election were therefore very poor. After some prompting from Clifford Sifton, Mackenzie decided the Dauphin seat should be saved for the Liberals. Consequently, a week before the election, a construction train moved into Dauphin. Work was begun on an important western extension. The local papers and the *Manitoba Free Press* gave the matter very extensive coverage. Burrows thus convinced his constituents that he could still get them the railways they wanted, and was re-elected with an increased majority. This was all achieved without violating Hanna's edict against active political participation by Canadian Northern employees, and without large campaign contributions.[32]

CASE TWO   Thomas O. Davis, the ubiquitous Liberal Member of Parliament for Prince Albert, regularly demanded Canadian Northern overtures toward a Prince Albert mainline prior to elections. When, indeed, the Canadian Northern decided to run its main line well to the south of Prince Albert, the promoters satisfied Davis by steadfastly referring to the Prince Albert line as a mainline, and Davis saw to it that this line received suitable federal guarantees as a mainline. With such devotion to the development of his constituency Davis was never defeated, and eventually went on to his reward in the Canadian Senate.[33]

CASE THREE   The provincial elections of 1909 and 1910 in Saskatchewan, Alberta, and British Columbia carried railway branch-line politicking to ridiculous lengths. In Saskatchewan, detailed maps were circulated which looked as if each government member had simply drawn in all the branch lines he felt his constituency needed or wanted. Constituencies foolish enough to return an Opposition member might, of course, endanger the desired railway construction.[34] The government, in each of these elections, was returned with an overwhelming majority.

CASE FOUR   In British Columbia an undefined commitment to build a new Canadian Northern line to the Pacific made everyone anxious to vote for government candidates, lest they offend and lose a prospective branch line or see the main line routed through a more deserving constituency. In the face of such tactics no opposition candidate could survive unless his constituency already had all the railways it needed, or he promised to outdo the government's already very extensive railway schemes.[35]

In light of these examples, it would be a mistake to conclude that Mackenzie and Mann seriously contorted their railway or construction programs to meet particular political requirements. The Canadian Northern's Chief Engineer, M.H. McLeod, was a thorough professional who ran surveys and had railways built where they best fitted into the larger systems and provided the most traffic. Even Davis's importunities, and serious doubts by Mackenzie and Mann, could not dissuade him from running the main line well south of Prince Albert,[36] and the most determined political representations failed to save Battleford when McLeod decided it would be much cheaper and better to build along the northern shore of the North Saskatchewan River. The best the Canadian Northern could offer in that case was to put the bridge where the Battleford residents wanted it, if the provincial or federal governments would provide a special subsidy to cover the additional costs.[37]

That is not to say that the railways built in accordance with McLeod's surveys and plans did not help local politicians. Often the most helpful gestures were small in scale. A well timed announcement, a subtle threat or a little sign of new activity, or a simple but well publicized greeting or discussion between the local candidate and the railway promoter could prove of great political value. Rural voters knew very well that even slight changes in the promoters' priorities could have very serious consequences in isolated communities. A politician with access to the railway builders was a great asset to most constituencies. Mackenzie and Mann's power was enormous for the simple reason that they actually built more prairie branch lines than anyone else after 1900. And they built these lines because they believed in the future greatness of the country.

Mackenzie and Mann very successfully imparted their belief in the Canadian Northern Railway and their vision of future greatness to associates and employees. Many Canadian Northern employees, particularly in the early years, identified strongly with the company and took great pride in every additional item of traffic added, in every construction or operating economy devised, and in every additional mile of track built.[38] The challenge of participating in a great venture, and of competing with and beating the mighty CPR on the prairies excited Canadian Northern employees as much as it excited the promoters.

In general, Mackenzie and Mann had little trouble with their employees. The wages and bonuses paid on the Canadian Northern were among the best on the continent.[39] Certainly Mackenzie and Mann had no sympathy for adversary or class-conflict theories propounded by the leaders of the labour unions. Their concepts of employer-employee relations were much more authoritarian and paternalistic. Employers and employees were partners in a great economic undertaking. They must both work to ensure its success. A good employee must come to identify himself with the company, not with a union bent on class warfare with management. Such an employee certainly deserved a good salary. Collective bargaining, however, was entirely unacceptable, as the one really serious Canadian Northern strike of 1902 clearly demonstrated. D.B. Hanna, the general manager, was very willing to discuss any and all grievances with workers' committees or delegations, but every employee's first loyalty must be to the company and to its success. This, in Hanna's opinion, was not possible if employees committed themselves to collective action dictated by international or national union leaders who might know little or nothing about the policies and problems of the company.[40]

In the generally prosperous years before the Great War a good worker on the Canadian Northern could therefore expect top wages and good job security. The company looked after its employees well enough that those employees sent a petition to the Prime Minister in 1917 opposing nationalization of the railway and strongly endorsing the old management.[41] They feared government patronage, and preferred the old system where the lazy, the incompetent, and the dishonest were dispatched without ceremony, but where good employees were valued and rewarded.

The most serious exploitation of labour often occurred in the construction camps and usually involved immigrant workers. In the case of the Canadian Northern many of the abuses were perpetrated by subcontractors. Mackenzie, Mann and Company Limited often did only the track-laying themselves, and tracklayers were always the construction workers closest to the amenities of civilizations and contact with the outside world. At times working conditions in the construction camps of Mackenzie, Mann and Company Limited were very difficult. Edmund Bradwin's *Bunkhouse Man* could certainly be found working for the Canadian Northern,[42] but the spirit and attitude in the construction camps was often quite different than that depicted by Bradwin. Even in the Canadian Northern construction camps there was a strong identification with the great project, considerable pride in every achievement, and even in many of the hardships endured. The peculiar Canadian mentality which takes pride in braving and surviving a bitter prairie blizzard, or of an old-fashioned threshing crew breaking some new record, is evident in the recollections of many former Canadian Northern employees. This attitude was very much encouraged by the promoters.[43] Sizable bonuses were given without request when workers completed an important project, set some new record, or marked a particular achievement. Good workers suffering an accident or disaster were assisted in ways not legally required, and, as a result, it was possible for a foreman like Rod Mackenzie to get almost anything out of his men.[44]

Serious difficulties and nasty confrontations between contractors and construction workers did occur during the war years. The financial difficulties of the railway company led to delays in paying the workers and in providing needed facilities. The resulting disorders earned all the railways a bad reputation, but this was a departure, under distressed conditions, from the generally amicable Canadian Northern employment policy. As former workers and contractors themselves, Mackenzie and Mann, and indeed all senior management in the early days, maintained fairly close contact with many of their workers. They reportedly knew, for example, which cook in the camps prepared the best meals, having themselves eaten with the men in many of the camps.[45] Here the fact that they were not "gentlemen" often stood them in good stead.

Mackenzie and Mann always expected that many of the construction workers would take up homesteads alongside Canadian Northern lines. On occasion they also tried to give work to local homesteaders who were in need of some hard cash to buy necessary implements. All such labourers had to be kept reasonably satisfied if they were to become settlers who would generate traffic for the Canadian Northern Railway.[46]

All this, of course, did not mean that the promoters could not be very harsh when occasion demanded it. Troublemakers were given short shrift, sometimes unfairly, and firings were common.[47] But the recorded recollections of those who served for any length of time nevertheless reflect a positive identification with the project.

Mackenzie and Mann's relations with their sub-contractors were generally as positive as those with their employees. It was expected that contractors would make a reasonable profit, and several became moderately wealthy working for the Canadian Northern. Yet to earn that profit all the terms of the contract had to be fulfilled, and Mackenzie and Mann were expert at detecting shortcomings. Few contractors managed to get shoddy work, improper measurements, and other shortcomings past the eagle eyes and sharp pencils of Mackenzie, Mann and Company Limited inspectors.[48] If, for reasons beyond his control, a subcontractor found he could not meet his commitments, Mackenzie and Mann, recalling a similar unfortunate experience of their own, would invariably pay sufficient additional amounts to allow the embarrassed contractor to break even on the operation. Mackenzie and Mann proudly maintained that no honest and competent contractor ever lost money on a Canadian Northern contract.[49] Conversely, no dishonest or incompetent contractor made large profits.

When Mackenzie and Mann left the service of the CPR in the early 1890's, Thomas Shaughnessy provided them with a letter of reference which is the essence of what they regarded as good contracting. "I take pleasure in saying to you that the very large amount of work which you performed under contracts with this Company was in every instance completed to the satisfaction of the Company and without quibbling when the time came for final settlement."[50] Nothing less was expected of the sub-contractors and contractors who built the Canadian Northern Railway.

All this suggests that the Canadian Northern Railway was a well planned and honestly, if perhaps sharply administered, project. Why then did it fail? The answer is essentially twofold: transcontinental expansion and financial stringencies after 1912.

Mackenzie and Mann believed the federal railway policy forced them to expand to the Pacific and Atlantic Oceans when in fact there was not sufficient traffic, at least not immediately, to support three transcontinental systems. As long as the Grand Trunk was only an eastern system and the Canadian Northern a prairie system, each could benefit from interchanges of traffic. Once the Grand Trunk Pacific was built, the Canadian Northern would be entirely dependent on hostile competitors for all eastern-Canadian connections. Unless it developed its own eastern system, the Canadian Northern would find itself "bottled up" in the West. Transcontinental expansion became to Mackenzie and Mann a matter of self-preservation, and the basic decision to expand was made in 1904.[51]

Lack of suitable government assistance and the incomplete state of the rival Grand Trunk Pacific led to delays, but in 1910 and 1911 contracts were signed to complete the British Columbia and Ontario sections.

It was clear to all concerned that the British Columbia, Ontario, and Quebec mileage of the Canadian Northern would not be profitable, at least not initially.[52] Only very substantial future development could possibly justify this construction. The prairie system, however, was very profitable, and Mackenzie and Mann fully mortgaged and committed that prairie system to the debts and obligations of the less promising projects. The Ontario, Quebec, and British Columbia and Nova Scotia mileage was kept under separate corporate identity, but the Canadian Northern Railway agreed to guarantee the bonds of the new mileage.[53] Perhaps if the Canadian Northern had remained a prairie system, it could have survived. G.R. Stevens was quite right when he wrote, "To an extraordinary extent Mackenzie and Mann lacked any sense of self-preservation in their financial affairs. They never adopted simple legal devises to protect their personal fortunes or the revenues of their prosperous properties against the inroads of their speculative ventures. It was all Canadian Northern money as far as they were concerned."[54] Heavy losses in British Columbia, Ontario and Montreal eventually swallowed up all the profits of the Canadian Northern and the entire personal fortunes of the two promoters.

Mackenzie and Mann knew that only future development could make their eastern and Pacific projects profitable. They expected initial losses, but hoped their excellent credit arrangements in London and the profits from the prairie system would see them safely through the difficulties. Instead the financial stringency that began in 1912 and intensified by the outbreak of war destroyed all their credit arrangements, while sharply escalating costs and fixed freight rates drastically reduced profits on the prairie system. Canadian Northern officials were virtually unanimous in blaming the war for their misfortunes. In 1914 the Canadian Northern found itself in much the same situation as had confronted the CPR in 1884. Instead of the fortuitous Riel Rebellion and massive new assistance from a grateful government,[55] however, the Canadian Northern found its credit arrangements destroyed, its costs sharply increased, and a government grown weary of requests for further help. The bond guarantees also committed the Canadian Northern Railway to carry a good deal of military traffic free for the government.[56] Mackenzie and Mann simply could not raise the money needed to complete the expensive transcontinental mileage, and they could not increase rates even to compensate for increased prairie operating costs. Prairie politicians were too well aware of the fact that increased rates were requested primarily to meet the heavy losses elsewhere and refused to authorize the increases which Mackenzie and Mann thought they would grant in order to avoid defaults on guaranteed bonds.[57]

Thus the great project was wrecked, but even in defeat the Canadian Northern officers steadfastly maintained their faith in the future of the country and in the importance of the railways in realizing that future. D.B. Hanna repeated the Mackenzie and Mann philosophy when, as president of the nationalized railway, he wrote, "the importance of impressing upon the people of Canada the true value from a national standpoint and the almost unlimited potentialities of the road cannot be overstated. Canada must acquire a new angle of vision; the measure of our future depends on it. . . . Great things can be accomplished if the Dominion is disposed to regard railroading in the same light as the private railroaders have done in the past, as a risk that must be taken to assure a big future."[58]

Six

RAILWAYS AND ALBERTA'S COAL PROBLEM, 1880-1960

A.A. den Otter

Measured in terms of its potential, Alberta's coal industry never achieved full production. While many factors prevented a constant, steady flow of coal from Alberta's collieries, one of the chief obstacles was the high cost of transportation and the peculiar connection of railways with the mining industry. Coal mining in Alberta was closely tied to the railways, for although the railways seldom invested directly in western mines, they sparked interest in coal development and became the chief consumers and sole conveyors of this natural resource. Yet ironically, the transportation problem proved to be the greatest barrier to stable operations because the mining corporations, unable to pay the high freight rates to Ontario, could not break out of the limited, regional market. Since the federal government refused to subsidize fully the movement of coal to central Canada, western desires for a national fuel policy, that is, self-sufficiency in coal, were not realized. Consequently, when the railways converted to diesel locomotives, the coal-mining industry, having no immediate alternate market, nearly collapsed.

To understand the close relationship between Alberta's coal mines and railways, it is necessary first to look at the development of coal mining in the Northwest Territories. As early as the 1870's the Geological Survey of Canada, stimulated by the plans for a transcontinental railway, conducted extensive explorations in the foothills and mountain areas west of Edmonton, a region thought to be in the path of the proposed route.[1] Although the surveyors uncovered "practically unlimited" supplies of coal, exploitation of the rich reserves had to wait thirty years, for in the spring of 1881 the omnipotent railway builders decided to route the railway across the southern plains instead of along the North Saskatchewan. Consequently, the attention of government prospectors like George M. Dawson shifted to the southern region. In 1881 Dawson enthusiastically reported that gigantic coal seams lay buried beneath most of southern Alberta, assuring a bountiful fuel supply for railways and settlers.[2]

Although the federal government had uncovered the coal reserves, the first large-scale development of this resource was carried out by a private promoter, Sir Alexander T. Galt, one of the Fathers of Confederation. Armed with the optimistic report of his own engineer and that of Dawson, Galt convinced a number of London financiers to form the North Western Coal and Navigation Company to build and operate Alberta's first coal mine near present-day Lethbridge, as well as a railway from the colliery to the Canadian Pacific main line at Dunmore. The project, completed in 1885, was only moderately successful, because the population of the Northwest did not grow as quickly as anticipated. Dr. Alfred Selwyn, of the Geological Survey, pointed out that "The population of the country is so scattered at present and the means of transportation so costly and difficult that were it not for the CPR, which uses immense quantities, the Company could not afford to work the mines."[3] While Selwyn's assessment was basically correct, the phrase "immense quantities" was misleading. C.A. Magrath, an official of the North Western Coal and Navigation Company, defined the problem more precisely. "The construction of the Canadian Pacific Railway had not brought to the West the anticipated prosperity. Our coal mines were busily employed for a couple of months in the winter only; in the summer it was a couple of days work weekly."[4] The limitations of the regional market were already evident.

Galt attempted to escape the restricted Canadian market by building a railway from Lethbridge to Great Falls, Montana. The Canadian portion of this road, like the Dunmore line, was aided by a federal land subsidy. The land grants, totalling over a million acres, were unprecedented because they were unusually large and were given to a resource-access road rather than a colonizing road.[5] Canada's prime minister, Sir John A. Macdonald, a personal friend of Galt, justified the government action by pointing out that the colliery was a timely contribution to his national policies since it would supply inexpensive fuel for settlers and railways as well as winter employment for idle farmers.[6] The generous subsidy enabled Galt to tap a large supply of British capital, permitting the construction of a large, efficient coal mine, and giving him an important competitive edge over other producers in the Territories.

For a number of reasons the Great Falls Railway, completed in 1890, did not secure an American market for the Galt collieries. A major obstacle was that the coal mines in Montana, which were owned by the Union Pacific and Great Northern Railways and protected by tariffs, underpriced Galt coal. In addition, the closure of the Anaconda smelting works and depressed market conditions continued to curtail exports throughout 1895.[7] Conditions began to improve slowly in 1896, and in that year the Galt collieries produced well over 50 per cent of the territorial output, or 120,000 tons, of which half was sold in Montana. But sales in the United States never rose significantly beyond this point, and for all practical purposes the American market was closed to Alberta coal.

Despite these disadvantages in the export markets, at the end of 1896 the Galt mines were still the largest producers of coal in the Territories. The second largest, the Canadian Northwest Coal and Lumber Syndicate on the CPR main line at Canmore, had begun prospecting work in 1890, and by 1895 its superior bituminous (steam) coal had replaced Galt coal on the Medicine-Hat-to-North-Bend section of the CPR. In 1896 Canmore produced sixty thousand tons, half of the Lethbridge production. Third in size was the colliery at Anthracite, near Banff, where as early as 1887 the Canadian Anthracite Coal Company had shipped anthracite coal as far as San Francisco. Besides these larger ventures a number of smaller concerns operated in the Northwest Territories. At various times small collieries extracted coal at Medicine Hat, Red Cliff, Midford and Cochrane, but because of poor financial backing and wasteful mining techniques their performance was poor and short-lived. Further north, the completion of the Calgary-Edmonton Railway permitted the small domestic mines in Edmonton to ship coal to Calgary; the amount was never large and in 1896 only four thousand tons were shipped to Calgary.[8] Calgary also received fuel from the Knee Hill mines but here too insufficient capitalization prevented any significant production of coal. In 1896 only two thousand tons were extracted and teamed to Calgary. In many other parts of Alberta even smaller mines, called "gopher holes", supplied local needs.

The chronic problems which were to plague the coal industry had emerged in the first stage of its development. The market was too restricted; tariffs prevented further expansion into the United States; and high transportation costs prohibited competition with other suppliers east of Winnipeg or west of the Rockies. The collieries, therefore, remained dependent upon the needs of the prairies where the slow and irregular influx of settlers and the resultant slow growth of rail traffic created a limited, fluctuating, regional market. Under these conditions only well-financed ventures could survive, and by 1896 the Galt mine, supported by a large land grant, was the only large producer left in the Territories. A classic example of the limited growth of the industry in the pre-1896 period was provided by the Canadian Anthracite Coal Company, whose production and transportation costs proved too high for effective competition in the California market. In the summer of 1888

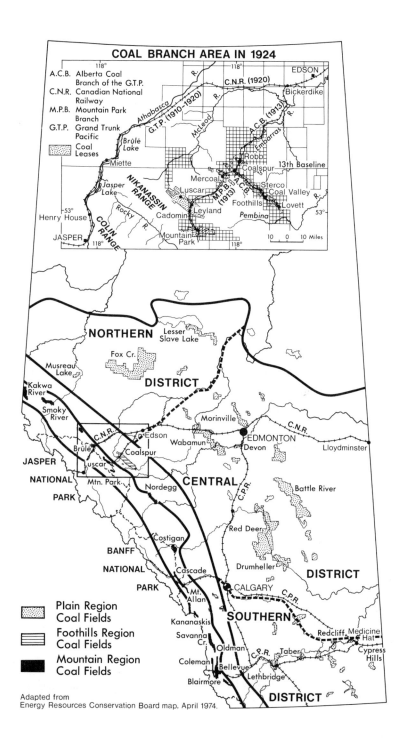

COAL BRANCH AREA IN 1924

A.C.B. Alberta Coal
        Branch of the G.T.P.
C.N.R. Canadian National
        Railway
M.P.B. Mountain Park
        Branch
G.T.P. Grand Trunk
        Pacific
        Coal
        Leases

EDSON

C.N.R. (1920)

Bickerdike

Athabasca R.

G.T.P. (1910–1920)

McLeod R.

A.C.B. (1913)

Brûlé Lake

Miette

Robb

Embarras R.

Coalspur

13th Baseline

Jasper Lake

NIKANASSIN RANGE

Mercoal

Luscar

M.P.B. (1913)

C.B.

Sterco

Coal Valley

Foothills

Lovett

Henry House

Rocky R.

Cadomin

Leyland

Pembina

JASPER

COLIN RANGE

Mountain Park

10 0 10 Miles

NORTHERN

Lesser
Slave Lake

Fox Cr.

DISTRICT

Musreau
Lake

Kakwa
River

Smoky
River

C.N.R.

Morinville

C.N.R.

Edson

Brûlé

Coalspur

Wabamun

EDMONTON

Devon

Lloydminster

JASPER

Luscar

NATIONAL

Mtn. Park

Nordegg

CENTRAL

C.P.R.

Battle River

PARK

Red Deer

Costigan

BANFF

Drumheller

DISTRICT

NATIONAL

Cascade

PARK

Mt.
Allan

CALGARY

C.P.R.

SOUTHERN

Kananaskis

Savanna
Cr.

Redcliff

Medicine
Hat

Oldman

Taber

Cypress
Hills

Coleman

Bellevue

C.P.R.

Lethbridge

Blairmore

DISTRICT

Plain Region
Coal Fields

Foothills Region
Coal Fields

Mountain Region
Coal Fields

Adapted from
Energy Resources Conservation Board map, April 1974.

the company ran out of funds, stopped production, and laid off two hundred miners.[9] Refinancing efforts proved fruitless and eventually the directors sold the properties to the H.W. McNeil Company,[10] which did not resume shipments until 1894. In 1896 the Company sold only twenty thousand tons of anthracite, a low production caused mainly by the inability to meet the competition from Pennsylvania coal.

The accelerating rate of settlement in the Northwest, beginning in the mid-1890's, generated a rapid expansion in the coal industry because the swelling ranks of settlers not only required more domestic fuel but also increased rail traffic. The extension of the CPR through the Crowsnest Pass in the late 1890's effectively began the second stage in the history of Alberta's coal industry. Although the existence of the rich coal seams had been well known since 1882, the fuel needs of the Kootenay smelting industry and the prairies were insufficient to warrant their exploitation. Not until the Great Northern Railroad threatened to build through the Pass did the CPR exercise its charter rights in the region. Included in the government railway subsidy were six square miles of coal lands at Hosmer in the British Columbia section, on which the Company built an elaborate colliery and coal-cleaning plant. Other companies established mines at Coal Creek, Morrissey, and Michel.[11]

The Canadian Pacific was not involved directly in coal mining on the Alberta side of the Crowsnest where development was relatively slow. The first colliery, the French-owned Canadian-American Coal and Coke Company, at Frank, commenced production in 1901 and by 1910 was extracting 132,000 tons of coal per year. The second large concern, the West Canadian Collieries Limited, also at Frank, was not opened until two years later. In the same year the International Coal and Coke Company began operation at Coleman, and by 1905 was producing over one thousand tons per day. The Hillcrest Coal Company began shipping small quantities of coal in 1905. And, the last large coal mine, the McGillivray Creek Coal and Coke Company, opened in 1909 and a year later extracted 53,000 tons. In comparison to earlier efforts, the Crowsnest collieries were giants, and, by 1910, coal production in Alberta had shot up to 3,036,000 tons and the industry employed nearly 6,000 miners.[12]

The euphoria of the western immigration boom also affected the coal industry further north. Sir Wilfrid Laurier, the Liberal prime minister, announced in July 1903 that the Grand Trunk Pacific, a subsidiary of the Grand Trunk Railway, planned to use the Yellowhead Pass for its transcontinental railway. The news revived interest in the coal fields west of Edmonton, and in 1906 D.B. Dowling of the Geological Survey explored the region intensively and reported favourably on the Big Horn, Brazeau, and Yellowhead areas.[13] Dowling's report and the start of railway construction triggered off private prospecting expeditions to the area, and in 1909 the Yellowhead Pass Coal and Coke Company leased five thousand acres on the Embarras River, but for lack of transportation produced little coal.[14]

To solve the problem of transportation, the Grand Trunk Pacific Branchline Company in 1911 commenced construction of the fifty-eight-mile Alberta Coal Branch Railway southward from the Grand Trunk Pacific. The Alberta government guaranteed the railway's bonds at $20,000 a mile. At the same time the Mountain Park Coal Company, destined to become one of the largest producers along the Alberta Coal Branch, built a branch line from Coalspur to its properties at Mountain Park which, when completed, was leased to the Grand Trunk. Within two years, over a hundred miles of track had been laid to connect the isolated mining camps with the outside world.[15]

With the completion of the railway link, development along the Coal Branch proceeded very rapidly. By 1914 the Mountain Park Coal Company employed over one hundred men and mined about three hundred tons a day.[16] In the next few years collieries opened at Cadomin, Luscar, Robb, Mercoal, Sterco, Coal Valley, Foothills, and Lovett. By 1929, the Coal Branch achieved the peak of its production, more than one and a half million tons per year or twenty-two per cent of the entire Alberta output. Practically all the coal was sold to the railways.

The last major bituminous region to be developed in Alberta revealed again the intimate relationship between railways and collieries. In 1906 Martin Nordegg, representing the Deutsche Canada Syndicate, visited Canada for the purpose of investing in some suitable Canadian enterprise. In 1907 Nordegg prospected the Brazeau area, accompanied by D.B. Dowling, who the year before had completed the government survey of that area. The men uncovered a number of coal seams whose value was confirmed by subsequent tests. By 1910 Nordegg had decided to commence construction, but, like the other promoters, first had to make transportation arrangements.[17]

To solve the problem, Nordegg approached the Canadian Pacific and Grand Trunk railways. He was rebuffed by both. Disappointed, he turned to the Canadian Northern, which was also building a transcontinental railway, and to his surprise the railway was not only anxious to help, but promised to buy more coal than Nordegg had expected to sell. If Nordegg had been better informed about the coal industry, he would have been neither disappointed nor surprised. The Canadian Pacific had sufficient independent suppliers in the Cascade and Crowsnest area and owned large mines at Lethbridge, at Bankhead near Banff, and at Hosmer in the Crowsnest.[18] The Grand Trunk, in turn, could purchase all its fuel requirements in the northern Yellowhead-Coal Branch fields.[19] But the Canadian Northern had no such provisions because it had always bought Pennsylvania coal. In a joint venture with Pittsburgh Coal Company it had erected elaborate docking and storage facilities at Port

Arthur.[20] The arrangement proved unsatisfactory, and as the railway spread farther and farther from its Winnipeg base, American anthracite became increasingly expensive. Consequently the company leased several coal sites in the Brazeau area, a region not yet controlled by its competitors; development of these coal seams would require expensive branchline and mining facilities. At this point, Nordegg fortuitously appeared.

A satisfactory arrangement was worked out. The Canadian Northern and Nordegg's Brazeau Collieries agreed to merge their coal leases on a fifty-fifty basis. The two companies agreed to share the cost of the colliery-railway project which was estimated to cost about ten million dollars. By the spring of 1910 most of the capital had been raised by Nordegg's friends in Brussels, London, Paris, and Berlin. Then, by a stroke of pure luck, Nordegg discovered an extremely rich seam near what eventually became the town of Nordegg, a site which would save some forty miles of railway construction. By 1914 a branch known as the Canadian Northern Western had been completed with the help of provincial bond guarantees and federal subsidies, and its ownership was then transferred to the Canadian Northern.[21] The next year the Brazeau Collieries were extracting fifteen hundred tons a day.[22]

By the end of the First World War all the major bituminous fields in Alberta were known and the larger mines were in operation.[23] The recently formed Canadian National system used Coal Branch and Brazeau coal along its lines in Alberta, Saskatchewan, and the western part of Manitoba. The CPR burned Cascade, Crowsnest, and Lethbridge coal on its prairie runs.[24] The pattern had been established by then: while the railways counted on these mines to supply the inexpensive coal, the collieries depended entirely upon the railways as consumers and carriers of their product; without the mines, the railways would only have to pay higher fuel costs, but without the railways the coal industry would have been small indeed. For example, in 1929 the Mountain Park section of the Coal Branch sold 90.8 per cent of its output to the railways. (See Graph One.) Unfortunately the needs of this major consumer fluctuated rapidly in accordance with rail traffic, the grain shipping season being the busiest time of the year. The lack of a stable demand had a detrimental effect, not only on the industry, but also on the labour force. Hence the aim of the operators, assisted by the government, was to leap beyond the confines of the western rail market.

The third stage in the development of Alberta's coal industry, from 1919 to 1929, was a decade of growth tinged with concern for the future. Immediately after the end of the War, production plummeted to less than four million tons but quickly recovered, and by 1928 output soared to over seven million tons per year. Yet the bright flush of expansion was marred by some distressing signs that all was not well. The Alberta government, concerned about an industry which was so important to the

GRAPH I

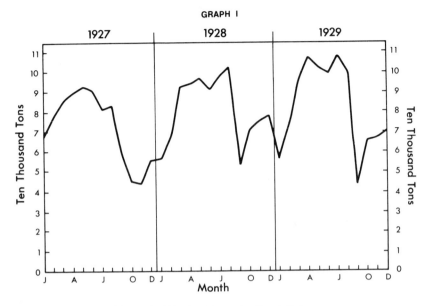

Monthly Fluctuations in Coal Sales
Mountain Park

province's economic well-being, appointed two commissions within six years to study the coal problem. The first, the Coal Mining Industry Commission of 1919, concluded that Alberta's market needed to be enlarged through better handling and advertising techniques.[25] The second, the Alberta Coal Commission of 1925, chaired by H.M.E. Evans, conducted a very intensive review of all facets of coal mining in the province and noted a "grotesque irregularity" in mine operations; it calculated that by operating at full capacity every working day of the year all the mines together could have produced six million four hundred thousand tons of coal; in reality they worked sporadically and extracted only half that amount.[26] The mine operators blamed the shortfall on the lack of orders. The commissioners, however, insisted that the industry was overdeveloped, and to prove their point, showed that while more than a thousand collieries had been opened in Alberta by December 1924, nearly seven hundred of these had been abandoned permanently. Although both sides essentially agreed on the nature of the problem, a difference in emphasis was evident in the solutions they stressed. While the commissioners would seek full production by restricting the multiplicity of separate operations, the mine operators wanted to expand beyond the confines of the prairie market into central Canada.[27]

Clearly a number of fundamental problems plagued the industry. It was equally evident, however, that one of the major obstacles to stable production was the high cost of transportation. Two thousand miles of prairies and pre-Cambrian rock separated Alberta from a voracious energy consumer, the industrial heartland of Canada, which was at that time being supplied by Pennsylvania coal.[28] Under a totally free enterprise system, Alberta could not compete with American coal; not only were its mines over sixteen hundred miles farther from central Canada, but, due to geographical conditions, they operated two to five times less efficiently than the Pennsylvania collieries.[29] Without government support, Alberta coal was no match for the superior Pennsylvania anthracite.

When assistance did come, it was from the provincial rather than federal administration. The Alberta government, recognizing that the limited regional market prevented expansion to full capacity, launched a publicity campaign in Ontario similar to an earlier successful effort in Winnipeg. In the fall of 1922 a few operators donated a load of coal which the province sent to Ontario and distributed there free of charge. The timing was perfect because a five-month strike in the Pennsylvania coal fields had caused an acute fuel shortage in the United States and Canada. Some Americans were disturbed that coal was still being shipped to Canada despite the coal shortage, and in turn Canadians worried about the agitation south of the border which threatened to cut off the fuel supply.[30] Canadians undoubtedly were startled by a New York *Times* editorial quoted in the House of Commons. "It is reasonable to ask Canadians why they do not use their own coal, which they have in Cape Breton as much as they choose to dig. . . . That they like hard coal better is no reason for pretending that they will freeze if they do not share our inadequate supply. Besides there still is wood in Canada. . . ." In reaction to the fuel crisis the House of Commons approved a motion in March 1923 which stated "that the time has arrived for Canada to have a national fuel policy in relation to its coal supply."[31] However, no real steps were taken to implement such a policy beyond the establishment of the Dominion Fuel Board to study the energy problem.[32]

Despite the lack of concrete federal activity, the provincial government continued in its attempt to break into the Ontario market. In 1923 it reopened its publicity campaign in Ontario and convinced the CNR to establish a special test rate of $9.00 per ton of coal moved from Alberta to Ontario. About twenty thousand tons were shipped under this program.[33] Meanwhile a second strike in the Pennsylvania mines spurred the Board of Railway Commissioners into action. In February 1925, the Alberta and Canadian governments each agreed to pay a $1.00 subvention towards the $9.00 per ton freight, a subsidy which the commissioners felt would make Alberta coal competitive in the Ontario market. A trial shipment of twenty-five thousand tons was made under these conditions but no record of costs were kept.[34]

In 1926, the governments of both Ontario and Alberta successfully convinced the federal government to resume the Railway Board's investigation. At this time a majority of two commissioners found the out-of-pocket cost for the transport of coal from Alberta to Ontario to be $7.22 a ton while a minority report, filed by Frank Oliver, an Albertan, lowered this figure to $6.50 a ton. Of greater interest than the discrepancy in these estimates was Oliver's argument. He wrote, "At an average f.o.b. cost at the mine in Alberta of say $3.50 per ton with a rail rate of $6.50 there would be a distribution of $20,000,000 of Canadian money among Canadians," for the same services now being provided by Americans.[35] Provided equipment was available, Oliver stated, Canadian rather than American mines and railroads should benefit from this large expenditure. The federal government decided on a compromise figure of $6.75 and agreed to pay a subvention for the remainder of the rail cost,[36] but it was still too low to encourage large shipments.

The stock market crash of 1929 ushered in the fourth period of Alberta's coal industry. The collapse of the Canadian agricultural and industrial economies slashed traffic on the national railways in half and consequently greatly reduced the demand for fuel. Thus the steam-coal mines were hardest hit, especially in the Crowsnest Pass where production figures plunged, causing massive unemployment and hardships.[37] At the depth of the Depression in 1931 the Mountain Park area extracted only fifty-six per cent of its 1929 output, and, although the slow recovery of global commerce in the mid-thirties stimulated the industry, production had returned only to sixty-five per cent of normal by 1938.

In an attempt to deal with the crisis, in September 1935 the provincial government commissioned Sir Montague Barlow of London, England, to conduct an inquiry into the condition of the Alberta coal industry. Barlow discovered that the reduced railway market was not the only factor in slumping sales; competition from natural gas, wood, illegal mining, and American coal also hurt the industry. Furthermore, the commissioner felt that high freight rates and tariffs precluded any incursions into the American market. Barlow put it very simply, "It cannot be too-often repeated that the principal problem before the Alberta coal industry at the moment is too many mines and too few markets."[38]

Throughout this critical period westerners called for a national fuel policy which would see Alberta fuel replace much of the Pennsylvania product. One moderate solution, presented by William Nordegg in *The Fuel Problem of Canada*,[39] chided the federal government for failing to formulate a coherent national fuel policy. While high transportation costs would prevent complete Canadian self-sufficiency in coal, Nordegg

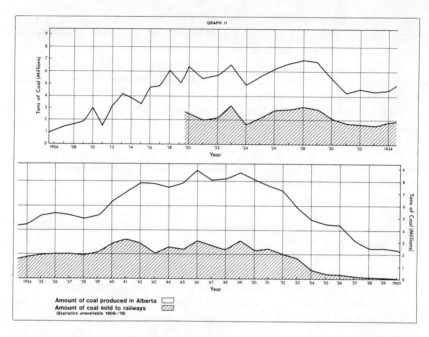

GRAPH II

Amount of coal produced in Alberta ☐
Amount of coal sold to railways ▨
(Statistics unavailable 1906-'19)

declared that many anomalies could be removed. Why, he asked, should it cost two dollars per ton more to ship coal from Fernie to Winnipeg than from Sydney to Montreal? Why should Canadian railways buy half their coal in Pennsylvania? Why, indeed, did the CNR operate a gigantic coal mine in the United States? Besides the removal of these aberrations, Nordegg proposed the discontinuance of subventions, but the reservation of the area west of the Lakehead for Alberta coal and a greater use of Nova Scotia coal in Quebec and Ontario. Canadians, wrote Nordegg, must be willing to pay a little extra for their fuel in the national interest.

The federal government nevertheless declined to ask Canadians to pay a little extra, and instead continued the interim policy of subventions. In 1932 the Board of Railway Commissioners re-examined coal freight rates, and upon their recommendation, the federal government increased the subsidy to $2.50 a ton.[40] Despite government assistance, the Ontario market remained nearly inpenetrable. In this period the largest shipment amounted to seventy-five thousand tons a year, or about 1.5 per cent of Alberta's entire output. The interim nature of the policy discouraged the majority of operators from participating in the plan.

The Second World War re-activated the Canadian economy, and with it revitalized Alberta's coal industry. (See Graph Two.) As the world plunged deeper and deeper into global war, increasing demands for agricultural and industrial goods stimulated rail traffic across the continent, and finally after so many years the need for coal matched the theoretical capacity of Alberta's mines; ironically, however, in their fifth stage, 1939-1948, the collieries could not meet rising demands because of the shortage of manpower. During the Depression years the mines had been allowed to atrophy, and thus when the industry finally approached maximum production, it no longer had the necessary manpower. In 1942, for instance, when production in Alberta shot up to a record 7.8 million tons, Canada still faced a serious energy shortage.

The federal government, in an attempt to deal with the fuel crisis, used several very powerful instruments. Reminiscent of the First World War, the government employed the Department of Labour, the Coal Administration, and the War Times Labour Relations Board in an attempt to prevent strikes in the nation's coal mines. In 1942 the Emergency Coal Production Board was established to stimulate production, control wages, and freeze prices. That same year the labour shortage was so acute that the federal cabinet placed miners under the Selective Service Act. The legislation prohibited anyone from terminating his employment without seven days notice, and furthermore forbade anyone with two or more years of mining experience to remain in any other job. After 1944 no miner could join the armed forces, and for the first time in the nation's history, women eighteen years or older were permitted to hold surface jobs in coal mines. To compensate for the hardships of frozen jobs and wages, the government authorized the payment of war bonuses.[41]

Despite record production during the war and afterwards, the Alberta government wanted further expansion of coal markets. In a brief to the 1946 federal Royal Commission on Coal, the provincial administration blamed the instability of the coal industry on the transportation problem. While the submission recognized that coal prices could be reduced by eliminating overlapping activities, avoiding duplication of equipment, and by improving regulations, it declared the root cause of Alberta's coal problem to be inadequate distribution rather than inefficient production: "An existing large market needs only to be made available and this can be achieved only through the establishment of a sound national policy of long duration and subject to alteration only at widely, clearly specified times by an Act of Parliament." Echoing the sentiments of many western producers, the report saw the vast central Canadian market as a panacea for the ills of the coal industry; if only, through a permanent national fuel policy, Alberta could wrest Ontario, and to a lesser extent Quebec, from the Americans, its production could be doubled and stability would be assured. Using a fifty-year-old argument the provincial government pointed out that the National Policy had for many years forced Albertans to subsidize Ontario and Quebec industries and insisted that the time had finally arrived for all Canadians to support the coal industry. The government also referred to the Ontario government's purchase of thousands of tons of American coal for its destitute citizens during the Depression, at a time when many Alberta miners were on relief. Why then, the brief asked, had this Ontario money not been spent on Alberta coal so as to reduce its welfare rolls? Justice demanded a national policy for fuel too, with high tariffs against American coal, and the long-term subventions which were so "necessary to the achievement of the supply of Canadian needs by Canadian coal."[42]

While it was willing to lend some support to the coal mines located in the extremities of Canada, the federal government would not accept Alberta's plea for a coherent and permanent national fuel policy which would give Canada self-sufficiency in coal. In pure economic terms, American anthracite was much cheaper than Canadian bituminous or lignite, and thus should dominate the central Canadian market. The Canadian government was very reluctant to force Canadians to pay a higher price for domestic fuel, be it directly through high tariffs against the American product or indirectly through full subventions.* Thus it rejected arguments based on patriotism, nationalism, and the economic benefits to be derived from an all-Canadian fuel supply;** instead, it elected to retain the temporary, short-term subventions.

Regardless of its merits or demerits, by the late 1940's Alberta's overture for a national coal policy was obsolete. The Leduc gusher of 1947 introduced the sixth stage in the history of Alberta coal, a period of rapid decline. In 1948 the CPR, citing lower overall operating and maintenance costs, commenced a policy of "dieselization". Eight years

---

*In 1946 the National Railway Commission rejected any policy aimed at making Canada completely fuel-independent on the grounds that in 1945 such a scheme would have cost the consumer an extra $5.00 per ton of coal, or about $100,000,000.00 annually. The Royal Commission of 1946, which cited this argument, felt that Alberta and Nova Scotia were entitled to some assistance because Quebec and Ontario industries enjoyed some measure of tariff protection and the national interest warranted a reasonable level of production which could prove to be of great advantage during an emergency.[43]

**The "coal romantics", as one writer calls them, felt that since coal mining was very labour intensive, subsidies would have a wide impact on employment in Alberta by bringing stability to the province's agricultural economy. In addition, they argued, greater subventions would expand coal-mining activities that were essential to the industrialization of Canada. One mining periodical protested further increases in freight rates because such a move would kill an industry needed for the defense of Canada. "Canada just can't afford to lose this industry at a time when the success of the whole defense effort of the Pacific may be entirely dependent upon it. And neither can one of the historic cornerstones of the western part of this country be kicked away at a time when stability is essential to defense and progress."[44]

later neither the CNR nor the CPR burned Canadian coal. A 13,000,000-ton market had disappeared.[45]

The Alberta steam-coal industry nearly expired. Although some collieries in the Cascade and Crowsnest fields survived, the Coal Branch and Nordegg mines disappeared completely. Adjustment was difficult for the miners who were skilled only in that occupation and received only token government assistance. Not until April 1954 did the provincial Coal Miners' Rehabilitation Act authorize the expenditure of $100,000 to meet the transportation costs of miners who had found work in other areas, but little was done for those without jobs.[46]

Even though nothing could have been done to prevent the railway's conversion to a more economic fuel, governments might have been better prepared for the change-over. Both the Evans Commission in 1925 and the Barlow Report in 1935 warned that the discovery of inexpensive oil could have serious repercussions for the coal-mining industry. Yet in 1946 the Alberta administration confidently predicted:

It will be noted that our railways have in the past been the greatest and most stable market, year in and year out, for Alberta coal. Great and stable as this market has been, it is our considered view that this market is capable of absorbing still larger tonnage and on a firmer basis than in the past.[47]

Only ten years later the railway market was extinct.

For eighty years the railways, as chief consumers and sole conveyors of Alberta's coal, had supported the province's mining industry. Unfortunately, while the collieries furnished inexpensive fuel, the railways never reciprocated by providing low rates to permit operators to break out of the limited regional market. Lower freight rates coupled to long-term subventions or high tariffs could have helped the mines to compete on the central Canadian market.* The emphasis, however, should not have been placed on railway and domestic consumption but rather on other stable users, namely industries and thermal generating plants. The

---

*To March 31, 1960, the federal government certainly had spent money on the development of Canada's coal resources but only a small segment of the total 203 million dollars in aid was spent to aid the movement of coal from Alberta to Ontario. Considerable amounts were spent on war-time subsidies [see footnote 41], research, and administration. Of the total amount spent, 135 million dollars went in aid of coal transportation subventions. Alberta and the British Columbia sections of the Crowsnest Pass received only 29.3 million dollars. In addition, the Canadian government paid 2.8 million dollars in subsidies to Alberta and British Columbia coal mines on bunker coal shipped to the Pacific coast. The largest beneficiary of federal subventions was Nova Scotia; she received a total of 99.4 million dollars in support payments.[48]

great tragedy of the coal-mining industry in Alberta, especially in reference to the fate of miners, was its total dependence upon the regional
railway and the domestic market of the prairies; when these disappeared,
the industry withered away. It was the Japanese smelting industry and
Alberta coal-fired generators which ultimately revived the dying industry.
Perhaps the current energy crisis will fully restore the coal-mining industry to its former status.

Seven

THE INSTABILITY OF
THE COMMUNITY OF GOODS
IN THE SOCIAL HISTORY
OF THE HUTTERITES

Karl Peter

On the 12th August 1899 the Governor General in Ottawa approved a report of the Privy Council saying that:

The Minister is of the opinion, under the circumstances and considering that the Brethren of the Hutterische Society would appear to be a most desirable class of settlers to locate upon vacant Dominion Lands in Manitoba and the North West Territories, that it is expedient to give them the fullest assurance of absolute immunity from military service, not only to those who have already settled but also to those who may settle in the future.[1]

A little more than two months later the Deputy Minister in the Department of the Interior wrote to the Commissioner of Immigration in Winnipeg, Manitoba:

Dear Sir,

I have your letter of the 12th instant, No. 21, 759, enclosing a petition from certain members of the Hutterite community in which they ask that in coming to Canada they may be assured of certain privileges.

(1) As to their request for exemption from military service, this question has already been dealt with, and I enclose you a copy of the Order-in-Council authorizing their exemption.

(2) These people will not be molested in any way in the practice of their religious services and principles, as full freedom of religious belief prevails throughout the country. They will also be allowed to establish independent schools for teaching their children if they desire to do so, but they will have to be responsible for their maintenance themselves. The children will not be compelled to attend other schools if their education is properly provided for.

(3) The law does not compel the taking of an oath in court by persons who have conscientious objections to doing so, and there is no compulsion as to voting for or holding offices, but the privilege of doing so is generally most highly prized.

(4) There will be no interference with their living as a commonwealth, if they desire to do so.

(5) The Dominion Lands Act makes provision for the locating of people as communities and their being allowed to live in villages instead of being required each to live separately on his own land.

(6) The privileges asked for in the last four sections cannot be more firmly established by any further official document than they are by the established laws of the country, and the members of the Society in question may rest assured that the statements made above are of as full value to them as they could be made by an Order of the Governor-in-Council or any document of that nature.

Yours truly,

(signed) Jas. A. Smart,
Deputy minister.[2]

These two documents spell out the privileges Hutterites have traditionally asked for and insisted upon throughout their history.

Exactly twenty years later, Canada's Minister of Immigration and Colonization, J.A. Calder, wrote to one of the Hutterite elders in South Dakota who inquired about the possibility of migrating to Canada.

Dear Sir:

I am in receipt of your letter of the 6th instant in reference to the removal of the remaining members of your community to Canada. I have noted carefully all you state respecting the separation of members of your faith, and can appreciate your feelings and wishes in this regard. However, I must advise you that after the most careful consideration of all the facts and circumstances, the government concluded that it would be inadvisable, owing to the general feeling prevailing throughout Canada, to continue to permit certain persons to enter Canada because their custom, mode of life, habits, etc., were such as to prevent them becoming readily assimilated. These persons included Doukhobors, Mennonites, and Hutterites. We have had so much trouble in Canada in connection with school and other matters in the colonies and communities of these people that their neighbours and people generally insist that no more should be permitted to come.

If in the future this decision should be reversed, it will depend largely, if not entirely, upon the conduct and mode of life of those of your people now settled in Canada. Unless they are prepared to become Canadian citizens in the truest and best sense of the term, and unless they are ready to assume all the obligations of citizenship including military service if called upon, it is extremely doubtful if any government in Canada would be prepared to admit them.

I trust I have made the situation quite clear. Should you desire any further information, or in case you wish to place any further facts before me, I shall be pleased to hear from you.

Yours very truly,

J.A. Calder
Minister of Immigration
and Colonization.[3]

Without changing the laws of the country, privileges granted under them at one time, were denied at another. Canada's official policy toward the presence of Hutterites, which in 1899 was one of ethnic tolerance and openness, had changed and become dominated by ethnic hostilities and pressure toward assimilation.

It is interesting to note the Minister referring to the general feeling throughout Canada; to the trouble connected with schools and other matters; and the insistence of neighbours and people, that no more Hutterites should be permitted to come. Unless the Minister distorted the case, certain sectors of Canadian society seem to have responded to the Hutterite presence in a most unfavourable way. As later events showed, particularly during the Second World War, a patriotic-minded section of the population, for which the Canadian Legion often adopted the role of official spokesman, resented Hutterites on national and cultural grounds. The German origin of Hutterites, particularly their use of the German language and their socio-cultural isolation, created an atmosphere of suspicion. There was also a feeling of deprivation by those who thought they were carrying the burdens of war and citizenship while they alleged that Hutterites gained materially at their expense.

Another sector of the population resenting Hutterites was, and still is, recruited from the Canadian western farm populations. The patriotic sentiments of these farm groups are somewhat secondary to their major concern, which centres around Hutterite population growth and the corresponding multiplication of Hutterite communities. Land and land acquisition, which during the pioneer days were taken for granted, have become problematic. The vast reaches of the western prairies have long been allocated, and the frontiers pushed into marginal regions. The structural adjustments from the homestead to modern mechanized farming repeatedly shook Western communities and the basic economic unit, the family farm, leaving both in a high state of anxiety and frustration. War, depression, overproduction, and increased technology eliminated many farmers and taxed the endurance of those who remained. Hutterites expanded into the economic vacuum so created, and although they were not the only group who did so, nor even the most threatening, at least they were the most visible and therefore could be singled out as a target of resentment and hostility. There are many factors which helped to generate feelings of ethnic hostility toward the Hutterites. Their net reproduction rate, for example, has been remarkably high and stable for the last hundred years, leading to a doubling of the population every seventeen to twenty years. From 1880 to the present, the number of Hutterite communities increased dramatically from three to approximately two hundred today, that are widely distributed over Alberta, Saskatchewan, Manitoba, South Dakota, Montana, Washington, and Minnesota, with high concentrations in Alberta, Saskatchewan, and Manitoba.

In the face of such growth patterns, it was not surprising to see even serious commentators engaged from time to time in calculating the day when all agricultural land in Alberta, or the West as a whole, would be absorbed by Hutterites. A whole series of restrictive Acts in various jurisdictions, beginning with the Land Sales Prohibition Act in the 1940's, and culminating in the currently defunct Communal Properties Act, attempted to deal with this problem of Hutterite land expansion.

Fear, it seems, is the prime originator of irrational action, and fear has the ability to feed on itself, giving rise to prejudice and discrimination. Obviously, there is some need for concrete information regarding past, present, and future growth patterns of Hutterites, which might form a basis for public policy as well as public opinion. This chapter attempts to fill this need in part. It proposes to look at growth and decline throughout the social history of Hutterites and tries to analyze the conditions, and to assess the interaction of various social factors under which growth and decline took place. A cautious look into the future will be taken at the end of the chapter.

It should be noted at the outset that the community of goods is the most essential element in Hutterite life designating a close spiritual bond between God and man, and between man and man, validated by a

1535   16|85   17|61   18|18   18|59   1974

Figure 1: The alternation of the Hutterite community of goods and the
           Hutterite family.
           The shaded periods designate the dominance of the community
           of goods.
           The light periods designate the dominance of the family.

rigorous sharing of social and material properties and submission to a
communal authority structure. It is commonly assumed that the Hutterite sect has experienced a continuous existence, with regard to these
communal characteristics, since the years of its founding in the 1520's
and 30's. This is not the case.

From 1535, when the Hutterite sect was founded, to the present time
(a total time span of 440 years), the Hutterite community moved
through five phases, alternating between the dominance of the community of goods and the dominance of family property relations similar
to those of their host society at the time. The above graphic presentation
of these phases shows the alternating pattern.

In its first phase, which lasted for about 150 years, the *Gueter-
gemeinschaft* (community of goods) dominated. For the next 85 years
the family became the dominant structure. In the year 1761 the community of goods was revived, lasting for only 56 years. From 1819 to
1860 the family again dominated, only to be replaced by a second revival
of the community of goods in 1861 lasting up to the present time. In
terms of population, Hutterites grew from a few hundred persons in 1535
to more than 13,000 in 1622, only to decline to less than seventy persons
in 1760. During the next century, the population slowly increased to
five hundred and assumed a stable growth from 1880 to the present time.
The total number of Hutterites today is somewhat higher than in 1622,
totalling approximately twenty thousand members.

This chapter hypothesises that the recurrent processes of change
within the Hutterite sect were, in large part, due to an irreconcilable
struggle between the Hutterite community and the Hutterite family.
This social dialectic pulled the community so that one time when the
family relations were dominant, the absence of the community of goods
created ideological and spiritual stresses leading to attempts to recreate
the community of goods.

The Elimination of Alternate Explanations

To prove successfully that the dialectical relationship between the
Hutterite community and the Hutterite family is in fact accountable for

the successive historical changes in dominance of one by the other depends first on the elimination of alternate factors of explanation.

Factors most often associated with patterns of change in sectarian groups are war, persecution, economic and technological development, and growth. There is no question that the Hutterite sect was greatly affected by war and persecution throughout its history. The migratory route from Germany to Moravia, Hungary, Rumania, Russia, the United States, and finally Canada, was initiated in every case either by warfare or by persecution, or a combination of both. Some historians have suggested that the disappearance of the community of goods in 1685 might have been due to the incessant warfare ravaging the countryside at the time that made it impossible for Hutterites to keep their communal storage places and eating facilities. While this is true to some extent, Hutterites in the years following 1547 survived more extensive and cruel forms of warfare and persecution than persisted around 1685. Moreover, when the sect gave up its community of goods a second time around 1818, neither factor was in evidence at all. If the retention or the disappearance of the community of goods at one time is associated with war and persecution and at another time it is not, then causal logic suggests that the two factors are neither necessary nor sufficient conditions to account for the social phenomenon in question. At best, they are contributory factors.

Economic and technological changes occurring throughout Europe similarly had great impact on Hutterite communities. The Industrial Revolution eliminated a great variety of crafts from the communities. Changing styles and techniques in pottery manufacture, for example, one of the main crafts of Hutterites, had a noticeable effect on the entire Brotherhood in 1685, when the community of goods disappeared for the first time. The crafts, however, continued. In 1818, when the community of goods disappeared for a second time, no economic pressures were in evidence. The sect had a number of flourishing crafts well capable of supporting the entire community adequately.

During the dominance of the family from 1818 to 1859 most crafts died out, so that the communal experiments which began in 1859 took place within the framework of a community entirely oriented toward agriculture. Although there were agricultural traditions, because the sect always maintained an agricultural base sufficient to its own material needs, the successful revival of the community of goods on the basis of agriculture (rather than crafts) demonstrates the adaptive qualities of the sect toward changing economic and technological conditions. If this is the case, non-adaptivity to changing economic and technological factors cannot be taken as a cause of the alternating patterns between community and family.

To move to the fourth alternative, growth patterns followed by the restructuring of the social group (as exemplified in a more complex hierarchy, and accompanied by centralization and specialization in structure and functions) cannot be taken as the source of the changes and fluctuations observed in Hutterite history. Hutterites never tried to form social structures beyond *Gemeinschaft* relations. Nor did they ever insist on territorial consolidation or on one particular host society. While growth in population has occurred and is particularly evident at the present time, such growth patterns did not lead to the emergence of more complex structures. In fact, the division of labour in Hutterite communities today is much simpler than it was 450 years ago when Hutterites maintained a great variety of crafts organized on a semi-industrial basis.

Further evidence lies in those social structures superordinate to the individual communities, such as the "convention of preachers" which were kept structurally simple by dividing the whole population into three largely autonomous and endogenous groups. The preachers' convention of each of these groups was able to maintain primary and face-to-face interaction of all preachers. Thus population growth as it occurred was channelled into the multiplication of identical community structures, thereby preventing the emergence of higher differentiated and specialized structures, and subsequently avoiding the stresses and strains associated with changing social structures.

Taken either singly or in combination, war, persecution, technological changes, and growth therefore cannot be taken as causes of recurrent changes; however, they must be considered contributory factors facilitating or inhibiting the unfolding of contradictions internal to the structure of Hutterite communities.

The Dialectic of Community and Family

The elimination of factors to which the community-family fluctuations of the Hutterite sect perceivably could be imputed does not in itself, of course, lend credibility to the assertion that the source of such fluctuations ought to be sought in the dialectic between community and family. A separate argument must be made to establish the reasonableness of this hypothesis.

Given the nature of the Hutterite religious ideology at the time of the group's founding, only one social structure containing primary forms of interaction between individuals – the community – was of interest to the members. Their religious teachings strongly favoured a communal living arrangement under cultural conditions prevalent in their host society, giving the family authority over property ownership, child socialization, and mate selection. In practice, therefore, there always was, and there continues to be, a visible alternative to the primary relations of the Hutterite community of goods. The controversy between the family-oriented Mennonites and Amish on the one hand and the community-oriented Hutterites on the other hand emphasizes precisely this alternative. These sectarian groups whose overall religious-ideological systems are so similar are nevertheless split on the question of whether the family or the community ought to control property, production, socialization, and mate selection.

This historical interface shows that Mennonites and Amish, supported by a family-oriented religious ideology, have in fact always maintained family prerogatives of property, socialization and mate selection; while Hutterites supported by a community-oriented value structure alternated between family and community. It seems that the family-oriented ideology of Mennonites and Amish provided stability of relations in practice while the community-oriented ideas of the Hutterites promoted social conditions inherently unstable in practice. It is therefore reasonable to assume that the existence and the maintenance of the Hutterite community of goods depends to a high degree on a strong ideological commitment which in turn reinforces its communal structure. If this religious ideology is weakened and loses its grip on its members, the alternate structure to the community of goods – the family – becomes a practical possibility. In contrast, Mennonites and Amish do not suffer from similar contradictions because their family-supporting religious ideas do not create social tensions leading toward the creation of a community of goods.

Looking at the other side of the coin, it is also reasonable to assume that Hutterites living under family arrangements but maintaining a communally oriented religious ideology suffer from considerable psychological strains if their religious commitment is high. When certain social conditions lead to a strengthening of the previously weak religious commitment one would expect them to make attempts to move from their family arrangements to the creation of communal structures. The dialectic between the Hutterite community and family, therefore, can be summarized in two more precisely defined hypotheses:

(1) *Hutterites having a communally oriented religious ideology and living under communal arrangements have a tendency to transform their communal living arrangements into family living arrangements when the religious ideology loses its central significance and weakens;*

(2) *Hutterites having a communally oriented religious ideology but living under family living arrangements, tend to transform their family living arrangements into communal living arrangements when the religious ideology attains greater significance and strengthens.*

A look at the following data will explicate the conditions under which these contradictions occurred at least four times during the social history of the Hutterites.

The First Phase, 1535-1685

Because the Hutterite community assumed the right to control property relations, production and consumption, child socialization, and mate selection, the family was never mentioned in Hutterite dogmatic writings or in primary historical data. Hutterites spoke of marriage, not the family. Marriage was first a union of God with men and women, and secondly a union between a man and a woman. Marriages were arranged twice a year by the local preacher who took great care to instruct that such worldly considerations as love and affection did not interfere with the divine nature of marriage. Soon after birth, children were handed over to community nurses and the mother was required only to nurse the child when necessary. Later, when the child was weaned (for which a definite time was set community-wide), it was educated and cared for entirely in the community kindergarten or the school until it reached the prescribed age of entry into the community labour force. No private property of any kind was allowed, either for the individual or the marriage partners. Man and wife participated throughout the day in work groups separated by sex. They were allowed to sleep together at night. These practices indicate that the control of the sex urge and procreation were the only functions granted to marriage partners. In addition, these communal practices denied the emergence of intimate parent-child relations and instituted instead adult-child relations characteristic for the community as a whole.

The source of the religious strength creating such social practices is to be found in the overwhelming conversion-experience which motivated the founding members of the Hutterite sect. So strong were their convictions that nothing but an extreme type of the community of goods would save their souls that they practically abolished all traditional and conventional family relations and allowed only the most primary husband-wife relations.

It is most interesting to note that with the passing of the founding generation, several processes made themselves felt which began to alter these original relations.

In the first instance, the enormous sense of conviction and sacrifice which characterized the founding generation could not be maintained when people were born into and socialized by the communities. Extensive recruitment of new members on other than religious criteria weakened the faith even further.

Simultaneously with the weakening of religious convictions, more intimate family relations began to reassert themselves. Hutterite community ordinances, representing a codification of moral laws, appeared shortly after 1560 and increased greatly the variety of social areas covered and the intensity of their exhortations.

The reassertion of family relations occurred principally in three areas: production and distribution, socialization, and mate selections. Those masters of crafts or managers who had access to, or control over, the resources of the communities began to expropriate goods, materials, or money for themselves, making their families the principal beneficiaries. Those excluded from sharing these resources reciprocated by refusing to work. By 1650, such practices had diffused to all individuals in the communities, so that the common consumption through redistribution became increasingly impossible because goods were appropriated by individual families before they could reach the communal pool.

Coinciding with this trend was an ever increasing readiness of parents to circumvent the austere environment of the kindergarten and the school. Parents would take their children home for longer periods only to spoil them, whereupon on their return to school they would experience difficulties. As the school responded to deviant behaviour with harsher and harsher measures, parents searched for ways and means to keep their children out of school altogether. Those parents having authority in the communities were the first to use their power and influence to do so, only to initiate a trend which soon diffused to all members, rendering the Hutterite school ineffective.

Mate selection posed an even greater problem. The preachers who were supposed to match marriage partners according to divine criteria found themselves unable to do so for their own sons and daughters, whose affections for certain partners were well known. Increasingly, they were unable to deny to others what they could not deny to their own offspring. The matching ceremony, therefore, became a meaningless ritual justifying mate selections which were in reality made on the basis of affection.

This decline of social controls was facilitated by the creation of wealth in communities for which no legitimate use could be formulated. Up until 1622, Hutterite elders expropriated all genuine surpluses for a common treasury intended to provide safeguards against war, plunder, and famine. In fact, this common treasury saved Hutterites from extinction in 1622, when they were thrown out of Moravia and all their material properties were confiscated by the authorities.

Since equality in access to common resources is easier to maintain under conditions of scarcity than of affluence, and since the expropriation by the elders absorbed the accumulated wealth of the communities entirely (except for working capital and capital needed for expansion), the diversion of profits by families was kept in check.

After 1630, when the newly-built communities in Hungary had overcome the hardships of their exodus, no surpluses for a common treasury were expropriated. As a result, the community was exposed to the diversion of competing family factions.

The social dynamics created by a declining religious commitment were accompanied by an increasing family appropriation of goods and a coincident undermining of the socializing system. These forces in turn led to a progressive erosion of the community of goods and an increased reassertion of the family which eventually absorbed all these functions when the last community of goods broke up in 1685.

The final outcome, therefore, proved to be inescapable. War and persecution provided only the challenges, acting like snares for the spiritually and socially weakened communities and bringing them to ruin.

The original structural design of the Hutterite community of goods by the over-zealous founding fathers was psychologically too demanding of parents and children alike. So much so, that when the religious convictions moderated, as was inevitable once children were born and raised in the communities, Hutterite parents and children were left in a state of psychological tension which drove them to reassert the traditional family relations. The reassertion of the family, particularly as an economic unit, destroyed the egalitarian qualities of the community of goods, and while there is no evidence at all that the Hutterite membership wilfully weakened their communities, the trend became irreversible when the economically and socially debilitated communities failed to overcome the external challenges of the time.

The Second Phase, 1685-1761

Of the Hutterite communities in Hungary and Transylvania which discarded the community of goods in 1685, only five were able to maintain their religious ideology and consequently survive for the next seventy-five years. The others assimilated. These communities were organized around the family as a basic unit, but maintained a number of community functions for which the families assumed responsibility. Each family had its private home, and economic pursuits were a private affair. Property was held in the name of the family. The preacher was elected from the male population and his upkeep was provided for through contributions by the various families. Schools were maintained on the same basis as the church. Welfare measures for widows and orphans likewise were provided for by contributions of families. Individuals grew up in families and early, as well as later, socialization apart from schooling was predominantly a family affair and certainly a family responsibility. Mate selection took place on the basis of individual choices channelled and modified by family preferences. All in all, none of the far-reaching and strict community prerogatives characteristic of the first phase was maintained during the second phase.

The simultaneous occurrence of two processes led to the re-establishment of the community of goods. First, religious persecution of these remaining Hutterite communities led to the conversion of most, but not all, Hutterites to the Catholic faith. Secondly, while this conversion progressed among Hutterites, the religious ideology of these same Hutterites was adopted by some recent Lutheran migrants from Carinthia. These people had been deported to Transylvania because of their Lutheran convictions.

All of these Lutherans were converts who had voluntarily chosen the hardship of forced migration rather than religious acquiescence. They had lost all their friends, relatives, and belongings in Carinthia. The Catholic authorities had given them ample time to make up their minds. They were kept in prison for four months and a simple recantation would have freed them and restored their property to them. While some did recant, those who were finally shipped off to Transylvania formed a group of strong-willed religious converts ready to suffer for their convictions. A further selection took place when the Lutheran officials in Transylvania (where the Lutheran religion was tolerated) demanded that the migrants take the oath of loyalty to the Austrian Crown. A small group refused to do so. They were punished and forcefully dispersed over the countryside.

Some of these Lutherans found work among the equally persecuted Hutterites and consequently came in contact with Hutterite religious ideas, to which they became strongly attracted. After a short while, they consolidated into a group with some Hutterites, who were also ready to defy the authorities, and together they spontaneously reinstated a community of goods among themselves.

Here one observes a self-selective mechanism which distilled from a group of persecuted Lutheran and Hutterite immigrants those personality types which were the religiously most committed and most extreme. Or, in other words, the religious ideology of the newly formed group was strengthened through reducing the membership of two larger groups down to their most orthodox members. For this orthodox remainder, the community of goods as it had existed two hundred years earlier was the right model, and they proceeded to copy rigorously the old structures and the old customs. It is for this group of orthodox members that the processes in our second hypothesis seem to hold true.

The Third Phase, 1761-1818

In order to escape persecution, the newly formed community of goods, which again called itself the Hutterian Brethren, first migrated to Wallachia and finally settled in Russia, northeast of Kiev. The community of goods began to flourish after the group reached Russia in 1770. Within a few years, goods and monies lent to them were repaid. The various crafts proved to be extremely productive and profitable. The community became a showcase of success for peasants and nobility in the area, and the members of the community earned a reputation for honesty, good work, cleanliness, and morals.

In 1808 they were able to acquire Crown land and consequently set themselves up under even more favourable economic conditions. This remarkable trend toward prosperity and independence, however, suddenly reversed itself, and within the next few years the community of goods collapsed.

The assistant of the Office of Trustees for Foreign Settlers, Fadjeew, who was ordered to investigate the difficulties of the Hutterite community, reported in March 1818:

I noticed already at the beginning of my investigation that the root of the disunity of the Mennonites (the group was officially called Mennonites) *was to be found in the contradiction between the principles that were supposed to govern this group and the real concrete social conditions characterized by the corruption of the brethren. . . . I found that the rules of ethics and indestructible single-mindedness which the founders of the community regarded as a duty were not observed any more. These duties were in full force and produced a rare example of unity between several dozen families as long as their number was smaller, as long as they did not have their own land, and as long as they had to divert some of their earnings to pay their local nobleman. However, when the brethren began to occupy their present location which put them into possession of . . . good land and produced several other advantages for them, surplus was created within the group. Under conditions of an increasing population, several persons began to discover that it was possible to live by the work of others. Among the fifty families several began to neglect their duties and lived on the products of the diligent. At this time the tendency emerged to obtain private property and secure earnings of one's work to the advantage of one's own family. . . .*[4]

Another contemporary observer reported:

The masters which headed the various economic branches of the community demanded independence. Each of them withdrew from the common treasury and opened businesses of their own. They bought raw materials and sold the goods independently. Instead of handing over the revenues to the community, they just presented the invoices. . . . the tendency to enjoy the good life . . . brought apathy, hostility, envy, and dissatisfaction into the Gemeinschaft, and, step-by-step, caused the disintegration of the group.[5]

Hutterite reports written during this time indicate that the last founding fathers of the community of goods in 1761 died between 1800 and 1810.

When the leadership of the community was transferred to members born and socialized in the system, "They had neither the loyalty, integrity, nor the diligence to conduct the offices and duties with which they were entrusted."

The community of goods disintegrated a second time, insofar as its internal processes are concerned, in exactly the same way as in 1685. Two social processes were simultaneously occurring and developing side-by-side. On the one hand, families began to expropriate communal resources for themselves to the exclusion of others, while those who were excluded from sharing those resources correspondingly lost their motivation to participate in the productive processes of the community; both these processes took place when religious restraints were low, allowing such tendencies to be expressed openly.

Inequality among members and relative deprivation between members, facilitated by a low religious commitment under conditions where distributable wealth was available, led to the disintegration of the community of goods and the reassertion of the Hutterite family.

The Fourth Phase, 1818-1859

For several decades, those Hutterite families who had abolished their community of goods in 1818 lived in considerable poverty and social disorganization. In 1842, however, the Russian authorities allowed all Hutterite families to re-settle close to some Mennonite villages, assigning about 175 acres of land to each family and providing some capital for a new start. The settlement quickly flourished and three years later was already able to repay the loan it had received.

In 1846, the first group of families asked for permission to form a community of goods. When such permission was finally given in 1856, a complicated series of communal trials, followed either by failure or success, began. Employing the same self-selective process already observed in 1761, one group of Hutterite families after another got together, pooled their resources, and instituted the community of goods. Those groups which failed eliminated those members which were socially, psychologically, and religiously unable to adapt to the conditions in the community of goods. As more communal trials followed, the whole population sorted itself out in such a way that only those people were left to carry on the community of goods who possessed the required dedication, enthusiasm and conviction to endure the restraints which the community of goods imposed on them. Three such groups distilled themselves out from the larger population by such self-selective processes: the *Dariusleut*, the *Lehrerleut*, and the *Schmeidenleut*. Those who failed, and those who never tried, came to be known as *Praerieleut*. When all four of these groups migrated to the United States between 1874 and 1879, the three former groups formed the nucleus of all North American

Hutterite communities, while the *Praerieleut* were culturally and religiously absorbed by the larger society. *Again, a weakened religious ideology was strengthened and made central through the elimination of members until the committed remained. When only committed members were left in the group, the community of goods became socially possible and continued successfully.*

This phase, therefore, shows a variation of the same self-selective processes already observed prior to the first re-establishment of the community of goods in 1761. There is, however, one important difference. The self-selective processes of 1761 emphasized religious convictions and consequently led to the formation of groups consisting of religious converts – or revival personalities who then proceeded to establish a community of goods satisfying their religious convictions.

The communal trials following 1856 were social experiments where people actually lived together communally. Depending upon whether they failed or succeeded, they sorted themselves out in such a way that the community of goods which survived these trials not only satisfied the religious convictions of its members, but also incorporated such social variables as leadership, personal compatibility, and individual satisfaction.

The Fifth Phase, 1859 to the Present

As a result of the processes of the previous stage, the community of goods in force at the present time does not conform to the extreme models of 1535 and 1761 but is in fact much more sophisticated and balanced. Socialization of children is a responsibility divided between community and the family, so that the severe psychological strains of the early socialization practices are avoided. Mate selection is largely left to the individual channelled by family preferences. The role of the community is confined, providing the opportunities for meeting potential mates rather than determining the choice of the mate as formerly practiced.

The restrictions on property ownership are somewhat relaxed, allowing for private possessions in the form of clothing, furniture, dishes, books, and other personal belongings.

This more moderate community of goods largely avoids the contradictions which the former extreme types suffered after the death of the first generation of believers.

In today's Hutterite community a relatively low commitment to the communal religious ideology, which is largely ritualized, is congruent with a relatively moderate version of the community of goods. It would, therefore, be unreasonable to expect our hypothesis to be applicable to the present situation.

The interesting question arises as to whether or not Hutterites have learned from their past failures how to avoid the unstable relationship between community and family. The answer to this question is: Yes and No. They do avoid the dangers creating the instabilities in the past but in doing so they have chosen to follow a narrow and demanding route which creates new contradictions in which the family plays a new and decisive role.

The age-old question of the community of goods is this: how to maintain the equality of members and how to motivate members to participate in a system which produces considerable wealth, but refrains from redistributing it and instead allows differential access to at least part of the social and material resources. The solution which Hutterites have implemented today has four answers: first, Hutterites have institutionalized a system of socialization which teaches every male member to entertain high hopes for advancement and social privileges; second, they fulfill these hopes through a system of automatic promotions based entirely on age; third, they make these promotions possible through an unprecedented growth in identical communities which offer these promotions; fourth, they allocate all surpluses to finance their own growth.

A clarification must be made regarding the reward system in today's Hutterite community. First in importance is the system of social rewards in the form of social status and prestige positions. The importance of the hierarchical order in Hutterite communities, and the emphasis on even very small status differentiations and the significance of the behavioural validation of status attainment in all aspects of the daily life of the communities demonstrate the existence and the extent of this motivational reward system. The second reward system consists of a limited, but legitimized, access to material resources and other privileges stratified according to the status positions obtained in a community. These privileges are limited because, in contrast to earlier models of the community of goods which supported a great variety of crafts and trades facilitating decentralization, specialization and independence, the present community of goods is centralized in its division of labour as well as in its accounting system.

If, as we have maintained, social rewards in the form of status positions constitute the crucial variable in regard to the motivation of the individual and ultimately the maintenance of the unity of the community, and if these rewards are obtained and distributed through growth, all these processes ought to be reflected in forms of behaviour associated with the pattern of growth.

Let us then take a look at the status distribution and how it is affected by growth.

The reward system in terms of the total number of status positions in each community is of course limited. Given the high population increase of Hutterites which doubles the population in seventeen to twenty years, every community must "branch out" within this given time in order to create new status positions with which to reward status applicants who come of age.

Hutterite communities have minimum and maximum terminal points as to population size. A new community is hardly ever set up with less than sixty members and is equally seldom allowed to grow beyond one hundred and forty members. The regularity of this process in combination with the data of a stable population growth mentioned earlier allows us to calculate the status distribution in a Hutterite community at these minimum and maximum points.

When a new community is started, there are normally only twelve males over the age of twenty. They have to share between them a division of labour that must distribute from twelve to twenty advanced positions. Most likely, every male over twenty-five years of age will obtain an advanced position or, if one of the older males holds more than one position, as is often the case, the younger members have a reasonable chance that with increasing age they will obtain such a position. Moreover, the community has the possibility of increasing the number of vital positions to its maximum size of twenty as more manpower becomes available. The opportunity structure for Hutterite males at this stage is wide open and promises reasonable advancement for any Hutterite male.

One generation later the opportunity structure has reversed itself. An adult male population that has reached twenty-eight must share the maximum division of labour (twenty positions) possible in the community. At least eight adult males cannot obtain advanced positions and cannot entertain much hope of ever obtaining them. Those who started the community twenty years ago are only in their forties and early fifties and quite unwilling to remove themselves from the scene and hand things over to a new generation.

The opportunity structure of the community at this stage is closed.

A closed opportunity structure, on the other hand, can quickly generate dissatisfaction, frustration, and suspicion on the part of those men excluded from advancement in the economic and social hierarchy.

It is at this point that a conflict between family and community interests becomes operative, leading to inequalities and relative deprivation.

Status positions are distributed by the vote of all baptized male members, and family members tend to vote for each other; therefore families with the most votes can favour their members to the exclusion of other families. Despite all attempts to keep the mechanism of motivation and reward strictly egalitarian, status positions are indeed often distributed not according to accepted criteria of seniority but according to the powers wielded by a particular family. Unequal access to community resources and unequal distribution of privileges and prerogatives, however, lose their legitimacy when they are backed up by nothing more than the accident of a family's voting power. The individual tends to tolerate inequalities as long as there is a realistic hope that one day he himself will obtain certain privileges. In cases where such hopes are shattered because of the unequal distribution of votes which will lead to his permanent exclusion, his motivation for participation drops and gives rise to actions of frustration, obstruction, and conflict.

There are a number of additional factors which must be assessed in this connection. If, as we have asserted, a Hutterite community must establish a daughter community within one generation in order to reward its members, who otherwise would become a source of social conflict and disunity, the community must accept the responsibility for making the establishment of the new community financially possible.

The expropriation of community surpluses and severe restrictions on consumption are necessary to obtain this goal. Furthermore it is evident that the establishment of a new community requires the acquisition of more property, and this property must be bought from members of the respective host society.

With one of the world's highest rates of natural increase, Hutterites have managed to finance each successive generation for the last 100 years in such a way that its equipment and holdings are at least equal to, if not better than, those of the preceding generation. This feat is only duplicated by the most highly technologically developed societies, which all have a much lower rate of population increase than Hutterites. In fact, Hutterites score a lonely first among the world populations in terms of population increase and ability to finance their own expansion quantitatively as well as qualitatively.

Therefore the motivation of individuals in terms of status expectations, the high population increase, the maintenance of the reward system under legitimized conditions plus the acquisition of land and the financial capacity to acquire it, all acting together and properly timed, produce a social dynamic which has allowed Hutterites to make possible what no other population in the world was able to do over any extended period of time.

At the same time, these factors expose the vulnerability of the system. The partial or complete inability to perform any of these functions at the proper time can put serious strains on the system and might promote various forms of social disintegration. The consolidation of the Western family farm in terms of maximum size, manpower, level of technology, and institutionalized succession will invariably lead to a situation not unlike the one the Amish sect is faced with in Lancaster County, Pennsylvania. A well consolidated farm population maintains its hold on the land and enters into competition with the Amish over the relatively small amount of land which is vacated. Such competition puts land out of reach for those groups with the lesser powers of raising capital. Although the Amish or the Hutterites are able to save more than their neighbours in absolute terms because of their greater restrictions on consumption, their population increase creates a much greater need for capital and puts them at a disadvantage relative to a more slowly increasing or even declining population.

The fact that Hutterites moved into Saskatchewan, Montana, and Northern Alberta during the last two decades indicates that these competitive processes are already at work. There is no question that most Hutterites would like to continue the type of farming found in Southern Alberta for which they have the greatest experience as individuals as well as communities. But only the very wealthy communities were able to stay in the area, while the others moved into less competitive regions.

Many Hutterite communities during the last decade were unable to finance their own expansion. Consequently, they resorted to loan or share-cropping arrangements. In either case the difficulties of one generation to generate the necessary capital for expansion are simply put off to the next generation. If the rate of natural population increase remains constant the financial difficulties of these communities will compound during the next fifteen to twenty years.

At the same time, restrictions on consumption, the main means for Hutterites to raise capital, are becoming more difficult to enforce. Expansion of consumption takes place in many legitimate areas like the acquisition of technological equipment for communal use, even though these do not necessarily contribute to the efficiency of production or to health services for Hutterite individuals. While Hutterite communities were almost self-sufficient thirty years ago, the variety of goods and services necessary today has increased dramatically. Incoming cash revenue has of course increased at the same time, but the general move from economic self-sufficiency toward interdependence with the larger economic market means that Hutterites today are sharing more of the economic problems of the prairie farm population than ever before. This trend is still increasing.

Another factor which accounts for the powers of raising capital among Hutterites is the pooling of human resorces, which enables them to escape to a large extent the cost-price squeeze from which other western farmers suffer. The existence of crafts supporting the agricultural operations in the community and the profitable use of these crafts during the off-season is still a major competitive advantage for the Hutterites.

This trend might be effectively offset by the greater per capita overall efficiency of the well established western farm family. The pooling of human resources in Hutterite communities also creates social responsibilities from child care and education to old age. These services are carried on the Canadian societal level, while Hutterites insist on discharging these responsibilities on the communal level, thereby placing an additional burden on themselves.

Given that the consolidation of prairie farming continues, the competitive advantage of the Hutterites relative to other western farmers will correspondingly erode and will most likely lead to a closing of the real-estate market from them. Each new Hutterite community requires the consent to sell from five to ten farmers whose holdings must satisfy certain qualitative and geographical requirements. Such a combination of factors will be harder and harder to obtain as farmers generally become more unwilling to sell.

In such a situation Hutterites have a number of choices. They may allow the loss of members, to ease the population pressure. This solution would be most dangerous because loss of membership would only be possible if members are allowed to doubt the validity of the whole religious-socio-cultural system. Once this process of doubt gains momentum, it will be difficult to stop the flood from overwhelming the whole group, and bringing about large-scale disintegration; therefore, this choice is not very likely to materialize.

The second choice is to migrate to new frontiers. Although the frontiers of this globe are rapidly disappearing, for a limited period into the future it might be possible to find such places. But Hutterites in the past have never migrated unless direct and overt threats against their beliefs and practices were made and even then they migrated with great reluctance. The experience which certain Mennonites and other sectarian groups have had in South America is not altogether encouraging, and it is extremely doubtful that the present Hutterite generation in fact has the necessary pioneering spirit to enter into such drastic and upsetting experiments.

A third, more likely, possibility is to continue to search the western plains of Canada and the United States, avoiding highly competitive areas and settling in places where the pooling of manpower and resources in combination with considerable agricultural skills provides Hutterites with competitive advantages. Such a move would lead to a wider dispersion of the sect in North America and the avoidance of concentric settlements as found in Alberta and Manitoba.

Another possible, but presently not very likely, move which Hutterites might undertake is a change in regard to their division of labour and their productive skills. Hutterites unable to acquire land for agricultural expansion might resort to industrial and semi-industrial expansion. Food processing, furniture making, carpeting, and constructing seem to be the most likely areas where already accumulated experiences exist. Such a diversion of skills would shift the competitive struggle from the agricultural to the industrial level.

The last possibility, and probably the most likely, is birth control. There probably will be no change in the official religiously approved group sentiments, but individuals, particularly the younger generation, have already responded to a change in attitudes. Knowledge about birth control methods has long found entry into Hutterite communities through medical channels for the older generation, and peer-group relations for the younger. No drastic drop in the net reproduction rate can be expected because children are still a valuable group asset putting relatively little inconvenience on individual parents. But many young parents are becoming aware of a number of factors which previously carried little weight. As parents become more self-centred rather than community-centred, this cannot help but have some influence on the birth rate of the group.

It was not, of course, my intention to compile a catalogue of factors which foretells the doom of the Hutterite sect. Nor can I offer any consolation to the prejudiced who might hope for a quick assimilation or drastic reduction in the expansion of Hutterites. On the contrary, I believe that Hutterites probably will outlive most, if not all, ethnic groups presently in Canada, with the exception of Jewish communities and the bicultural group of French Canadians.

The inherent instability of the community of goods which has plagued Hutterites in the past is by no means absent at the present time, but it is extremely well managed through highly dynamic, goal-oriented, direction-giving patterns of growth.

Yet these patterns of growth are so demanding of the population and are dependent on so many interacting and properly timed factors which are not controlled by Hutterites (and therefore cannot be taken for granted in the future), that a change in these growth patterns is a highly probable inference.

The most likely change, as indicated earlier, will be a wider distribution of Hutterite communities over the western plains of Canada and the United States, combined with a gradual slow-down in population growth.

Of equally high probability is my further inference that no sudden collapse of the Hutterite community of goods is in evidence at this time. The creative powers and the collective wisdom of this socio-cultural group is of such a nature that the Hutterite tradition and the Hutterite way of life will successfully exist for many generations to come.

Eight

CHANGE AND TRANSITION
IN HUTTERIAN SOCIETY

John W. Bennett

Economically speaking, the Hutterian presence in North America is a
story of the response of a sectarian people of sixteenth-century origins
and Eastern European village background to the evolving commercial
agricultural economy of North America from the nineteenth into the
twentieth century. Hutterian culture, then, regardless of whatever else it
might be, presents a problem of social and economic development and
change, perhaps comparable to the emerging countries of Asia, Africa
and Latin America, but equally, a part of the agrarian transition in
North America.

However, the problem has its complexities insofar as the Hutterites
have a unique social system that differs in key institutional features from
the general system of North American society. This means that the
effects of developmental change on Hutterian life are bound to differ
from those observed for non-Hutterian rural society. In the most fundamental sense, they will differ because the Hutterian system is "inten-
tional"; that is, it is a self-conscious experimental social order, held
together by deep social conviction, religious faith, and objective social
planning – all with full awareness of the differences as compared to the
general system. Change, therefore, in Hutterian life is accompanied by
attempts to control and direct that change; Hutterites, like the rest of
us, may be powerless to control the major vectors of socio-economic
change in a modernizing society and a growing economy, but perhaps
to a greater degree than most of us, they are able to anticipate and
control its local effects.

My own experiences with the colonies should perhaps be mentioned:
in 1964 and 1965 I conducted a study of six colonies in southwestern

Saskatchewan with special emphasis on their economy and decision-making system, that was eventually published in articles and a book (see bibliography). Since that time, I have maintained contact with these colonies, and in 1972 did a re-study of the same six, plus some others that had settled in the region since the initial research, as well as three or four colonies in Alberta. In 1973 I conducted a survey of Montana colonies that involved brief visits and discussions on economic and social matters with most of the colonies in that state. All of these later studies have emphasized the change process. My 1965 baseline is conservative, since in that initial study I emphasized the *Lehrerleut* more than the *Dariusleut*, and the former are considerably more conservative. This chapter does not present the definitive analysis of Hutterian change, but shall be regarded as tentative and descriptive only, rather than the finished statement that will hopefully follow when the work is complete.

An assumption, and some historical-geographical facts, underlie this chapter. First, the facts: in general, change and innovation in Hutterian life has been more marked in the colonies in Manitoba and in the United States than in Saskatchewan and Alberta. The changes I outline in this chapter are taking place in colonies in these two Western Canadian provinces where I have done my research. Many of the innovations described here began earlier in the south and east.

The assumption, which is related to the foregoing, is this: that change in Hutterian institutions is related to the development of the colony's economy. By this I mean that Hutterites resist change in any social field, and in consumption habits, until they feel the colony's economy has reached a satisfactory level of development. When this takes place, they begin investing in consumption, and also seem, in many cases, but not all, to relax personnel policies and the rules governing social life. The western Canadian colonies in Saskatchewan are just entering this stage, since they began as daughter colonies of Alberta Hutterites during the past fifteen years. But in addition, all colonies in western Canada, because of the refractory climate and other resources, as well as the relative slowness of growth in the Canadian economy, have been less prosperous than colonies elsewhere.

The above comments are included to help the reader who may know Hutterite life elsewhere to understand that the colonies in my purview have been in many respects less inclined to accept innovations.

Economic Change and Development

First of all, it is important to note that nearly all the colonies I have looked at since 1971 have experienced a satisfactory economic growth rate which equals, or exceeds, the rate of cost inflation. I have taken this rate (this is written in February 1974) to be approximately five per cent per annum – a figure representing the increase of costs in doing agricultural business. That is, the colonies I have seen, with three or four exceptions, have maintained their competitive economic position, and have not suffered a drop in consumption. In fact, simply by maintaining a growth rate equal to or in excess of cost inflation, they have increased their measure of affluence and collective consumption, since they have been able to build on assets already in hand. I take this as evidence of the favourable economic adaptation represented by Hutterian culture and economy: the impressive savings permitted by communal property, consumption austerity, and the large scale of operations gives the colonies considerable protection against economic uncertainties and high interest rates. The Hutterian performance in the past decade thus suggests that the collective adaptation to a capitalist market arrangement in agriculture can be an extremely effective one, providing that discipline and commitment are maintained. I am convinced at the time of writing that even if cost inflation should reach an annual figure of ten per cent or above, Hutterites would continue to maintain a favourable position, although their growth might slack off as markets constricted. It is admitted that their continued growth in the current period is due in large part to sustained markets for grain and livestock, despite inflation of costs of production.

This growth in the past decade has also meant that the colonies I have surveyed have experienced an approximate doubling of their net worth or capital value. A colony with a net worth of five hundred thousand dollars in 1965 is worth at least one million dollars today; a colony with a gross income of two hundred and fifty-thousand dollars in 1965 doubled that income in 1973; while others show net worth and gross income increases of much larger magnitudes. Net incomes are of course not proportionate to these increases in gross, because costs have risen. The following stylized and somewhat idealized figures represent the trends I have encountered:

Item	1965	1973
Colony gross income:	$250,000	$500,000
Operating expenses:	200,000	350,000
Net income:	50,000	150,000
Debt retirement:	15,000	—
Domestic expenditures	10,000	100,000
Cash savings:	5,000	10,000

These figures are interesting, because they show that income has kept up with increases in costs, not only at the operating level, but also in domestic consumption and maintenance. The consumption figure includes installation of interior plumbing and other conveniences – a widespread innovation in the 1970's. Not all colonies are in this fortunate a position, but this certainly represents a trend. As already indicated, whether this can be sustained if agricultural markets experience a serious decline is another question.

Every Hutterian colony fissions when population reaches a certain level: the precise figure has steadily dropped in the past quarter-century, reflecting both sociological pressures to maintain a smooth collective communal decision-making apparatus (Hutterites feel, rightly, that communes function best with relatively small numbers), and also the need to maintain a given consumption level at current costs. Hutterites have been increasing their collective consumption level despite inflation not only because their rate of growth gives them more cash (as shown in the sketchy figures above) but also because the average colony is smaller due to earlier division.

However, it must be noted that this favourable position has been maintained in part at the expense of the surrounding community, since there are now more colonies. As colonies increase in number, land for continued expansion grows scarcer, and the existing colonies move toward competition with each other. In other words, the relative affluence and high growth rate does not mean that all problems are solved. There are certain social costs associated with this process which may have to be paid at some future date. But even here, it must be remembered that Hutterites have shown considerable willingness to undertake daring and unusual solutions when needs require. If they are blocked from further expansion in western North America, they may move toward Mexico or the sub-Boreal lands, where room for expansion will remain available for a long time to come. Such colonization, however, would mean a return to earlier, more rugged and deprived conditions.

And of course there is another cost associated with early fission: the strain on the cash reserve. Colony division means that the new colony is financed in considerable part by withdrawals of cash, which can penalize the home colony. This can be particularly serious when growth requires consistent and sustained investment in order to maintain a given income level – a situation common enough in all enterprises, agricultural or other, in an era of inflation. It is possible that the present favourable situation could change if costs should increase further, markets become depressed, and land becomes scarcer. Colonies will have to find some way to maintain larger populations, which can contribute to internal stress and the need to accomodate lower levels of consumption. In other words, the picture is not entirely bright, and Hutterites are well aware of the dangers.

Still another problem must be faced. If colonies divide sooner, it increases the total number of small, undercapitalized colonies. In order to move rapidly toward solvency, such colonies must enter highly specialized production with high rates of return (e.g., turkey production, or large-scale livestock feeding). Since land is increasingly expensive, these small new colonies will not have large acreages, further underlining the need for intensive, specialized regimes. This has its vulnerabilities to market conditions as well as a rapid growth rate. It has an important sociological implication in that it means that a large proportion of the population of the new, small colonies is involved in management. That is, the colony becomes equivalent to a commercial farm or agricultural enterprise – more so than in the past, when the managerial group was a distinct minority. Thus the adaptive responses to the changing national economic situation will have their sociological implications, and the precise adaptive responses to these cannot be predicted confidently at the moment.

Increasing Domestic Consumption

Perhaps the most dramatic change in the colonies since the early 1960's has been the installation of a series of "modern" (the Hutterite term) collective consumption items: complete interior plumbing, including private bathrooms for each nuclear family unit; central heating systems, with propane probably the most common; the use of pre-cut and in some cases, fully prefabricated structures of all kinds, especially dwellings; more lawns, flower beds and other exterior adornments; and more interior adornment in the form of plastic flowers, coloured curtains, vinyl-covered floors and walls; and new or used factory-made furniture. The rapidity and universality of these improvements constitute a virtual revolution in Hutterian lifestyle toward a town or farmhouse middle-class standard.

When interviewed on these changes, Hutterites have a number of routine responses:

"It's the modern way – all the colonies are doing it."

"They all do it – you have to go along."

"There is nothing different here – we just have enough money to do what we wanted"

"The women want it, so we have it."

"We told the men we had to have more conveniences; the old ways, like those wood floors, make too much work."

In sum, Hutterites tend to view the consumption gains as a matter of deferred gratification, and they also see them as rewards for their adherence to the general standards of the sect, and of the wider community. Their posture is a familiar one: they too have shared in the general increase in prosperity of Great Plains agricultural communities.

At the same time, the improvements have not made important inroads into the remaining taboo against excessive *personal* possessions and consumption (with the partial exception of interior objects of adornment, like bouquets of plastic flowers, and, in some colonies, more factory-made toys and clothing for children and young people). The colonies continue to draw the line on what they see as the most important source of corruption by the "World System": personal acquisitiveness. The consumption gains are mainly in the sphere of collective benefit – if one family gets an indoor toilet, so do all the rest. The configuration provides another example of the Hutterian adaptive strategy of allowing for rising expectations but holding the line on the basic rules.

Studies of labour allocation in several colonies suggest that the increased installation of interior bathrooms, the building of new structures of all kinds, and the installation of lawns, sidewalks, and flowers and trees has been facilitated by labour freed by automation and the use of efficient machinery. The mechanization of Hutterian agriculture has proceeded at the same rate or slightly faster than on the surrounding individual farms and ranches in the Northern Plains. This has meant more production, but in many colonies there has been a net saving of labour time. In slack periods made possible by more rapid planting and harvesting with better and more machines, the male labour force can concentrate on making improvements. In the early 1960's it was unusual to find numbers of men engaged in construction of dwellings, or in adornment tasks, but this was common in the early 1970's. Again, Hutterites did not perceive this as a change in policy, but simply as a shift in labour allocation made possible by time saving.

The innovation of pre-cut fabricated structures has been due in large part to promotion of the technique by construction companies in Regina, Saskatchewan, and Calgary, Alberta, who have offered to prepare the materials in accordance with Hutterian specifications, and deliver them to the colony for a unit price. The price would decrease with more colonies using the service. This arrangement has been successful for everyone concerned: the colonies, who cannot really turn down a bargain, especially in necessities, get everything supplied for the building, and can save considerable time formerly spent in negotiating with different suppliers and in cutting and shaping the materials themselves; the appearance of the buildings is more uniform, more "modern"; and many of the technical arrangements for accomodating the new plumbing and heating systems are taken care of in advance. Although the Hutterites make a point of the time-saving, they do not seem to be aware that this is in apparent conflict with the fact that more time has become available through labour-saving devices, as noted previously. The writer has concluded tentatively that the bargain aspect of the system, plus the more professional finish of the resulting structures, has been the major attraction, and not labour-saving.

The "deferred gratification" aspect of these developments suggests that Hutterites possess a hierarchy of values concerning the domestic and economic activity spheres which do not emerge clearly unless the colonies are studied over a period of time. My interviews, for example, made it clear that lawns and flowers are not new ideas, but are anticipated improvements. However, they must wait until a satisfactory level of capital investment in the farm has been reached. The situation is exactly the same for the majority of the individual farmers in the region: our studies of their management and domestic economy strategies show that among a majority the "farm comes first." However, the differences between the Hutterites and non-Hutterites show up in the greater sense of restraint in the former: the standards are not individual, but collective, and the number of adornment innovations is carefully controlled.

Increased Liberalization of Personnel Policies

This trend is more visible among the *Dariusleut* than the *Lehrerleut*; it is simply a continuation of a long-standing difference between the two *Leute*. However, at the present the difference is increasing, as the *Lehrerleut* continue to resist liberalization in what appears, in some colonies, to be a last-ditch clinging to conservative definitions of individual autonomy and expressiveness. While no detailed figures are available, most Hutterian experts agree that the defection rate among the *Lehrerleut* has increased greatly in recent years, and may now be double that of the *Dariusleut*.

Hutterian policies restricting public education to grade eight reflect a well founded belief that exposure to peer groups in the society at large will lead to devastating emigration by the young. In fact, in their early years in North America, Hutterites were more relaxed about education, and permitted high school and college experience in the initial South Dakota sojourn (1872-1917), after which they left the United States for Canada. (Colonies have now re-entered the United States, including South Dakota, where many of their old colonies were held by the state government and sold back to the Brethren.) These early experiences with public education were unfortunate, and the restrictive policies developed as a response.

Currently policies are beginning to change toward greater tolerance of educational experiences beyond the eighth grade. Many colonies now permit, and some encourage, correspondence-course high-school training, and a few have permitted teacher training beyond high school. The *Dariusleut* colonies in Montana, which represent a liberal wing even among the *Dariusleut*, are moving in this direction – not rapidly, but, one feels, definitely. One might hazard the guess that within a decade or two nearly every child will have some high school, and a small percentage a year or two of college. There are similar tendencies in South Dakota, and among the *Schmeindeleut* in Manitoba.

Travel has increased greatly, largely as a simple consequence of an increasing reliance on the automobile. The habit of searching out bargains in large machinery and appliances, like refrigerator plants or bulldozers, has meant an increased proclivity to travel long distances. A fairly common sight in the Northern Plains is a Hutterian truck loaded with a massive machine, on its way back to the home colony hundreds of miles away. The increased business visits to nearby service-centre towns has meant that a larger number of women and young people have had greater opportunity to shop and visit. In a few colonies increased movement is becoming a problem for the colony and its neighbor colonies, but the relaxation is general. Hutterites are more verbal about travel, they are eager to discuss their travels and sightseeing with visitors, and they present a more cosmopolitan profile than a decade ago – and all these changes are showing up in the colony culture in the form of more magazines, souvenirs, maps, stories, and communication with other Hutterites.

Many of these changes have influenced the role of women more than that of the men. Since the female status in Hutterian society has been constrained, there was room for change, and any alteration in consumption habits or personal movement is bound to have its effect. Hutterian women are responsible for much of the consumption change – the men say so openly, and outspoken women likewise. The Hutterite woman's ability to influence colony policy has always been important, as it is in all male-dominated societies, and numerous male informants have told me that the women have been quite assertive in recent years, and have applied various subtle sanctions to obtain their ends – which are generally an easier life and more adherence to the middle-income living standards of the larger society. Women have successfully campaigned for indoor plumbing, covered floors, electric floor-polishing and spray-painting equipment (traditionally women have been the painters, and have come to resent the job), better kitchen equipment, the right to do some cooking in the family domicile, more latitude in buying certain items of clothing for the children, more decoration inside and outside the houses, and in general, nearly all of the consumption changes previously described. It is not that men have been uninterested in these; many of them have joined the women in their campaigns for increased capital allocations to the domestic economy. But in many colonies the initial pressure came from the distaff side. Some of my male informants are secretly proud of this, and seemingly welcome this assertiveness on the part of the women.

These changes also mean increased autonomy for the family. This is a trend of long standing; Hutterite life, in the context of a commune, has always recognized the integrity of the nuclear family unit (the Israeli kibbutz has had a similar history). Hutterian society combines reverence for the sexual bond of husband and wife and their love and affection for their own children, with the communal socialization principle expressed as schooling for the children from pre-school age. The separate eating facilities for the adults and the children have also emphasized the principle of communal socialization. However, these institutional separations are "daytime"; all children have returned to the nuclear apartment for the evening and sleeping, and this experience has provided abundant opportunity for familial experiences and socialization.

The installation of private bath and toilet facilities tends to strengthen these family ties and domestic unity; this change, spreading rapidly through the colonies, may have unforeseeable effects on the delicate balance between the commune and the nuclear units which compose it. It is too early to predict ultimate consequences or sweeping changes (no change is ever "sweeping" in Hutterian society), but there is no question that the nuclear family has shown increasing strength in the past decade – at least in these Western colonies. This tendency joins with the increasing agrarian professionalism cited earlier – the "commune" tends to function more emphatically in the sphere of agrarian management, and perhaps somewhat less so in the social relational; while the family, and blood kinship ties generally, begin to appropriate more of the social and expressive functions.

Something is happening to the Hutterian population. The enhanced autonomy of the women, and the increasing integration of the nuclear family, has meant a growing awareness of the population situation. Hutterian families appear to be getting smaller; women are terminating their child-bearing earlier; and many men seem to accept, or at least not to oppose, this trend. The colonies are well aware of the increasing restrictions in colony expansion and land purchase; if they wish to remain in the West, and to avoid new adventures in colonization elsewhere in the world, or into the less well-endowed regions of the Americas, they will have to control their rate of increase. Their collective consumption gains may also be playing a role in this possible "demographic transition" in Hutterian society. Hutterites will deny that any change in attitudes or practices pertaining to family size have taken place, but checks on the situation strongly suggest that a quiet program of controls has been developing.

Wider External Contacts

Increased travel and mobility have already been dealt with in part, but there is another aspect: the Hutterian sect now shows signs of becoming a movement. There are now colonies claiming inspiration from Hutterian protocols and beliefs in the Philippines, Japan, India, and several European countries. The North American Hutterites have not formally acknowledged these groups, but the *Dariusleut* have held serious discussions about the possibility of sending delegations to the Japanese groups, in order to determine the extent of their adherence to Hutterian principles. The issue is clear enough: Hutterian society has been a kinship system as well as a sect, or a communal entity. Hutterites have to be born into the fold. If the foreign groups are recognized, a new principle of membership will have been adopted, and the consequences of this, like other things, are incalculable.

In 1972 a persistent rumour was circulating among the colonies concerning an affiliation between Hutterites and Old Order Amish – inconceivable geographically, technically, and culturally, but indicative of the expansive mood of some of the Brethren. The Bruderhof people – the first of the Hutterite convert groups, and once partly recognized as Hutterian by the colonies – have shown an interest in returning to the Hutterian universe, and becoming an Eastern U.S. branch or separate *leut*.

Many of the "new communes", formed during the commune craze in the mid-1960's, have shown increasing interest in the old communals, the Hutterites, and have made numerous visits to the colonies to exchange information and obtain pointers. Some of these groups have adopted Hutterian social policies and governing methods, with greater or less degrees of success. The "Jesus People" have shown similar interest, although interaction between them and Hutterites is generally strained – in some instances they have had the temerity to censure Hutterites for a lack of true Christian piety, (a criticism levelled at the Hutterites in the past by other fundamentalist groups, who have seen the colonies as profit-making enterprises masquerading as Christian brotherhoods).

The Shape of the Future

No one can predict in detail what will happen to Hutterian life in the next generation or so, but certain very general tendencies seem reasonable enough, given the processes described in this paper.

First, the Hutterites will continue to develop awareness and understanding of the structure of non-Hutterian society, and their own role in that larger world. Hutterites – at least most colonies – have ceased during the past decade to view themselves as isolates, as a separate people existing alongside a vague outside world which they acknowledge minimally. Many Brethren clearly articulate the dangers of this viewpoint: it leads directly to criticisms of the Hutterites as an arrogant, aloof people, out to exploit the majority society for all it is worth. Hutterites will continue to move into the larger world, and their personalities will become more accessible, more articulate as they do. But there is no good evidence at the present time that this will diminish their faith, nor that it will destroy the communal colony frame of their existence.

This movement into the world, or at least closer to it, involves a trade-off of a certain amount of freedom, or isolation, for greater security and greater acceptance by the non-Hutterian community. This will involve choices; it is not a simple matter of opening up the colonies to more outside involvement, or of merely spending more time in town, visiting friends, accepting social invitations, joining clubs, or becoming involved in agricultural politics. A Hutterian farm boss in Saskatchewan accepted election in 1972 as a regional representative of a hog-producers' association, an event that was censured by elders from other colonies, and was agreed to by the man concerned only after considerable soul-searching. He realized that it meant a break with the time-honoured policy of non-involvement in the institutions of the Outside, but he felt that his colony's own hog business, a massive and specialized operation, justified his decision. He recognized that the colonies could no longer remain aloof when in some communities they had become major producers.

There is also a growing tendency toward more variation between colonies. This is most obviously represented by the trend toward economic specialization. Individual colonies are becoming known as turkey farms, livestock feeders, hog producers, dairymen – although in every case the production program continues to show considerable diversity. It is simply that a choice is made to invest more than the usual amount in the most productive activity, given the market situation. The trend is general; it is affecting all agriculture in the Great Plains, and the colonies are only following the pattern.

Colonies will also begin to differ in size. Variations in population policy, as well as in consumption expenditures, are bound to result in varying population size. The colonies have been remarkably uniform: in recent decades 150 to 120 has been the size at fission; but this is dropping in a great many colonies, who feel that anything from 65 to 100 is an optimum size. The older, very large-acreage colonies will probably continue to permit population to expand to over 100 and even larger before dividing. Here again the forces are the familiar ones affecting all producers, individual or collective: increasing costs of production and rising standards of living mean that trade-offs need to be made between population and wants, with high-return specialized production becoming the means. Various solutions can be found; the differences in resources requires variation.

Colonies will also continue to differentiate in terms of personnel policy and relationships with the Outside. Despite difficulties with their young people, *Lehrerleut* colonies will try to hold the line, and these colonies will continue to be known as "old fashioned". Hutterites – *Dariusleut* people generally, and the more liberal *Lehrerleut* individuals – are increasingly articulate about this, which is a change in itself, since a decade ago Hutterites were extremely close-mouthed about colony and *Leut* differences, preferring to give the impression of an absolutely uniform sect and society. Against this differentiation, of course, are powerful forces for homogenization in Hutterian culture, such as the constant communication between colonies, and mutual surveillance to insure adherence to the rules. However, there is some evidence that communication has become more specialized; that the "liberal" colonies are less inclined to maintain ties with "conservative" colonies. If this trend continues, it will become the first decisive horizontal sectioning of Hutterian life. It will cut through the *Leute*, because inevitably, many *Lehrerleut* colonies will reject the strict regulations and begin to follow more liberal paths.

In the last analysis, one cannot foresee any drastic changes. So long as Hutterites retain control over children's education, and so long as family autonomy does not begin to seriously threaten the collective management of the colony economy, the Hutterian way will continue along its traditional path. Consumption is bound to continue to rise, but so long as the line is held on individual possessions, collective consumption can rise almost indefinitely before threatening basic beliefs and life styles. Most of these investments are directed toward general comfort and convenience, not luxury. A colony installs a standby power plant, which eliminates outages and cold in the long winters; this is increased consumption, but for the benefit of the whole, and without any real effect on possessions or relevant lifeways.

Finally, one can foresee continued economic competence and relative prosperity. Hutterites are here to stay, economically; the collective management and impressive savings make them unbeatable competitors. Sooner or later the individualized agrarian society of the Great Plains is going to have to emulate them, at least introduce more risk-spreading institutions – or else see Great Plains agriculture pass into the hands of impersonal, outside companies. In a sense, some Hutterites are becoming these "companies", but as Albertans have come to realize in recent years, they are preferable as neighbours, and as patrons of local business, to the outsiders. The tide has turned, certainly in Alberta: Hutterites are coming to be seen as the desirable alternative to Big Agribusiness.

Nine

HUTTERITE EDUCATION
IN ALBERTA: A TEST CASE
IN ASSIMILATION, 1920-70

Robert J. MacDonald

In the cultural development of Western Canada, notwithstanding the fact that some groups have retained such aspects of their culture as language, it could be said that the predominant patterns which have emerged have been derived from the precepts of Britain and America. That is, the predominant system of government and law, including many customs stemming from law, has been British, while the pattern of agriculture has been American. And English became the essential language to be spoken by all. For much of the history of the Canadian plains, the official *leitmotiv* has been the assimilation of the various immigrant ethnic groups to this Anglo-American norm. In his article "The Roots of Prairie Society", J.E. Rea suggests that during the 1880's in Manitoba, the migrants from Ontario quickly imposed their cultural views on the province. In doing so, they severely limited the political and cultural rights of the French Canadians. However this "fragment majority", having broken off from the Ontario base, faced its biggest task in absorbing the hundreds of thousands of immigrants who poured into the Canadian plains during the first decades of the twentieth century. Rea suggests that for Manitoba at least the "fragment majority" viewed the immigrants as a cultural and economic threat, and by extension the same could be said for the other prairie provinces, Accordingly, the dominant Anglo-American elite openly made the immigrant "aware that his language and his culture were his badges of inferiority and a continuing obstacle to assimilation."[1]

One of the instruments of this assimilation has been the public school. In a report to the Manitoba Legislature in 1948, a Select Committee stated "The public school is the great melting pot from which emerges the model Canadian citizen. It provides the means whereby the individual may obtain a better enjoyment of life and may become a more useful citizen and may make some contribution to the community in which he lives."[2] Several ethnic minorities have resisted this assimilative trend to a greater or lesser degree; the Hutterian Brethren have been prominent among those groups which have been most stubborn in their resistance. In this chapter, the cultural and educational conflict between the Brethren and the larger society of Alberta will be discussed. Specifically, this chapter will examine the attempts by the non-Hutterian community to assimilate the Brethren through the public-school system, and thus remove the cultural and economic threat which the Hutterites posed. As will be indicated, these attempts have failed. Although the Hutterites are spread throughout Alberta, Manitoba, and Saskatchewan in Canada, and Montana, North and South Dakota, Washington, and Minnesota in the United States, the largest single concentration has been in Alberta, and it is in Alberta where the conflict has been sharpest, particularly when a government body, the Communal Property Control Board, gave opponents of the Hutterites a forum to express their views.

Opponents of the Hutterites have seen the public school as the means to break down Hutterite culture. In 1947, the United Farmers of Alberta recommended government action "to cause the Hutterite people to conform to Canadian ways, at least to the extent of compelling their children to take the same education training as Canadian children of surrounding districts, with a view to their ultimate assimilation as Canadian citizens, speaking our common language."[3] Eleven years later, the New Dayton branch of the Farmers' Union of Alberta complained:

It is generally regarded as the object of our public schools to provide the training whereby individuals may become effective citizens and render service to their community and country. In this regard the existing educational facilities established for Hutterite colonies must be said to be unsatisfactory for they do not appear to be in any way developing effective citizens in the accepted sense of the term."[4]

By contrast, the Hutterite philosophy of education and social thought rejects for several reasons the school system adopted by the larger society. First, the Hutterites consider that aspects of the public school's curriculum (such as the implied advocacy of individualism, individual competition, and "Darwinism") threaten their communal life-style. This fear is legitimate in view of the significant place that salvation has in their world outlook. Secondly, the Hutterites view educational integration as the first step towards the gradual destruction of their culture. And finally, they suspect any public-school education beyond the bare essentials, since their life-style is one of agricultural production. Yet, in speaking of the Brethren and education, one must not think that Hutterites are opposed to schools, for their own kindergarten, German school and Sunday school are designed to inculcate Hutterian values in the children and make them aware of the essential religious philosophy behind their social organisation. Rather, the Hutterian Brethren are suspicious of the public system and all that it implies.

Perhaps the most striking aspect of Hutterian belief is the overriding concern to obey God and to achieve salvation. The theme of other-worldliness pervades Hutterite theology from the sixteenth century to such modern spokesmen as Paul Gross of the Espinola Colony in Washington, who writes: "Yet we are not of the world although we are surely in it, and subject to its vicissitudes the same as anyone else. We do not plan this world as our permanent home but seek a future home in the great beyond. We have to make the best of it here in this life, for there will be no other time for our trial. We show our citizenship in another world by living excluded and separated lives in this world."[5] This concern for salvation pervades the *Weltanschauung* of Hutterites in Alberta, for Reverend Walter of the Thompson Colony stated "just because we do not take part in the so-called society, and their way of life, or let our children integrate with the world, I as a true Canadian and Hutterite, a servant of God, cannot see how a life like that will bring our children to Heaven."[6]

Given such a world-view, it is easy to see how the Hutterites distrust the public-school system. Above all, that system is seen as godless, and the Brethren see a distinct link between the godless secular system and the unemployment, crime, juvenile delinquency, and even alcoholism or cancer as characterised in the "outside world".[7] Without a moral and ethical Christian base, modern society has permitted the diverse moral, ethical, social, and technological elements to drift apart. The unity of the educational "process has become fragmentalized into various often-antagonistic subprocesses, teaching incompatible elements to the growing generation. The result of this fragmentalized educational process is ambiguity, alienation, and often cynicism in the younger generation."[8] Hence, the elders believe that they must establish the proper environment for their children, an environment which creates spiritual, moral, and physical unity, an environment which is nurtured in fear of God, which is, they suggest, the beginning of true wisdom.[9]

It is argued that the child must be taught discipline, so that he will not become self-willed and unmanageable. He must thoroughly understand the importance of parental love and parental obedience, as well as his duties and responsibilities to others. The Brethren contend that the public schools do not provide this discipline, and point to the increased student unrest, delinquency and withdrawal from the values upheld by the public school. Consequently, they suggest, other people besides the Hutterian Brethren have set up private schools and colleges to provide a wholesome atmosphere in which to educate their children.[10] And in answer to the charge that they do not support higher education, they turn the argument around and suggest ". . . it is the world which opposes the full and complete and higher education of their children." By "higher" they mean spiritual and moral, rather than higher in terms of level of difficulty, as outside society understands the term.[11]

Given this outlook on the purpose of life and the failure of the public-school system (at least in their eyes), Hutterites clearly see the obvious social and spiritual dangers if they relinquish control of their children's education. Edwin Pitt in his 1949 study indicated that an earlier experience when they sent four men to secondary and normal school backfired when the men failed to return to the colony.[12] Consequently they are sure that the communal way of life will be destroyed by allowing off-colony schooling. According to a 1964 Hutterite pamphlet,

Many parents who have sent their children away from their homes into the cities to attend high schools to further their education have stood by and suffered sorrow and heart-break, for their children drifted into the cesspools of iniquity, turning completely away from their home training and parents. Therefore, why should we throw our children intentionally into perdition, when they see, hear, and learn all manner of godless things 'till their souls finally perish in misery?[13]

It would appear then that basic to any argument, whether in criticism of public schools or with respect to past experience, the central consideration of salvation and God's commandments still emerges paramount.

This philosophy is reflected in the means by which the Hutterites have resisted the imposition of public schools. The first way has been to insist on schools on the colony, where the full weight of Hutterian philosophy can be brought to bear on the child. He is surrounded by a special environment. In 1970, the Pleasant Valley Colony refused the offer of Lacombe County to provide room for Hutterites in an existing school. Whenever a colony school has been refused by the local school authority, Hutterites have been prepared to establish private schools. The further reduction of the secular influence of the public school has been effected by resisting the centralisation of Hutterite schools. It is said that busing would interfere with the religious education, and consequently proposals in Warner County (near Lethbridge) in 1958 and Wheatland County (near Calgary) in 1966 fell on deaf ears.

Another means by which the Brethren have resisted the inroads of the public school has been to insist that the school be held in the colony church. According to the Brethren, this is necessary in order to facilitate a Christian upbringing. But certain practical difficulties ensue for public instruction. For the English teacher, dual use often means that pictures and drawings must be removed everyday to make room for the German school and hence put back up the next day. There are other obstacles to instruction by the English teacher: curtains placed over the blackboard often erase work left on by the teacher; elders' benches at the front prevent effective use of the blackboard; and the prohibition on use of audio-visual aids means a traditional – or obsolete – teaching style has to be adopted by the English teacher.

Finally, the Brethren control the environment through their own system of schools. Since the sixteenth century, the Brethren have maintained their own schools, the German School. It was one of the main ways by which the Hutterite values were passed on to the young. Around the age of two and one-half to three, the child is sent to the *Kleinschule* or kindergarten. Here, along with the other children, he learns to play together and eat together with the others at the nursery school. Generally this is supervised by older women, and the early use of prayer and song is learned as well at this stage. When the child enters the English school, he is handicapped with no knowledge of English, and indeed some elders have requested that German be used to teach in Grade One.

At age six or seven, the child graduates to the German school. For up to an hour before and after the English school, the German teacher gives lessons in High German; the various sayings of Hutterite leaders; songs, largely from the sixteenth and seventeenth centuries; and essentials of Hutterian belief. At various stages of the school experience, the children are required to be able to recite these sayings by rote memory. At age fifteen, the child becomes an adult. Girls receive a hope chest, and both girls and boys receive a copy of the Bible. They also no longer eat separately from the adults. While this aspect of formal education is over, the children continue to attend Sunday school until baptism, generally around the age of nineteen to twenty-one.

This *counter-indoctrination* is designed to give the child an essential fear of God, and fear of disobeying His law. The individual begins his commitment of a life-long service to God, to ensure his salvation. His daily activities as a Hutterite are interpreted as fulfilling God's plan, as laid down in the Scriptures. The effect of the Hutterian education is thus to minimize the effects of the English school.

The cultural and philosophic conflict between the larger Alberta society and the Brethren has been centred in the controversy over public schools ever since they first came to the province in 1918. When the Hutterites first began to feel the pressures of conformity to the American society, the elders looked toward the opening Canadian West as a possible refuge. As a result a colony moved to Dominion City, Manitoba, although the experiment was short-lived. But in a letter dated 27 October, 1899, the Dominion Government agreed not to interfere with their religious beliefs. A significant concession was "They will also be allowed to establish independent schools for teaching their children if they desire to do so, but they will have to be responsible for their maintenance themselves. The children will not be compelled to attend other schools if their education is properly provided for."[14] Though they had had generally satisfactory relations with school authorities in South Dakota, by the time they moved north to escape persecution in 1917-18, provincial control of education and a philosophy of assimilation through the schools had emerged as threats to the Brethren's way of life.

As they moved into the Lethbridge, Macleod, and Rockyford areas, inspectors were sent to explain Alberta education laws. The desirability of establishing a school and finding a capable teacher "who would give the children the training that would best fit them for citizenship" was impressed upon the leaders.[15] Not surprisingly the elders co-operated, for they had been used to having outside teachers during their stay in South Dakota, and were themselves not opposed to education as such. Moreover, under the law they could set up their own one-room schools which were not too different from the rural schools around them. Consequently there was no real conflict as far as the Hutterites were concerned. In 1920, inspector Hutchison at Macleod reported that the Brethren gave no evidence of being opposed to Alberta's system, and indeed the elder at one colony "displayed a deep interest in the school and inquired closely into the progress the children were making in school, especially in the learning of English."[16] Attendance was regular, and the colony's co-operation was good.

Despite the apparent success of the early schools, the first stirrings of complaint by the outside community were felt that year. Generally, when the Hutterites moved into these areas, school districts had already been established and sometimes consolidated under recent legislation. Hence the established settlers objected to paying taxes to a school district set up to cater to "foreigners".[17] They refused to send their children to the Hutterite school, and succeeded in having their lands withdrawn from the school district.

Seven years later, the issue again broke into the open, but in somewhat reversed circumstances. Hutterites from the new Pincher Creek Colony proposed to withdraw their lands from the consolidated school district of Pincher Creek. There was an outcry from the other residents. The MLA Earl Cook (U.F.A.) was among the first to protest that such a move would put an additional burden on the rest of the land. Moreover, he hinted at the possibility of taking the children into the existing schools and perhaps assimilating them.[18] Resolutions opposing the Hutterite move were passed by several groups. Similar beliefs desiring assimilation of Hutterites were voiced by the Provincial Legion. Nor was the situation at Pincher Creek unique, for apparently comparable cases had occurred at Gleichen, Taber, Cardston, and Macleod.[19] In Pincher Creek, joint meetings were held to discuss the situation, and as a result, a special citizens' committee was set up to deal with the matter. Cook himself continued the fight through letters and meetings with Premier Brownlee and Perren-Baker, the Education Minister.

The issue dragged on into the next year, and a public meeting on 7 December, 1928 passed the following resolution:

WHEREAS, *the aim of State education is to ensure an intelligent use of the ballot, and*
WHEREAS, *the Hutterites disclaim all intention of ever swearing allegiance to the Crown, thereby depriving themselves of the rights of citizenship, and*
WHEREAS *these Hutterites, an alien people who seek to remain alien, have asked for privileges never before granted to our people under the circumstances, and*
WHEREAS *the granting of these privileges would work a hardship on all Canadian citizens residing in the community, and which, if granted, would undoubtedly result in a large exodus of our native sons to the United States*
THEREFORE *be it resolved, that the special committee appointed to pass upon this matter, advise the rejection of the proposed scheme placed before us by the Hutterites*
AND FURTHERMORE, *we recommend that steps be taken to enforce the law in the matter of school attendance.*[20]

Unfortunately for the complainants, the Hutterites had the right to set up their own school districts, particularly since the colony was three and a half miles from the existing school, and twenty-two of the twenty-six children were under ten and hence could not be forced to attend the existing school. Indeed, there was always the possibility of setting up a private school.

The conflict continued to simmer and on 19 May, 1930, the United Farmers of Alberta of Pincher Creek passed a resolution demanding the Hutterites be sent to existing schools.[21] By this time assimilation had failed. The Hutterite insistence on small colony schools and their own educational system combined to limit the influence of the English school. However, they appreciated the need for their children to learn English and basic arithmetic. Consequently inspectors reported favourable progress and co-operation from Hutterites.[22]

During the Depression, the Department continued to look favourably upon progress at the colony schools. With the worsening economic plight of the area, the rural municipal debt accumulated. In the Lethbridge inspectorate, twenty-one districts had arrears less than the current taxes, the same number had arrears the same as current taxes, while some forty-five had arrears double current taxes. In contrast to other school districts, some were notably free of indebtedness. These were the three Hutterite colonies near Magrath.[23]

In relative terms, financial considerations did not seem to hit the colonies too hard, for in 1935, inspector Owen Williams at Lethbridge was organising three new districts of colonies, and arranging for furniture and supplies as well as suitable teachers.[24]

But even the thrifty Brethren were not unaffected by the economic and social pressures of the Depression. In August 1935, at the Daly Creek School near Granum, the ratepayers were faced with a request from a nearby colony that, since it paid local taxes and was unable to maintain its private school, Hutterite children be admitted to the Daly Creek School. Reluctantly the Board turned down the request on the grounds that the increased enrollment would put an extra burden on the teacher, and that sufficient books, supplies and desks could not be found. The teacher concerned, Edwin Pitt, suggested desks could be obtained from the Hutterite school, and the problem of books presented no great obstacles. Moreover, he saw in the request an opportunity for Hutterite children to learn "Canadian ways". He concluded by saying, "It is through the children that we will break up these colonies, these islands of isolation within our midst, and eventually bring about a true assimilation of the Hutterites into Alberta and Canadian society."[25] Although the ratepayers seemed pleased with this idea, the Hutterian elders withdrew their request. Obviously they did not want assimilation, nor did they want the schools to be used for that purpose.

With the onset of war in Europe, agitation against the Hutterites increased. Led by farmers' groups and the Legion, the opponents of colony expansion succeeded in influencing the government to enact the Land Sales Prohibition Act of 1942. In brief, the legislation forbade land sales to Hutterites and enemy aliens. Due to the reference to aliens, the Act was disallowed, but it was renewed again in 1944 with specific reference only to Hutterites and Doukhobors. Instrumental in the passage of these bills was Solon Low, Provincial Treasurer and M.L.A. for Cardston, centre for Alberta's Mormon population and surrounding clusters of Hutterites. It may be in this instance that the clash between two religious beliefs helped to exacerbate problems dealing with land and patriotism.

During the twenties and thirties, economic factors had tended to be secondary in the conflict between the Brethren and the outside community. The larger society saw the threat of the colonies more in cultural than economic terms. Local groups objected to the Brethren's value system, especially the communal way of life and the failure to take on the usual responsibilities of citizens. However, by the beginning of the forties the rural community was increasingly concerned about what it perceived as unfair economic competition by which the colonies could purchase land easily. In addition, the Brethren were charged with failing to support local businesses. And, as the economy became more complex and rural school consolidation developed, complaints were made about the low educational achievement of the Hutterites and their one-room schools.

Increasing controversy led the Alberta Legislature to appoint a committee on 21 February, 1947 to investigate the Land Sales Prohibition Act, which was about to expire, and to report on the Hutterite problem in general.[26] According to the report, almost all briefs pointed out the inadequacy of the situation as far as on-colony public education was concerned. Included in the criticisms were complaints that instruction in German in kindergarten hindered the teaching of English, and that audiovisual equipment was discouraged. Poorer teachers tended to go to colonies, as superior teachers preferred to avoid the frustrations of teaching there. Some school divisions suggested colony schools had slowed the trend to centralisation.[27] But above all, the briefs repeated the longstanding belief that the schools ought to be used to assimilate the Brethren. In its brief, the Alberta Association of Municipal Districts objected to the slow progress in assimilating the Hutterite children, and was concerned that the flag was removed after the English school was over for the day. The brief went on to recall a resolution of 1946 which summed up its views:

That the Hutterites be given to understand that the present situation will in any event be continued until the several colonies demonstrate a readiness to identify themselves more fully with our common language and our national habits and customs of life. People who are not prepared to assume the burdens, liabilities, and duties of citizenship should not be entitled to claim all the benefits and privileges of the State. That special agents of the Government be appointed to work with them with a view to encouraging them to assume more fully the responsibilities of citizenship.[28]

The Brethren, in defence of their way of life, were represented by L.S. Turcotte of Lethbridge who stressed the fact that the Brethren had indeed supported the war effort both by donations to the Red Cross and by labour in work camps. The most important piece of evidence in this defence was a letter from Owen Williams, inspector at Lethbridge, to Premier Brownlee on 12 January, 1934, supporting Hutterite schools, and testifying to their generally high quality. Moreover, there were depositions of thirteen teachers at Hutterite colonies, reaffirming the inspector's view on the quality of education obtained at Colony Schools.

While the committee made no specific proposals on the education of Hutterite children, its tone suggested that it agreed that legislation and regulations on education should be more strictly enforced, and that since the education received was inferior, steps should be taken to improve the situation.

The Legislative Report recommended keeping the restrictions on the colonies, particularly in their purchase of land. Although the Legislature was not unanimous in supporting the committee's recommendations, the desire to restrict land expansion did cut across party lines. But the tone and significance of the report would lie more in the fact that two of its members would become cabinet ministers with direct responsibilities over Hutterites. Ivan Casey, chairman of the committee, was the featured speaker at a meeting of the High River Canadian Legion, which opposed the intended Hutterite settlement in an area northwest of town. Within a few months, Casey became the Minister of Education. In August 1949, he announced that in future, all Hutterite schools would have to deal directly with the Department of Education, not the local school boards. He indicated that the Department was attempting to develop a uniform province-wide set of regulations which would govern colony schools. The ostensible aim was to avoid the multiple and often contradictory regulations set up by local school boards. Apparently the Department was prepared to give firm direction to the matter. The other committee member who would have direct contact with the Hutterites was L.C. Halmrast, later the Minister of Agriculture, who would consequently be concerned with the problem of land expansion and related fears and prejudices in rural Alberta.

During the 1950's, those Hutterite private schools and Hutterite public districts which remained were brought increasingly under the control of the School Divisions. In 1951, there were six separate Hutterite private schools (Felger, Ewelme, Granum, O.K., Thompson, and Hutterville). In 1956 O.K. and Granum had joined their respective Divisions, to be joined by Thompson in 1957, Felger in 1961, and Ewelme and Hutterville by 1962. However, the controversy over land expansion continued, and on the report of the Minister of Municipal Affairs (A.J. Hooke, an opponent of Hutterite expansion), an Order-in-Council of 8 September, 1958 set up an Investigation Committee which had, among its responsibilities, ". . . to determine whether or not the existing educational facilities established for Hutterite colonies are satisfactory, especially in the matter of instruction in the responsibilities of Canadian citizenship . . . [and] any other matter relevant to the orderly and harmonious integration of the Hutterian Church into local communities."[29]

It would appear by the terms of reference that the government had shifted its priorities from assimilation to integration. But the issue of citizenship remained a cardinal feature of government policy. The committee hearings were witness to the fact that rural attitudes had not changed so easily. The briefs repeated familiar complaints. According to the Lethbridge School Division, "there is no possibility of Canadianizing these people until their education is standardized with ours, away from the domination of the elders." As a consequence, it proposed a centralized Hutterite school built by the Division so that the full resources of the Division could be brought to bear on the problem.[30] In addition, assimilation was at the heart of briefs such as that of the New Dayton U.F.A., which suggested that the only way the Hutterites could be gradually integrated into the social and economic life of the country was through the educational system. Finally the economic conflict was illustrated by the Nanton and High River Legions which suggested "any community adjacent to a segregated group, such as the Hutterites, tends to deteriorate in relationship, one with the other. Therefore integration would be to the benefit of all."[31] Perhaps the oddest suggestion came from C.F. Bentley, Professor of Soil Science at the University of Alberta, who suggested that all Hutterite children be required to attend non-Hutterite schools, in order to learn about birth control. In reply, one of the Hutterites in attendance at the hearing said "and this is what a university education does to you."

As in 1947, the Brethren had their defenders. R.A. Kimmitt, former school superintendent of the County of Warner, encountered angry shouting and hooting when he tried to suggest that school attendance was good and technical education received on the colonies was excellent. He also cautioned the committee against suggesting that the Hutterites be forced into the larger society, and spoke of the price Canadians had paid to protect their freedoms during the recent war. Others asked if the non-Hutterians had any better system or society to offer the colonies. H.D. Mann, representing the Rockyford Colony, maintained that the Hutterites had the right to educate their children on colony schools with qualified teachers. He also praised their work as farmers and good citizens.[32]

In its report, the committee, headed by Charles Hayes, referred to a master's thesis on education in the County of Warner done by W.D. Knill. Knill had concluded that up to grade four, Hutterite children were on a par with or exceeded the national norms, but that "the Hutterian students fall behind in their achievements between grades four and six."[33] The committee decided that there was no substance to the charges that the Hutterites were subnormal in intelligence. Moreover, the committee polled school superintendents who had charge of Hutterite colony schools, and the consensus was that the elders would resist any attempt to abolish colony schools. The members of the committee also opposed the integration into the public schools, since the resultant Hutterite moves would merely remove the problem from the supervision of the school boards. "A more subtle approach, aimed at ultimate integration" was recommended. The first requisite was capable, personable teachers who could stimulate the children. Secondly, "it is recommended that scholarship rather than age should determine when children may leave school."[34] By this means standards could be raised.

The report went on to recommend, moreover, that all colony schools should be placed under the jurisdiction of a capable superintendent, trained in anthropology, who could use his position to improve educational standards. Correspondence courses, night schools for older pupils, adult education, and extension courses would also assist in the process of "integration of Hutterite people with those of the dominant culture of the country." In conclusion, the report indicated:

Throughout this report the Committee has endeavoured to emphasize that the assimilation of a religious sect exhibiting such strong social cohesion as the Hutterian Brethren will take time and patience. Official restrictions placed on these people over the centuries would seem to indicate that the process of integration has been retarded rather than advanced by such measures.[35]

Thus whatever the subtle nuances of the words "assimilation" and "integration", the ultimate aim appeared to be to break down the Hutterite culture.

The Hutterite reaction to the report came in a series of briefs to the provincial cabinet and legislature in 1960. In a submission to the Agricultural Committee of the Legislature on 24 March, 1960, the Brethren reiterated the fact that they had the right to their own schools, and that the continuation of their own schools in colony buildings saved School Divisions money, as the committee itself had admitted.[36] With respect to withdrawing children at the age of fifteen, the Hutterites took "no course except what is open under the law to all families in the province." By citing the Cameron Report on Education, the Brethren stated that fifty per cent of the children in Alberta left school with grade nine education. And many of these children were unprepared for employment, while the Hutterite children would be prepared for agricultural production, under the tutelage of their parents. "One thing certain is that the Hutterites would not be joining the ranks of the unemployed nor will they be competing for positions in the professions elsewhere." Finally, the question of parental right in determining the kind of education to be given the children was examined. Thus, to single out the Hutterites for special treatment beyond age fifteen would be discriminatory.[37]

The view that "the same basic educational standards and emphasis on citizenship be required in Hutterite schools as in all other Alberta schools" seems to have been accepted by several groups. The Alberta Teachers' Association, at its annual meeting in 1961, passed a resolution sponsored by the executive council, that a study be made of the possibilities of integrating Hutterite children in Alberta schools.[38] Whether or not anything was done with the A.T.A. resolution was another matter. In March 1960, Gordon Taylor, Minister of Highways, endorsed the proposal that education standards be enforced, while L.C. Halmrast, Minister of Agriculture, advocated centralising Hutterite schools, although he recognised the need to treat the Brethren differently.[39]

During the 1960's, other incidents accompanied the establishment of new colonies by the Hutterites, despite their approval by the Communal Property Control Board and the Provincial Cabinet. Typical of these was the incident with the Athabasca Hutterite Colony, north of Edmonton. In the spring of 1962 children from the colony were attending the nearby Lahaieville school. The elders were unable to build a colony school, due to financial considerations. Consequently, after a request to use an empty school room was turned down by the County Council, the eleven pupils were mixed with other children. The teachers of the children reported no problems; the Hutterite children worked well and diligently in school and participated in sports. Of course, the parents were determined to end such integration as soon as they could afford to build their own school. A.J. Hooke, Municipal Affairs Minister, saw this as an indication "they have seen the light," and were accepting the responsibilities of Canadian citizenship. Soon afterward, the parents withdrew their children.[40]

The *cause célèbre* of the period, however, was the Brant case. Six Hutterites and nine non-Hutterites were charged with circumventing the Communal Property Act by selling land to individual Hutterites who then turned the property over to the Rock Lake Colony. The case was seen as a test for the constitutionality of the Act, something which lawyers for the Brethren and civil rights advocates had been asking for years. In a legal battle lasting several years, the Supreme Court of Canada upheld the Provincial Government.

More important for the question of public attitudes of assimilation was the concern of the people of Brant, a small village east of High River, at the western edge of Vulcan County. Paramount in their minds was the fear that their small school would be reduced even further by the loss of potential children from the colony. Under the leadership of Steve Dixon, the Southern Alberta Development and Protective Association was formed, largely to combat Hutterite expansion. At a meeting in September 1966, the Association urged the Hutterites to upgrade their colony schools to the full status of private schools, or else force their children to attend regular schools. The latter was clearly the preference.[41]

Dixon carried his fight to a meeting sponsored by the Foremost Chamber of Commerce on September 21, 1967. Denying that he was conducting a hate campaign, Dixon claimed that the Vulcan district farmers paid over eight thousand dollars a year to support the "private" public schools of the Hutterites. He even suggested that school boards which permitted this sort of situation to exist could be charged with the return to the voters of the monies misused. As a result of the meeting, a resolution was passed asking the Foremost Chamber to consult with other Chambers of Commerce with a view to forcing Hutterite children to attend public schools.[42]

The following year, the Vulcan County School Committee reaffirmed its decision not to open a school on the colony, stating that all children of school age resident on the "colony" should attend Brant school.[43] The Hutterites refused, saying that the situation was "unacceptable." They told the Minister of Education, Raymond Reierson, that they intended to set up a private school and had advertised for a teacher. Meanwhile the Department of Education said that the Brant Hutterites would be considered private families, pending a Supreme Court decision on the

Brant case and The Communal Property Control Act. However, Reierson indicated no public support would be given to a private school, in essence disputing Dixon's claims that the colony schools were private.[44]

In the spring of 1969, the Brant Home and School Association introduced a resolution to the Alberta Federation of Home and School Associations' annual convention. After discussing the poor educational standards on colony schools, the lack of audio-visual aids, and the duplicate school systems which the colonies inevitably cause, the Brant Association wanted the Department of Education to halt the opening of "segregated Hutterite public schools" until a basic plan could be drawn up with the eventual "objective of integration."[45] The resolution was accompanied by background material which purported to show that the colony schools did in fact cost the public some $12,000 a year per colony. The material stated, moreover, that little or no progress had been made with regard to upgrading the standards on the colonies since the 1959 report and that all government action had done was to appease the Elders. Other groups had the same right to set up public schools, and thus the whole system would be fragmented "as integration is postponed, [and] it becomes more difficult."

In the ensuing debate before the Federation, Dixon again suggested that the children were not encouraged to learn. He even suggested busing: "Why should the Hutterite schools be allowed to exist while other schools are closed?" In bringing up the issue of school busing, Dixon noted what had been a growing grievance in rural areas, especially since rural depopulation and school consolidation which had taken place since the Second World War, a grievance that was increasingly mentioned in almost every dispute over Hutterites. One of the Hutterite Elders, Rev. Jacob Waldner of O.K. Colony, replied that the Brant resolution was discriminatory. "We appeal to you, do not allow this resolution to be carried lest you be acting against God."[46] The vote on the resolution was thirty-nine to sixteen opposed.

The following year, the same resolution was up for debate, but a compromise was reached by the resolution, "That a Committee be set up that represents the Divisions, Counties and Department of Education to meet with the objective of arriving at a basic plan for all."[47] It is significant that no mention was made of Hutterite representation. By March 1970 the County of Vulcan was reconciled to the location of the Hutterian Brethren of Brant.[48] This did not mean, however, that the County was willing to establish a school on the colony.

When the school-leaving age was raised to sixteen, certain problems arose, for according to Hutterite custom, children became adults (though not full-fledged members of the church) at age fifteen. John Wurz of Wilson Siding Colony said "when they raised the school age from fifteen to sixteen, it threw our system out of kilter."[49] The 1969 Annual Report of the Department of Education suggested as much in its statement that:

"Most children attend school without compulsion. Raising the age limit to sixteen years, therefore, caused problems for only two groups of people: Indians and Métis, and Hutterites."[50] It went on to suggest that under Section 400(1)(g) of the School Act, school boards could permit exemption where no suitable school programme was available.

Subsequent court cases indicate that not all boards granted exemption immediately. In March 1969, Rev. Martin Walter from the Springpoint Colony chose to spend ten days in jail when he was convicted of refusing to send his fifteen-year-old son to school. His lawyer, Garth Turcotte, suggested that some school divisions prosecuted under the Act while others ignored it or even issued certificates to fifteen-year-olds. He argued that greater consistency was needed in the application of the Act, something of which the department officials were already aware.[51]

After a new School Act was passed in 1970, the issue was again brought to a head at High River, when Paul Stahl of the Cayley Colony was charged with the failure to send his daughter Martha to school, under section 131 of the School Act. In fairness to the Board, it is possible the officials wanted to get a legal opinion about the application of the new Act.

During the trial, on 3 March, 1971, John Wurz of Wilson Siding Colony testified on behalf of the defence. In his statements he repeated the general Hutterian beliefs about the need to preserve colony schools, especially the view that the system operated in obedience to God's law. According to Wurz, the elders had set up the communal organisation according to the word of God and the Holy Spirit. Consequently, "The Hutterite faith is a faith that God told us to live. . . . We believe that through living this faith we get into eternal life. And if we don't live up to it, according to the teachings of the Bible, we are losing eternal life." In bringing up children, the Brethren stressed that spiritual well-being was more important than physical well-being. Since the teaching of evolution and atheism were prevalent in the non-Hutterian schools, to integrate into off-colony schools would go against the teaching of God. On practical grounds the Brethren resisted sending children to school after fifteen. Wurz contended that at age fifteen, the child became an adult, ". . . and if these children are kept in school, this throws the whole . . . wheel out of its balance." Moreover, from experience he related how higher education had caused people to leave the colony and hence threaten their salvation. Finally it was stated that education to age fifteen was sufficient for this life on earth. Since the Hutterian way was based on the law of God, to obey the law on age-sixteen school-leaving was against Jesus Christ. Under cross-examination, Wurz stated that Stahl really had no choice but to withdraw his child, for it was not his decision but had been determined when he became a Hutterite, that is, when he was baptised. In case of conflict with secular authorities, "God's law comes first."[52]

Stahl was convicted on 30 March, 1971. Judge Collins rejected defence contentions that it was an Act of God which prevented the child from being sent, since in law the general as in section 134(b) takes its meaning from the specific, so *unavoidable cause* meant instances such as sickness or natural catastrophes. Immediately an appeal was launched. Conversations with the School Board continued, as did representations to the Minister of Education. Trial evidence showed the Department tended to relegate responsibility to the local School Board, with the Minister Robert Clark continually pointing to section 134(f) permitting exemption if there were no suitable programme on the colony. Finally, in August 1971, a verbal agreement between the Superintendent and the Cayley and Macmillan Colonies permitted the children to withdraw at age fifteen, but only at the end of term.[53] The appeal was dropped and pending cases against two other parents were dropped.

Throughout the more than fifty years the Brethren have been in Alberta, the conflict between the Brethren and the larger society has remained consistent. Economic grievances and value differences have led opponents to demand the Hutterites be forced to attain the educational standards of other Albertans, and in this way it was hoped the culture would break down. At the same time, the Brethren have kept firm control on the education of their children. The only difference in the modern dispute has been the fact that Alberta has become urbanised, so that the rural areas have less political influence and thus feel increasingly alienated from provincial policies. And gradually, the political leadership of the government has moved from a position of assimilation, to integration, to tolerance and concern for individual liberties.

But the basic conflict remains, and will likely continue to manifest itself. The high birth rate of the Brethren coupled with their agricultural orientation dictates a constant need to establish new colonies. As they purchase the new land, they come into competition with local farmers. And, as the rural de-population continues and farms become larger, demand for increasingly scarce land leads to continued conflict between Hutterites and the rural society of Alberta.

Since their appearance in Alberta at the end of World War One, Hutterites have been perceived as threatening the larger Anglo-American society of Alberta. Initially the threat was almost exclusively cultural, with the communal way of living, the German language, and the refusal to take the responsibilities of citizenship being points of contention. But since the Depression, the colonies have emerged as economic threats to the rural way of life.

With mechanization, farms have grown larger and there is competition for available land. But the spartan living of the colonies, it is argued, gives them economic advantages over other farmers, and permits them to outbid local farmers for land. Throughout this period, the public school has been seen as the means to end the threat and to assimilate the

Hutterite. But attempts at assimilation have failed. And though govern-ment has recognised the folly of trying to assimilate the Brethren, in areas of rural Alberta the demand for doing exactly that has not lessened.

Ten

OJIBWA, CREE, AND THE HUDSON'S BAY COMPANY IN NORTHERN ONTARIO: CULTURE AND CONFLICT IN THE EIGHTEENTH CENTURY

Charles A. Bishop

Introduction

The purpose of this chapter is twofold: at the empirical level, I wish to present some new data relating to the history of northern Ontario involving change processes among the Cree and Ojibwa during the eighteenth century; and simultaneously, to challenge the idea of *persistence* with regard to structural continuity in Northern Algonkian Indian culture.

The method employed is generally called *ethnohistory* by anthropologists. In many respects this method is identical with historiography; what most distinguishes ethnohistory from historiography, however, appears to be the application of ethnological concepts and methods. In recent years, anthropologists have paid greater attention to the historian's techniques for evaluating and employing written records in order to understand long-term change processes and to acquire sufficient information about early-contact native cultures so that meaningful cross-cultural comparative research could be undertaken.[1] Yet in the past, and to an extent even now, sub-Arctic anthropologists have relied almost exclusively on materials gathered in the field to reconstruct what are assumed to be baseline contact conditions. While there is no denying that certain cultural elements have persisted or have been retained in modified form from earlier times, to assume that all or most of prehistoric northern

Indian culture, as a functioning entity and an adaptive system, can be reconstructed through oral testimony alone is naive in the least, and has led to what M.G. Smith has termed "The Fallacy of the Ethnographic Present." According to Smith:

By means of this fallacy, the initial exclusion of change, whether current or historical, is taken as proof that change does not occur; and current processes of change and development are either ignored where recognizable, or where unrecognized, as often happens, they are represented as contributions to the maintenance of changeless conditions.[2]

The Northern Algonkians of sub-Arctic Ontario are an excellent case in point, since the seeming isolation and remoteness of the Boreal Forests have created an illusion of timelessness prior to the late nineteenth century. We now turn to the data.

Geography

Geographically, the area under consideration extends from the north shores of Lakes Huron and Superior westward to Lake of the Woods and Lake Winnipeg, and northward to the shores of Hudson Bay and James Bay. This vast region can be broken into several sub-zones. Coastal James Bay and Hudson Bay is relatively flat and treeless, yet provides an excellent feeding place for migratory waterfowl. A short distance inland and extending to the Canadian Shield, the country is enshrouded in a dense coniferous forest broken only by the major river systems which in the past provided travel arteries to and from the interior to the coast. North of Lake Superior extends the Shield country with its numerous lakes and streams. Faunal densities tend to be somewhat greater here, and as one proceeds further south to the east and west of Lake Superior, the forest cover changes to include hardwoods and wild rice. Within this area live two main tribal groups, the Cree and the Ojibwa. The former occupy most of the Lowland region to the coast, whereas the Ojibwa are restricted mainly to the Shield north and west of Lake Superior. However, tribal boundaries today are quite different from what they were three centuries ago. In order to comprehend these changes and others, it is first necessary to establish an early-contact baseline derived primarily from the historical source materials but interpreted within an anthropological framework.

Outline of Early-Contact Ojibwa Culture

The historical evidence does not support the view that the aboriginal Ojibwa were a true sub-Arctic people. When first visited by French ex-

plorers during the mid-seventeenth century, they appear to have occupied a series of animal-named (totemic) villages extending along or
near the north shore of Georgian Bay and at the east end of Lake
Superior.[3] These Ojibwa villages, numbering about 150 persons each,
were occupied semi-permanently from about May until November, and
were supported by the rich game and fish resources. With the annual
depletion of food caches (usually about December), village sites were
vacated as members dispersed northwards to hunt moose, caribou, and
deer. It has been argued that these villages formed patrilinear, exogamous clans linked to each other through cross-cousin marriage, periodic
multi-village feasts, and a common language and culture.[4] There were
perhaps between forty-five hundred and five thousand Ojibwa in all,
forming about twenty separate groups during the mid-seventeenth century. It is evident from more recent census data, then, that a population
"explosion" occurred during the historic period.

Outline of Early-Contact Cree Culture

To the north of the Ojibwa extending from Lake Superior to the coast
resided a number of Cree bands. The French called them *Christinaux* or
Kilistinon from which the name Cree is derived. The English Hudson's
Bay Company traders, however, generally applied the term Kilistinon or
"Cristeen" in a more restricted sense only to those groups residing inland
on the Shield north of Lake Superior.[5] The Christinaux were also distinguished from those nearer Port Nelson by Claude de la Potherie, who
said that the former lived on the lakes in the interior some 160 leagues
(about 400 miles) from the shores of Lake Superior.[6] Nicolas Perrot in
the 1660's mentioned that the Christinaux "often frequent the region along the shores of Lake Superior, and the great rivers, where
moose are commonly found. . . .", while Father Claude Allouez reported
that they lived by hunting, fishing, and collecting wild rice.[7] This or a
related division of Cree bordered on the Wood Assiniboine, who during
the early decades of contact resided along what was to become the International Border west of Lake Superior.

The groups of Cree nearer to the coast were smaller in size and more
nomadic than those further inland. Father Gabriel Marest said of the
coastal Indians: "They range the woods continually without stopping
anywhere, winter or summer, except when the chase is good." In contrast,
the Cree inland on the Shield were "greater in numbers . . . and are at
least sedentary for three or four months."[8] La Potherie also mentions
this sedentariness:

*When the ice in the lakes and rivers begins to break up, they assemble,
sometimes twelve to fifteen hundred, on the shore of a lake which is the*

meeting place, where they make all preparations for their journey to Port Nelson.

The chiefs point out the needs of the tribe and call upon the young hunters to look after the public interest, imploring them to take charge of the beavers in the name of their families. . . . For the time being the whole tribe forms a society for mutual admiration. There is a general renewal of alliances. Joy, pleasure, and good cheer prevail. . . .

When the Indians are ready to go down, they choose among the hunters several chiefs to take charge of the trading for the tribe.

La Potherie was unable to make an accurate census of the Cree on the Shield at this date since many were involved in warfare with the Dakota in Minnesota and did not come to the post. Ordinarily, however, "a thousand men, some women, and six hundred canoes may arrive."[9] Whether these large inland gatherings were a post-contact phenomenon replicating the situation among Ojibwa and other central Great Lakes Algonkians who coalesced at Sault Ste. Marie and Michilimackinac during the late seventeenth century is hard to say. The fact is clear, however, that the environmental potential permitting such large gatherings prior to the ravages of the fur trade has been grossly underestimated. Actually, it would appear that the Cree residing on the Shield northwest of Lake Superior constituted what Helm and others have designated a regional band numbering perhaps fifteen hundred persons, and composed of a number of smaller winter local bands which, at least during the seventeenth century, united to renew alliances and travel to the trading post.[10] Probably local groups were linked to each other through cross-cousin marriage, and they may have been exogamous entities. However, mobility in the quest for food may have inhibited the development of territorially based unilinear descent groups. While some Cree bands of this era are given band names, these lack the totemic connotations characteristic of Ojibwa groups.[11]

There were also other fairly large regional bands living inland from the coast. One was the Monsoni band, which may have originally lived in the upper Moose River drainage area but which was near Lake Nipigon in 1700. Another group was the Sturgeon band, which by the latter date resided somewhere west of Lake Nipigon.

Nearer the coast lived a number of smaller nomadic groups each consisting of several extended family units.[12] One such group was the *Ouerebigonhelinis* or "Sea-side" Indians, who occupied the area between Port Nelson and the Severn River. Another similar group consisting of "50 Men, Women and Children . . . in 22 canoes . . . of the Nation called *Pishhapacanoes*" arrived at Rupert's House in 1671. This latter group was reported to have been a poor miserable people, a description fitting other bands near coastal areas. J. Oldmixon, citing Thomas Gorst's journal of 1671, gives a description of coastal Cree social organization:

The Indians *of certain Districts, which are bounded by such and such Rivers, have each an* Okimah, *as they call him, or Captain over them, who is an old Man, Considered only for his Prudence and Experience. . . . He is their Speech-maker to the English; as also in their own grave Debates, when they meet every Spring and Fall, to settle the Disposition of their Quarters for Hunting, Fowling, and Fishing. Every Family have their Boundaries adjusted, which they seldom quit, unless they have not Success there in their Hunting, and then they join in with some Family who have succeeded.*[13]

While post-nuptial residence patterns may have been a matter of expediency, there appears to have been a matrilocal emphasis. La Potherie in describing marriage patterns remarked:

The greatest consolation that a father of a family can have is a number of daughters. They are the support of the house, whereas a father who has sons only may look forward to being abandoned by them when they have grown up.

Upon a marriage, the son-in-law must

reside with his father-in-law, who remains the master of his hunting until there are children born. Usually he spends the remainder of his life with her father unless some trouble arises.

A man who was a good hunter or who had many relatives was a desirable mate. Having many relatives "is one of the best conditions for an alliance because, if they should suffer distress, they would have recourse in their necessity to the relatives of their son-in-law."[14]

In a sense, coastal Cree groups were microcosmic versions of the interior Cree regional bands. Nevertheless, there were differences that preclude generalizing for all Cree. Variation in early historic Cree socio-territorial organization reflects not only seasonal economic activities but also a geographical gradient from the coast to Lake Superior in population density and group size, if not certainly in complexity. The overall Cree population in the area circumscribed may have been about forty-five hundred persons, three-quarters of whom resided on the Shield. This estimate, like that for the Ojibwa, falls considerably below earlier estimates by Kroeber and Swanton that the Cree numbered 20,000 and the Ojibwa 35,000.[15] The evidence then indicates a marked population growth among both the Ojibwa and Cree between the seventeenth and nineteenth centuries, despite disease, malnutrition, and warfare. Any appraisal of organizational changes in socio-territorial groupings must consider demographic shifts as well as ecological changes and acculturative influences. We now turn to these changes which first began further south with the expansion of the fur trade into the Great Lakes area during the mid-seventeenth century.

Population Movements and Trade: Contact to 1800

Although trade goods had probably reached the Ojibwa by 1610, it was not until the 1640's that large numbers of Indians began congregating at Sault Ste. Marie to trade for European wares and to participate in inter-tribal feasts. Following the Iroquois raids of mid-century, French traders began exploring the area west of Sault Ste. Marie in hopes of luring more distant groups. Either to maintain their lucrative middleman position with groups to the west, or to avoid encounters with the Iroquois, some Ojibwa and Ottawa had expanded almost to the west end of Lake Superior by the 1660's, while Nicolas Perrot reported "that the Nepissings and Amikouets [Ojibwa of the beaver clan] were at Alimi-begon [Lake Nipigon]."[16]

Until the 1670's, the Cree and Assiniboine traded through Ottawa and Ojibwa middlemen. But this monopoly was broken when the newly formed (1670) Hudson's Bay Company erected several posts on James Bay and Hudson Bay. According to Louis Jolliet in 1679, the English were sending presents to the Assiniboine "to win them over", thus threatening the French trade.[17] To prevent the Assiniboine and Cree nearer Lake Superior from trading at the Bay, the French established a series of forts north and west of Lake Superior,[18] while between 1686 and 1713 they were able to capture and hold a number of the Hudson's Bay Company posts. Most of the Cree of the Shield were trading either at Port Nelson, then in French hands and called Fort Bourbon, or at sites closer to Lake Superior. Meanwhile, the trade at the English-controlled Fort Albany post suffered from French competition. For instance, in 1706 Anthony Beale reported the arrival of only two canoes of "Cristeens", "which is all we have had of that sort of Indians this summer." The following year Beale said that "all the Christains that way [to the west] was gone to the Warrs therefore no more would come and Trade here this Year."[19] At this time warfare with the Dakota was luring the Cree and their Assiniboine allies toward the International Border west of Lake Superior, while the French were encouraging the Indians to kill the English, "with a promise of 40 Beavr for Evry Scalp of y English they bring them." By the 1720's, the only Indians who could be relied upon to bring furs to Fort Albany were the local "homeguards" (Cree living in the Lowlands near the post). It would appear that the Cree population north of Lake Superior was beginning to shift to the west in the van of the expanding trade, and was lured to war with the Dakota. Cree living great distances inland from Fort Albany were reluctant to make the journey due to food shortages on the trip, and to threats from the French-incited Ojibwa, who were expanding north of Lake Superior by the 1720's. For instance, in 1726 some Cristeens stated that "ye Echee-poes [Ojibwa] threatened to kill them if they came here." These Ojibwa began to locate in the upper Albany River region just east of the Cristeens. According to Joseph Adams of Fort Albany in 1733:

The French Cannyda Inds [Ojibwa] have several of them wintered with the uplands inds [Cree] having some places fortified with Trading Goods in them about two hundred Miles from this place – Intercepting the Inds that use to Come here and trading with those that are unwilling by Cumpulsive Methods.

Some of these "Oachiapoia" began to trade at Fort Albany, while the "Cristeens" were only able to do so "by Stealth."[20]

West of Lake Superior by the 1730's there were large groups of Cree, Monsoni, and Assiniboine.[21] By 1735, several more groups of Ojibwa had moved north to settle near French encampments, while the next year a group of Ojibwa had settled at Vermilion River near Rainy Lake.[22] By 1740 some Ojibwa began trading fairly regularly at Fort Albany, while relations with the Cree improved. For example, in 1741 some Ojibwa were given presents to take to the Cristeens "for its a 11 Years Since any Clisteen hath ben Downe.[23] The Cristeens were now referred to as "foreign" Indians by the Fort Albany traders, since the emergent Northern Ojibwa had come to occupy the eastern half of their territory. By the 1740's, the Ojibwa occupied the area extending to the Albany River from perhaps the Ogoki River to Lac Seul, and along much of the International Border to Lake of the Woods.

Trade competition between the French and the Fort Albany post intensified in 1742 when the former established a post at the confluence of the Albany and Kenogami Rivers to intercept both Ojibwa and Cree. Although the post was vacated in the spring of 1743, the English erected Henley House, their first inland post, in the same location that year. The English regained some of the trade until the early 1750's when the French were again reported to have been swarming all over the country north of Lake Superior. In 1754, some Indians massacred the Henley House traders, with the result that the location wasn't re-settled until 1759. That same year it was attacked by about twenty warriors, after which it was abandoned until 1766. By the late 1750's, problems in Quebec and the English threat prevented the French from competing north of Lake Superior, and the period lasting until the late 1760's saw large "gangs" of Northern Ojibwa travelling annually to Fort Albany. By this date, most of the Cristeens had shifted west of Lake Winnipeg, although a few pockets remained along the east side until the 1770's.[24] By the late 1770's, the area occupied by Ojibwa in northern Ontario and eastern Manitoba was essentially the same as at present.

Freedom from competition was short-lived for the Hudson's Bay Company, since by the mid-1760's traders from Montreal (now including Scots, English, and French) began moving into the area north of Lake Superior and disrupting the flow of furs. For instance, where Fort Albany traded 21,556 made beaver in furs in 1761-62, the trade fell to a mere 5,940 made beaver in 1768-69.[25] The decline in the fur trade is also reflected in the number of canoes arriving at the post. Whereas about one hundred canoes of Ojibwa visited Fort Albany annually during the early 1760's, the figure dropped to twenty-seven canoes in 1769, and to about four the following year. The trade loss was so keenly felt that the Hudson's Bay Company was forced to establish a series of inland posts in the area occupied by the Northern Ojibwa during the next three decades. This inland trade marks the beginning of a new era, one characterized by intense competition and extensive exploitation of the environment by Indians.

We have seen how the Ojibwa gradually replaced the Cree living inland north of Lake Superior. However, little has been said about what was happening to Cree culture nearer the coast.

Effects of the Fur Trade on Lowland Cree Culture

By the early seventeenth century a fairly stable trade was operating with Cree groups within 150 miles of Fort Albany, while more distant inland bands vacillated between the English and French according to the vicissitudes of the fur trade. The term "homeguard" was applied to these nearby bands.[26] In April 1717, for example, there were 109 homeguards (men, women, and children) awaiting the spring goose hunt.[27] The size of the four or five bands near Fort Albany can be estimated at about thirty to forty persons each. However, it would seem that band members formed single settlements only during the spring and fall while at the goose hunting camps or during the summer when food was more abundant. Winter units approximated extended families ranging from seven to twenty persons, although on occasion slightly larger groups were reported. The establishment of the trading post and the reliance upon Indians to hunt geese in the spring and autumn seems to have altered aboriginal seasonal movements. The autumn goose hunt was particularly disruptive since the homeguards were obliged to hunt until mid-October. Thus they had little time to prepare a larder of food for the winter while the formation of ice in the rivers hindered them from travelling inland to hunting and trapping areas. They were also growing increasingly dependent upon the trading post, which was to the advantage of the Company. According to Joseph Isbister in 1741, the debt system of trade was first introduced "as a bridle to making them more dependent on the Settlement for our Necessary Subsistence."[28] The fall goose hunt provided a considerable amount of food in winter for the twenty-odd traders as well as relief for starving Indians.

Among the trade items received were guns, powder, shot, bayonets, ice chisels, axes, knives, needles, awls, kettles, twine, coats, caps, shirts, cloth, blankets, tobacco, brandy, vermilion, mirrors, combs, and beads. After the fall hunt when the homeguards received their payments and winter debts, they would disperse inland to trap and hunt game. Although there were a few small herds of caribou in the James Bay Lowlands, Indians relied primarily on hare, fur bearers, and grouse for subsistence. Indeed, subsistence was precarious, and mention of starvation is a prominent entry in the post journals. For example, in 1703 John Fullerton stated that "a bundance of the poor Indians perishd and were so hard put to it that whole familys of them were kill'd and eaten by one another."[29] Throughout the century hungry Indians would gather at the post in winter if they could reach it to beg for food. There they obtained surplus fish and geese which they themselves had killed, or European foods such as oatmeal, peas, and prunes.

In April when the homeguards gathered at the post for the spring goose hunt, a feast was held with food from the store, after which the hunters prepared their stages in the marsh. The hunt was led by a goose-hunt captain, who maintained his position for life. The goose hunters received a pound of powder and shot for every fifteen geese killed. Hunters employed two guns, three or four geese being killed with every shot. Usually one man could kill one hundred geese in a day.[30] By early June the geese were gone and Indians, after receiving payment, dispersed to fish or kill caribou or small waterfowl. The summer was also the time when the James Bay Cree went on their "Eskimo hunt" to the Great Whale River area. Following a war dance, a number of homeguards from Fort Albany would set out in July, picking up recruits at Moose Factory and Slude River. Encounters with the Eskimo favoured the Cree, who were armed with guns. Traders tried to discourage these raids since they feared that the goose hunters would fail to return for the fall hunt, which was critical to the maintenance of the post.

Adaptation to trapping, goose hunting, and trading-post dependency had considerably altered mobility patterns and group size by the 1730's. After this time the names of original bands ceased to be mentioned in the journals, as the trapping economy favoured the dispersal and autonomy of extended family units. Augmenting this trend was the rather rapid depletion of beaver and game nearer the post.

The re-establishment of Moose Factory in 1730 reduced the core of homeguards associated with Fort Albany, while at the same time Cree further inland were shifting ever westward in the van of the expanding fur trade. The re-establishment of Fort Severn in 1759 lured away about forty more Fort Albany Indians. By the 1760's, Fort Severn was attracting both Cree (including some Christinaux) and Ojibwa, who took advantage of the herd of several thousand caribou that annually crossed the Severn River each spring. For instance, Andrew Graham reported in 1774 that one band "brought upwards of three hundred dryed Deer's tongues."[31] This large herd was virtually exterminated by the 1780's by the Indians and traders who captured the animals in a "deer hedge".

Toward the end of the century conditions at the coastal posts had stabilized, while the bulk of the furs were obtained at the newly established inland posts. Goose-hunting techniques became more efficient when battaux loaded with shot, powder, and salt for packing were sent directly to the marsh instead of having Indians return to the post each time they ran short or had filled their canoes. The annual goose kill at Fort Albany increased from about three thousand during the 1740's to about eight thousand by the 1780's. With the establishment of inland trade, there were more chores for Indians to perform during summer months, such as loading and unloading boats, and accompanying them part way inland. Trapping also became a more efficient occupation with the establishment of family hunting territories by the 1780's, and as Indians were taught conservation techniques. While life in the bush remained difficult, the improved conditions evidently permitted a population increase. The Fort Albany Indian population grew to about 200 persons in 1790 from about 150 at mid-century, and by 1829, it had increased to 259 Indians.[32]

The most interesting aspect of coastal Cree cultural history is the subtlety of change. After 1700, there was no radical reorientation in social organization until the twentieth century. Rather, changes were accretive and cumulative. The cultural history of the James Bay Cree, however, is in marked contrast to that of the Ojibwa.

Effects of the Fur Trade on Ojibwa Culture

During the late eighteenth century, groups and perhaps lineages or even whole clans of Ojibwa shifted westward along both the north and south shores of Lake Superior. Although for a time Indians returned to Sault Ste. Marie to fish and trade, there is evidence that by the early 1730's some groups were establishing themselves north and west of Lake Superior in areas formerly occupied by Assiniboine and Cree.

The picture of Ojibwa social organization during the mid-eighteenth century, however, is blurred by fragmentary reports of traders whose own residence in a given area was itself temporary. The very dynamics of the situation are nevertheless reflected in these data. The animal-named bands of Ojibwa who came to occupy the Shield northwest of Lake Superior were few in number but large in size, often numbering eighty or more persons.[33]

These large bands were highly mobile. In summer they frequently travelled to Minnesota to fight the Dakota with their Assiniboine and Cree allies, while winter saw them back in the northern forest trapping and hunting the still-abundant game supply. The termination of competition between the French and English during the late 1750's resulted in a further expansion of smaller groups of Ojibwa to the edge of the Shield in the wake of the Cree evacuation. Andrew Graham during the 1770's remarked that the *Nakawawuck* nation extended as far northwest as the Nelson River:

They are the most northern tribes of the Chipeways. It is our opinion that they have drawn up to the northward gradually as the Keiskatchewans receded from it.

These Keiskatchewans at the time of contact with the Hudson's Bay Company "inhabited the country from the sea-coast up to the Lakes. However, they moved west to the buffalo country in search of furs and new food resources."[34] Thirty years later Duncan Cameron also mentioned the Ojibwa expansion north of Lake Superior.[35]

The Ojibwa did not, however, come to occupy the Lowlands, since the Cree of this area were well adapted to the less-productive conditions prevailing there. The establishment of trading centres by Montreal traders and slightly later by Hudson's Bay men during the late eighteenth century led to the stabilization of Ojibwa groups in the northern interior. When trade goods became readily available near their encampments after the 1770's, treks to the coast or elsewhere ceased. About this time, the Northern Ojibwa (except for those nearer the International Border) ceased warring with the Dakota. By the 1780's, group size had shrunk to about thirty persons per winter settlement due to the immediacy of trading-post competition, and to the fact that the environmental productivity was rapidly declining through the uncontrolled slaughter of beaver and large game for both Indian and trading-post requirements.

There is also evidence that the Ojibwa population was on the increase, a development that accelerated the slaughter of game. Where during the 1730's there were probably no more than about 400 Ojibwa north and west of Lake Superior, by 1800 the number had grown to about 1,500. The game decline continued after 1800, accompanied by the process of fission among groups and a continuous growth in the population. By the 1820's these processes had led to the total destruction of the clan except as a marriage-regulating mechanism, as Indian families separated and dispersed to eke out a meagre existence on their trapping territories in much the same fashion as their Cree brothers of the Lowlands. While the population density was greater west of Lake Superior than in the Lowlands, convergent processes had produced a similar mode of existence throughout northern Ontario by the middle of the nineteenth century.

Conclusions

In this chapter I have tried to summarize the demographic and socio-economic dimensions of aboriginal Cree and Ojibwa culture, and how these were related to the environment. The basic socio-territorial unit of the aboriginal Ojibwa was the clan village. A situation of relative ecological stability allowed this form of organization to function. The Cree to the north, however, demonstrated considerable variability in band size and mobility patterns, a fact related to regional differences in environmental productivity. On the Shield where large game and fish were fairly abundant, Cree local bands were able to coalesce and remain sedentary during the summer months. Nearer the coast, groups were smaller, more widely separated, and more mobile.

The expansion of the fur trade changed tribal boundaries and altered the social structure of all Indians. By the early nineteenth century all Indians north of Lake Superior were heavily reliant upon the trading post in a drastically altered environment. Despite hardships, adaptation permitted an increase in the overall population, the emergence of family-exploited hunting territories, and the formation of trading-post bands.

The processes of the above-noted socio-economic change parallel in certain respects those changes which occurred further west. Everywhere as the fur trade spread and took hold Indians came to depend upon European commodities. Everywhere there were demographic and socio-economic changes which can be related directly to the introduction of Euro-Canadian commodities, environmental depletions, and new diseases. These processes differed in intensity and quality from region to region, however. On the Plains, so long as bison remained the focus of subsistence activities, the introduction of the horse and new iron tools for awhile augmented Plains Indian culture and even ensured political independence. Nevertheless, these tribes succumbed, as had the Cree and Ojibwa, as the food supply dwindled and as trade goods grew increasingly important. Along coastal British Columbia, tribal societies suffered severe population declines after European diseases were introduced. The remnants were often unable to acquire sufficient foods until they began to cluster in single communities. Numerous new trade wares and status positions left vacant following epidemics led to status rivalries involving the potlatch. Thus their ceremonial organization shifted emphasis in accordance with demographic and trade changes. Further north in the western sub-Arctic, Athapaskans experienced much the same fate as the Cree and the Ojibwa. Trading post bands are in evidence by the early nineteenth century. However, where caribou and other food resources remained relatively abundant, groups retained a greater degree of autonomy even though relationships with the trading post and other peoples had significantly altered their aboriginal social organization by the middle of the last century. While we are aware of the end results of these processes, and to an extent the general trends, much historical research remains to be done on these more westerly tribes.

It should now be evident that any attempt to reconstruct aboriginal conditions from oral testimony alone is doomed to fail. The changes which the documents reveal were by no means trivial. While oral accounts of former events and conditions can and should be used in ethnographic reconstructions, they should and must be tempered by documentary sources where and if these are available. Otherwise, such reconstructions are liable to errors including inaccurate historical sequence. Worse still, "the Fallacy of the Ethnographic Present" may allow for change processes to be "represented as contributions to the maintenance of changeless conditions."

Eleven

WHITE 'RITES' AND INDIAN 'RITES': INDIAN EDUCATION AND NATIVE RESPONSES IN THE WEST, 1870-1910

Jacqueline Gresko

Canadian history textbooks tell us little about Indians other than their part in the fur trade, exploration, and wars of the first centuries of white settlement in North America. There is little if any need to mention Indians in later years, for, as a typical history of Canada puts it, the Indians passively accepted "the collapse" of their "primitive . . . tribal life" when "it met a more advanced civilization."[1] Almost all history texts thus omit the Indians' part in Canadian history after 1800, except for their defeat in the North-West Rebellion, and neglect to say that "Canada still has an Indian population, or that they are presently in-volved in a movement to reassert their identity . . . . "[2]

A few exceptions exist, such as Patterson's assertion in *The Canadian Indian: A History since 1500* that during the North-West Rebellion some Indians of Western Canada did protest treaty terms and the loss of the buffalo-hunting way of life, but punishments given leaders of these Indians intimidated other would-be protesters.[3] This study goes on to say that the Indians settled down on reserves in the post-rebellion years, "lost their political and economic autonomy and initiative," and hung on to some extent to their "remaining social and religious identities" despite a government policy aimed at their assimilation into white Canadian society. But the resurgence in the Indians' organization for identity and cultural survival did not begin, says Patterson, until the middle 1940's when provincial Indian organizations began to discuss Indian lands and civil rights with the federal government.[4]

Examination of the history of the Canadian Indian Industrial Schools policy and programs in Western Canada from an ethno-historical standpoint shows that the Indian peoples did not remain quiescent from the 1880's to the 1940's. They did not respond passively to government and missionary plans for them and their children. Rather, they persisted in their traditional patterns of life and resisted the industrial schools' programs with their own educative program. In the 1870's and 1880's, government officials and missionaries, discouraged by the results of their efforts to convert the older generation of western Indians, sought to pull the Indian youths out of the tribal way of life of their elders and to immerse these youths in the arts and industries of Christian civilization in industrial schools. In an anthropological sense, Indians were placed in a directed acculturation situation, and there forced through a new set of *rites de passage*. Meanwhile, Indian elders in southern Saskatchewan persisted in their own social and religious institutions in opposition to industrial-school programs. In the case of these Indians, an ethno-historical examination of the industrial-schools experience from government, missionary, and local records shows that their response to the acculturative programs of the white civilizers was to continue in their dances, their sports, and their traditional ceremonies. When young Indians returned home from the industrial school, they were once again involved in the dancing groups central to Indian society at seasonal dance gatherings, Indian "sports" days, and "picnics", despite the continuing objections of missionaries and government officials into the twentieth century. It might even be said that the efforts to transform western Indians into civilized Christians through educational programs did not halt but in fact encouraged native involvement in traditional social and religious institutions, stimulated resistance to the assimilative efforts of white government and missionaries, and encouraged the generation of modern Indian rights movements.

*   *   *   *   *

This chapter will be ethno-historical rather than strictly historical, in that anthropological and historical sources and perspectives will be used in a case study of Indian education policy and the native response in the old North-West Territories. The anthropologist, using historical sources on the development of Indian education policy to study Indian-white contacts, defines this as an acculturation situation, and would probably agree with Melville Herskovits's classic definition of acculturation as *those phenomena which result when groups of individuals having different cultures come into continuous first-hand contact, with subsequent changes in the original cultural patterns of either or both groups.*[5]

Shifts in group patterns of living can vary along a continuum from complete resistance to change by both groups, to complete conversion of one group and its assimilation into the other group, or can range between the extremes in some form of accommodation or integration of the two groups by an egalitarian amalgamation of them. Anthropologist Robert Linton distinguishes in this continuum two sorts of acculturation situations: the "non-directed", and the "directed" or "forced". In the latter context, one group predominates over another, which has lost its political autonomy.[6] Such a directed acculturation situation is to be found in the industrial schools through which government and missionary administrators intended to Christianize and civilize the Plains Indians.

To discover what were the Indian-white interactions in and through the industrial schools, and what were the Indian responses to its acculturative programs, a study will be made of one industrial school, the Qu'Appelle Industrial School, and its tributary reserves in what later became southern Saskatchewan. The history of this school, under the direction of the Indian Affairs Department and the Oblate Missionaries, constitutes an acculturation situation which includes both headquarters policy decisions and field developments, and the Indian response to both.

Attempts to answer these questions must depend primarily on documentary evidence – letters, reports, petitions – written by those who were trying to direct change among the Indian peoples. There is little documentary evidence, however, as to how the Indians as the objects of change viewed the process. The goal of the government and missionary administration was to bring about the assimilation of the Indians, because most aspects of the traditional Indian way of life were considered not only inferior to the white, Christian way of life, but also evil. Means had to be devised to pry Indians from their traditional ways of thinking and behaving. In a controlled milieu set apart from camp life and white communities, young Indians would be transformed by the skills and attitudes appropriate to the white world. At the optimum point of assimilation, they would be released either to return to their reserves as exemplars to others, or to circulate in white society at a level proper to their station in life, and perhaps even enter communities which would be separated but autonomous units within Canadian society.

The prevalent view of government and missionary administrators was that selected Indians should be guided from their youth from a state of impurity, incompetence, and ignorance, by gradual stages to a state in which they would function as adults acceptable to the white society. This process was not to be a simple secular inculcation of useful technical skills, but a mission designed by God to improve both the spiritual and the temporal welfare of less fortunate non-Christian peoples. The missionaries, employed as part of the "Standing Army of our Dominion" in the struggle for control of the North-West Territories, conceived their role in Indian schools in such messianic terms. They sought to instill in Indian youths "a nobler individualism, superior religion, and grander civilization,"[7] and thus to prevent their moral or physical annihilation by the evils of tribal life, the neglect or mismanagement of the government, or degradation by immoral, intemperate whites in western towns.

Both secular and ecclesiastical programs to transform the Indians were analogous to those ceremonial patterns van Gennep analyzed as *rites de passage*. According to van Gennep,

the life of an individual in any society is a series of passages from one age to another and from one occupation to another. Wherever there are fine distinctions among age or occupational groups, progression from one group to the next is accompanied by special acts, like those which make up apprenticeship in our trades.

For the semi-civilized peoples, van Gennep contended, such acts are "enveloped in ceremonies," since to their minds "no act is entirely free of the sacred," and "transitions from group to group and from one social situation to the next are looked upon as implicit in the very fact of existence." A man's life "comes to be made up of a succession of stages."[8] Van Gennep attempted to assemble all the ceremonial patterns which accompanied "a passage from one situation to another or from one cosmic or social world to another." He especially singled out transitional rites or *rites de passage*, and subdivided them for analysis of their underlying patterns into *rites of separation, transition rites,* and *rites of incorporation*. In each segment of the schema, there are yet other divisions "characteristic of all societies": the separation of the sexes, and of the "sacred" and "profane" spheres of social life. The pattern and hierarchy of divisions in van Gennep's *rites de passage* are convenient symbolic correlates in any discussion of church administration of Indian education for the state. More useful as an ethno-historical tool in examination of the secular aspect of Indian schools are his formulations on social transitions themselves. Within the various stages of such movements, as within the steps of a marriage, van Gennep distinguished "the existence of transitional periods which sometimes acquire a certain autonomy," such as the betrothal period.[9] A passage from one social position to another is therefore often marked by a territorial passage, a change of residence.

In this examination, then, the industrial-school programs for civilizing and Christianizing the Indians' children, as developed at Qu'Appelle, are stages in the social transition of a directed acculturation situation.

The schema of *rites de passage* provides convenient symbolic correlates for the missionary-administrator combination of spiritual and social passages for their students.

Why and how did the industrial-school policy and the programs come about? Who were the Indians who would be affected by the directed acculturation situation of Qu'Appelle Industrial School, and how was that situation predetermined by government and missionary administrators in the North-West Territories?

*   *   *   *   *

When Canada acquired Rupert's Land from the Hudson's Bay Company in 1870, she established treaties with the Indian peoples of her new territories to ensure that future white settlement there would be peaceful. The treaties guaranteed the Indians schools as well as lands and annuities. While negotiating Treaty Four with the Cree, Saulteaux, and Assiniboine around Fort Qu'Appelle on September 12, 1874, Lieutenant-Governor Morris said that the Queen would assist in laying out reserves, agricultural settlement, and send and pay for "schoolmasters on every Reserve," as soon as the Indians had taken up residence on those locations.[10]

The dominant linguistic and cultural group to adhere to Treaty Four were the Plains Cree, who, like their neighbours, had had no special educative institutions. The *"social group as a whole* was the school of every growing mind. . . . The practical and the religious, the manual and the intellectual, the individual and the social flowed as one complex integrated function within the Indian group."[11] And, according to descriptions of the Cree life given to ethnographer David Mandelbaum in 1936 concerning the time within the memory of his oldest informants in the 1860's and 1870's, the traditional Cree life style and educative system persisted to a great extent from the time "before the buffalo had disappeared."[12]

The highlight of the Cree year was the annual sun-dance encampment in late June or early July. Scattered "sections of a band, or even several bands converged . . . together for two weeks or even longer. . . . When the food supply ran low, the bands drifted apart, each towards its own territory."[13] Then came the summer and fall, the time for hunting buffalo, deer, and elk, for trapping small game, and for gathering fruit and roots. In January and February came the hungry days when food supplies ran low. With the spring came the fishing season; larger gatherings of Cree were held for buffalo hunting, and then again the summer sun dance. This meeting, which should properly be called a thirsting dance, often lasted three or four days, and occasioned great social activity: other dancing, gambling, games, courtship, displays of ponies or war trophies, and visits to relatives and friends. Just as the Catholic mass is central to the sacred and social rituals such as marriage, so was the sacred part of the sun dance central to the dance gatherings.

Contemporary white commentators did not often differentiate between the sacred and social aspects of these convocations. They failed to make distinctions between those seasonal dances encompassing sacred rituals – Sun, Smoking Tipi, Masked or Give Away dances, which certain Cree might pledge to host – and those "secular" or social dances which went on year round and did not necessitate a vow. Missionaries typically referred to them as superstitions and to the sun dance as "pour les sauvages un acte de culte public rendu au démon."[14] Similarly they disliked the warrior societies which policed the buffalo hunts and cared for the needy, but also arranged such feasts and dances.

During the post-treaty years the Cree underwent shifts from their former life patterns even though they had not all moved on to reserves. Game and fruit disappeared. Officials tried to stop the Cree's annual migrations. But the greatest change was in the indigenous educational system. Missionary attempts to convert and educate western Indians, begun at Red River missions in the early nineteenth century, were now intensified in order to prepare Indians for eventual assimilation with white settlers. By the mid-1870's most missions in the North West tried to run day schools, boarding schools, or orphanages for Indian children, and to teach them Christianity and farming. To cite an example, at the Roman Catholic mission of Saint Florent near Fort Qu'Appelle, Father Joseph Hugonnard, the assistant Oblate missionary, had founded a school at the mission by the time the Cree signed Treaty Four.[15] After the treaties the government granted western mission schools some financial assistance, but the annual per capita grants of twelve dollars were too small to support day schools for all the scattered Indian settlements on reserves.[16] Most missionaries, like Father Hugonnard, therefore, concentrated their efforts in boarding schools or orphanages run at the mission post in order to keep pupils in regular attendance and thus obtain the government grants.

More government aid for western mission Indian schools came only in 1878 and 1879 when the Macdonald Conservatives came back to power. By that time the buffalo had disappeared, and famine was prevalent among the natives. The Macdonald government's desire to build a transcontinental railway and promote white settlement in a tranquil west fitted with the government's humanitarian sympathy for the starving natives and made urgent their settlement on reserves and their training towards agricultural self-support. As Minister of the Interior and Superintendent General of Indian Affairs, Macdonald tried to reorganize the Indian Service of the North-West Territories. He sent Edgar Dewdney west as Indian Commissioner, with the responsibility of ensuring that treaty provisions, especially those in which the government promised to help the Indians learn farming, were carried out.[17] However, the attempts of the farming instructors to teach the Indians on reserves to be self-sufficient farmers generally failed, and resulted in poverty and high relief costs.

Discouraged by the results of both their agricultural instructors and the day schools on the reserves, Indian Department officials looked at the longer American experience with western Indians, and decided to institute off-reserve industrial boarding schools which would remove Indian youths from the tribal way of life and train them in the arts and industries of civilization. In December 1878, J.S. Dennis, Deputy Minister of the Interior, submitted a memorandum on the "native problem" to Macdonald and the heads of missionary bodies in the North-West Territories, recommending such American-style Indian schools.[18]

Consequently, Macdonald sent lawyer-journalist Nicholas F. Davin to visit the American Secretary of the Interior, Carl Schurz, and to investigate American Indian industrial schools. Davin did not visit manual-labour boarding schools or industrial institutes in Ontario since the Department already had information on them; their "civilizing" of younger natives had become known as a "long range policy", rather than a quick and inexpensive assimilative process.[19] In his "Report on Industrial Schools for Indians and Half-Breeds," Davin noted that American experience "is the same as our own as far as the adult Indian is concerned, little can be done with him." But the industrial boarding schools conducted through the agency or contracted to one of the Churches had "happy results," since some of the schools even had large herds of cattle. To Davin, the best example of the results of industrial schools was the progress of the five "civilized" tribes (the Cherokees, Chickasaws, Choctaws, Creeks, and Seminoles) in agriculture, self-support, education, and government.[20] Therefore Davin recommended that the Canadian government help establish three church-run industrial boarding schools. For all the schools, Davin advocated rewards to pupils and parents for attendance, future compulsory education, teachers of high moral and intellectual character, and inspection of the teachers' work. Further education as Department clerks or teachers ought to be available to bright native pupils.

On receipt of Davin's report, the Indian Service began negotiations with other government departments and the Churches for the establishment of Indian industrial schools. These negotiations dragged on for several years, partly because relief for starving Indians took precedence, and partly because of the Conservative government's desire to economize in establishing schools by utilizing missionary endeavour and, one might add, missionary competition.[21] By 1883, Indian Commissioner Dewdney recommended to Macdonald that arrangements be made to build three industrial schools: one for each of treaties Four, Six, and Seven, with the Treaty Four school at Qu'Appelle and the Treaty Seven school at High River under Roman Catholic management, and the Treaty Six school at Battleford under Anglican management. Father Joseph Hugonnard, O.M.I., was appointed by Macdonald as principal of the new Indian Industrial School at Qu'Appelle.[22]

At Qu'Appelle Industrial School, Father Hugonnard implemented the combined program of federal Indian education and Roman Catholic missionary instruction to train "savage" children in the "arts" and "industries of civilization". The characteristic of the industrial-school system that would differentiate it from its predecessors as well as its contemporaries, the boarding and day schools, would be its joint promotion by church and state. There would be a common set of government-assisted (but missionary-managed) boarding schools, an off-reserve location in or near "civilization", a comprehensive English-language training program, and a technical- and agricultural-oriented curriculum, all designed to make model brown white-men. Father Hugonnard saw the Indian childrens' baptism, confirmation, communion, and marriage as stages in a novitiate, paralleling their apprenticeship in civilization at the school. By the turn of the century, agent Graham agreed with Hugonnard that graduation and marriage, the final incorporative stages in industrial education, needed more supervision, and Graham helped both Catholic and Protestant principals to extend their programs to an ex-pupil colony.

In the 1880's, Father Hugonnard, together with his Oblate and lay assistants and the Grey Nuns, sought to remove Indian boys and girls* from the "savage milieu" and to convert these recruits to "civilized" habits through English-language classroom instruction,[24] through training in such industrial skills as farming, carpentry, and laundering, and through the Christian religion. Thus, according to Indian Department policy, the new, moral, self-supporting Christian citizens would be capable of amalgamating with the white community or of elevating the pagan and dependent reserve community.[25] The Roman Catholic Oblate missionary policy for the industrial schools likewise aimed to civilize and Christianize the young Indians "menacés d'être éteints par la démoralisation et les vices qu'ils copaient plus facilement que la civilisation et les bonnes moeurs," and to make of them "pour l'avenir, des chefs de familles catholiques, qu'iront s'établir dans les nombreuses réserves."[26]

---

*Although the Department of Indian Affairs had not at first intended to educate girls in industrial schools, the availability of devoted nuns at a very low rate of pay for Roman Catholic Industrial Schools brought a change in policy. Girls trained in domestic service fit the Department of Indian Affairs long-range policies of self-support and enfranchisement for Indians by providing wives for trained Indian youths who would otherwise "find wives among the uneducated women of their Bands and relapse into barbarism."[23]

Father Hugonnard consequently programmed the sacred transitional stages for the Indian children – baptism, communion, confirmation, and marriage – as the process of a catechumenate or novitiate, paralleling the apprenticeship in civilization of the secular sphere of the children's education. At the Qu'Appelle Industrial School, the children were first immersed in their new environment, and then trained to communicate in it as civilized Christians by learning English and such concepts as time, work, and order through classroom instruction or by "fatigues" in the garden or sewing room. Then the children were confirmed in the moral attitudes and industrial habits of civilization by stages leading through elementary education, agriculture, trades, and domestic training.

The educational programs at the Qu'Appelle Industrial School evolved as a result of official policy changes, Protestant competition, and Indian resistance to the school in the 1880's and 1890's. Two North-West Territory Indian Department officials, Inspector J.A. Macrae and Indian Commissioner Hayter Reed, toured Ontario and American industrial schools, particularly Captain R.H. Pratt's Carlisle,[27] in order to make recommendations on the extension of the much lauded[28] industrial schools in the North West Territories and in British Columbia.[29] Their reports paralleled those of Anglican Reverend E.F. Wilson of Sault Ste. Marie, who competed with Qu'Appelle Industrial School for pupils and funds using many of the same American programs admired by Reed and Macrae; and these became policy directives for all industrial schools.[30] To conform with these directives, and to survive Protestant competition, not to mention Indian apathy to the schools, the principal of Qu'Appelle Industrial School intensified the programs of religious and secular conversion. He arranged for intensified English-language teaching, and a student monitor system that required half of each senior boy or girl's day be spent in new and varied trades-workshops or in the kitchen, laundry, or dairy. He organized white recreations for pupils, such as cricket and football teams, chequer games in the evening, a brass band, and excursions to agency and town fairs.[31]

One might say, along a tangent of van Gennep's theories, that these and other exhibitions of student's progress constituted special ceremonies to mark their movement from apprentice status in civilization as senior pupils of the industrial school to journeymen members of the guild. Advanced pupils not only went to fairs, but sometimes (like those of Carlisle School) were hired "out to service among the settlers" as farm hands and household help.[32] This practicum or 'outing' was intended to confirm them at the end of their apprenticeship in the role and status of self-supporting Christian citizens, more thoroughly than could any visiting dignitary's examination of their work at school or the white settlers' approval of it at fairs and exhibitions.

Although Hugonnard consciously programmed the process of school leaving as a commencement and marriage ceremony into Christian civilized life,[33] he worried about the ability of ex-pupils to persevere as Christian farmers on their home reserve. Hence he co-operated with the equally concerned local Indian agent William Graham and the principals of the Protestant File Hills Boarding School and Regina Industrial School in extending Industrial School programs to an ex-pupil colony on the File Hills reserve. This extension seemed like the fulfillment of the dreams of the religious and governmental planners of the industrial schools policy. They had hoped for future parishes of self-supporting Indians and "colonies for pupils after school leaving," rather than have them return to reserves and retrogress to the tribal way of life or be immersed in eastern Canadian society.[34]

In the spring of 1901, agent Graham began to place boys "as soon as they had left school, on farms of their own, instead of allowing them to return to the teepee as formerly." Missionary principals assisted him in arranging marriages for ex-pupils and directing them to do parish work among the colonists at File Hills.[35] By 1907, Graham, who was now Saskatchewan Inspector of Indian Agencies, wrote "a special report" on the extension of "the training received by young Indians" at the Industrial School on the "File Hills ex-pupil colony." He considered the results of the colony "phenomenal" in light of his previous experience of seeing school leavers retrogress under the influence of the old Indians. The twenty young farmers and their wives raised children who spoke English only, produced good crops on their farms, and owned and operated their own steam thresher. Some ex-pupil colonists like Fred Dieter, a graduate of Regina Industrial School, had even hired white men as farm help. Another ex-pupil, Graham's former teamster and interpreter Mark Ward, was an alumnus of Qu'Appelle Industrial School, and was inspired by visits to the colony to join it voluntarily as a farmer. Thus, in terms of van Gennep's schema, the colony's extension of the school incorporative *rites* made the pupils apprentices in Christian civilization. And churchmen, journalists, and officials lauded the effectiveness of the colony incorporative 'rites' as if they were commenting on the perfection of a medieval guild.[36]

Although the extension of Qu'Appelle Industrial School programs to this unique ex-pupil colony seemed to vindicate the industrial-school policy, it was not typical of the federal Indian education policy which had been withering from congenital defects for years. Church-state tensions in the operation of Indian schools particularly affected the Roman Catholic institutions in the era of separate school questions in the West.[37] Government economizing during the depression of the 1880's and early 1890's had cut grants to all Indian schools. Local administrative economies perverted the half-day of trades instruction and the "outings" from their educational purpose to forced child labour for the sake of economy. A plethora of schools, industrial, boarding, and day, sometimes run by the same denomination, competed for pupils and government grants during the years of diseased and declining Indian populations.[38]

Just as they had arbitrarily begun and run industrial schools in the old North-West Territories without consulting Indian parents, after 1896 Indian Department officials promoted the end of that school system and the development of the residential school system in its place. Ostensible reasons for the end of industrial schools were the Indian Department's need to economize on Indian education, and the need to improve health conditions in the schools. But the greatest factor in their demise was probably Indian resistance and the persistence of traditional social and religious institutions, particularly summer dance gatherings. These dances took whole bands, including industrial school ex-pupils, away from settled individual agricultural enterprise during the season when farms needed attention in order to be productive.

According to the Regina *Leader* of January 15, 1903, the average school leavers' "retrogression", the persistence of dancing on reserves, and the "continued tale of exceeding slow progress . . . in view [of] the great effort and great expenditure" of the government, meant the "time has arrived . . . to lessen the Indian outlay." James Smart, Deputy Superintendent General of Indian Affairs, had already expressed similar sentiments. He did not think that the expense of educating Indian "children above the possibilities of their station" and creating in them "a distaste for what is certain to be their environment" could be justified to the taxpaying and voting citizenry of Canada. In addition, the elaborate Industrial School systems would be a "waste of money" that would do Indian children "an injury."[39] Consequently, the Indian Department phased out many Industrial School programs and combined former industrial institutions with boarding schools on or nearer to the reserves.

*   *   *   *   *

The failure of the schools experiment also had an internal aspect. During the heyday of Qu'Appelle Industrial School and the File Hills Colony, Indian peoples of Treaty Four had resisted the assimilative thrust of the educational programs, both secular and sacred. They continued in and adapted their own social, religious, and educational traditions and institutions, especially the annual sun-dance gathering. And, even when shunted on to and supervised on reserves, the Plains Cree had not conformed to missionary and government directives to stop dancing, or to settle down to farming year round, and send their children to school. Though children who were recruited for schools nominally conformed while there, the whole community went dancing annually.

Estimates of Indian childrens' school attendance, perhaps the best evidence of Indian resistance to schooling, are difficult to find or to establish. Official estimates rarely range above twenty-five to fifty per cent of school-age children in any given area. For example, in 1889, J.A. Macrae, a Protestant School Inspector, reported that of 107 children of school age at the File Hills Agency, only about 24 were in either the Catholic or Protestant schools. A table on Indian pupils of Qu'Appelle School in 1893 shows that few of them stayed at school longer than four years, and very few progressed beyond Standard V to any form of secondary education. At the same time, many Indian children died of forms of tuberculosis at school or on return home.

Why did Indians on Treaty Four reserves tributary to Qu'Appelle Industrial School resist assimilation? From the documents it is clear that the Cree and other Treaty Four Indians did not want to be separated from their children in this life or in the next. As Chief Piapot told Father Hugonnard in the 1880's,

Je ne veux pas qu'aucun de mes enfants à ton école prendre les habits et surtout la religion des Blancs. Nous sommes formés avec la terre noire et toi avec la terre blanche, tu as ta religion et nous, nous avons la nôtre, garde la tienne et nous gardions la nôtre. . . . Ce n'est pas sans raison que tu portes cette longue robe, si tu veux instruire mes enfants, viens bâtir une maison ici près de la mienne. . . .[40]

Only by "constant attention" did the Indian agents and the principal of Qu'Appelle Industrial School recruit pupils. According to the Indian Department officials, the parents' migratory life style, their dislike of corporal punishment for children, and their indifference to the occupational prospects of educated youths impeded the assimilation policy and programs.[41]

The government reports demonstrate most emphatically that the Cree did not want to have their children apprenticed in "civilization". Indian parents complained that although they may have wanted their children to learn to read and write, they did not want them to work as cheap or forced labour for the school administrators under the guise of "instruction in trades". Cree men probably considered instruction in or employment at year-round, individual, free-enterprise farming as tedious, womanish, and selfish – even though they did seem to enjoy those aspects of industrial-school training which were not too much at variance with traditional Indian patterns of life, such as plentiful housework for girls, and musical instruments and fancy uniforms for boys in the brass band.[42]

Because the Cree disliked government and missionary direction of their children's acculturation, they attempted to subvert it. They either did not send their children to industrial schools, or they let them go only intermittently to a reserve day school. And they often allowed only the female, sick, and orphaned to attend industrial institutions. Since Protestant schools at File Hills, Elkhorn, Round Lake, and Birtle sought pupils from the same homes as did the Qu'Appelle school, Indian parents played off one denomination against another, or manipulated agents in order to prevent their child's going to school or to promote his removal from school. Even the economic policies of the administrators were distorted to conform with the traditional economic patterns of life. Turn-of-the-century Qu'Appelle Valley Indians' high earnings and near self-support did not result from their farming profits, but from casual wage employment. Among the males the most common activities were hauling freight, selling firewood, raising ponies, and harvesting for white farmers; and among the Indian women, domestic labour, digging senega root, or tanning hides. These seasonal and casual labour occupations allowed for attendance at dances, even to those dances on distant reserves.[43]

The core of cultural resistance among the Cree, Assiniboine, Saulteaux, and Sioux were these annual sun-dance gatherings. There the "ideological rituals", as defined by Karl Mannheim, presented a means to protect and perfect the existing social system, in contrast to the industrial schools' "utopian rituals" which strove for revolutionary change in that system.[44] Treaty Four Indian groups went dancing with their children each summer despite, or in spite of, the school principals, the Indian agents, and the force of law. Officials, more optimistic than the missionaries, annually announced that through their "moral suasion," the "last" sun dance had been held.[45] The local press was perhaps more candid than the government officials about the disappearance of the dances. Qu'Appelle Valley papers reported how in 1885, in spite of the missionary schools and official warnings to stay on reserves during the North-West Rebellion, Indians from File Hills came down to have a dance at Fort Qu'Appelle. The April 23, 1885 issue of the Qu'Appelle *Vidette* told how "painted and adorned as usual . . . they said they were not afraid of the redcoats." On June 18, 1885 the same newspaper reported, as others would every year on into the next century, how Piapot's, Muscowpetung's and Star Blanket's bands held dances despite government proclamations against movement off the reserves.

Laws were introduced to stop the sun dance, and the North-West Mounted Police patrolled dance gatherings to prevent heathenish tortures, the consumption of alcohol, the spread of disease, or the presence of "trespassers" which might lead to pan-reserve political action. Yet, the Indians were as indifferent to informing on their fellow dancers as they were to sending children away to school. Even File Hills colonists, who had adopted the social clubs and church activities of the whites, still liked the old dances and held them secretly in their homes.[46]

The sun dance presented a parallel educational system designed to oppose that of the government and missionaries. The Plains Cree approach to teaching the arts and industries of their civilization had been to gather annually not merely for sacred rites, but also for the initiation of young braves, for marriage ceremonies, and for social reaffirmation rites such as visiting, boasting, and politicking. While the Indian Affairs Department and the missionaries tried to train, co-opt, or assimilate individual youths, the whole tribe went on with its "ideological rituals" designed to perfect and protect their own social system. The Cree adapted these *rites de passage* for separation of the younger age group, both temporal and eternal. Newspapers and missionary and government reports told how pre-schoolers, "truants", and school leavers accompanied family groups to the "races", "sports", or dances.[47] Children who came back homesick from industrial schools, or who died there, were the objects of the avowed dance ceremonies. Undoubtedly Crees returning from the United States in 1897, having been associated with the Ghost Dance, furthered the adaptation of dance gatherings in Canada.

In the early 1900's officials and missionaries clearly recognized that the Indians were persisting in dancing, and moved to discourage the practice by having the instigators prosecuted. Thus in 1903 the Saulteaux Etchease and the Sioux Standing Buffalo, who disobeyed Section 114 of the Indian Act forbidding immoral dancing, were arrested and tried.[48] Father Hugonnard, who had been saying for years that the dances "had confirmed them in all practices adverse to Christianity and civilization," voiced his complaints loudly in 1903-04 on the adverse affects of dancing on his ex-pupils:

[On returning to] the reservation from the school they have much to contend with if they persevere in civilized habits, as the old people and dancing set bitterly oppose all progressive ideas and actions these are abandoned – on account of the ridicule they provoke from the dancing set – for gambling, debauchery and slothfulness. . . .

[Only those who have] studied the evil effects of pagan dances as they affect the moral and physical welfare of the Indians, realize the important step taken by the department in the total suppression of such dances in this district. Usually the dance was the first downward step . . . of ex-pupils, as when once they become dancers, progressive ideas and actions are abandoned. . . .[49]

In March 1903, Hugonnard wrote directly to Indian Commissioner David Laird on the "restless" feeling caused by local Indians' holding of dances contrary to the prohibition of the Indian Act and their not being punished by the courts when apprehended. He exhorted that "Indians unless punished in some visible way when justly arrested, consider their release a victory over the N.W.M.P. and Government authorities. . . ." According to Hugonnard, "Clemency in their eyes was a sign of weakness."[50]

By December 1903, Commissioner David Laird forwarded to Ottawa

a letter from Father Hugonnard "relative to evils connected with danc-
ing on the reserves," and also included supporting statements of the
Roman Catholic Archbishop of Saint Boniface, Methodists Dr. Suther-
land and James Woodsworth, Brandon Industrial School Principal T.
Ferrier, and Presbyterian Thomas Hart. These men all swore their agreement with Hugonnard's letter on the evils of dancing for the welfare of
Indians, particularly for the ex-pupils of industrial schools.[51] Archbishop
Langevin of Saint-Boniface, writing to the Minister of the Interior,
Clifford Sifton, on December 26, 1903, recommended that the government "amend the law" if necessary against the Indian dances. He
reiterated Father Hugonnard's lament that even children educated at
"high expense in the Industrial Schools of the Government" practised
such dances, "the means of opposing all efforts made by the Government
and the Missionaries to civilize the Indians . . . to earn a living by farming or by raising cattle."[52]

Clifford Sifton replied to the Archbishop that he had "fully sustained"
the position of agent Graham and Father Hugonnard against dancing.
Deputy Superintendent General of Indian Affairs Frank Pedley wired
the Mounted Police Corporal at Fort Qu'Appelle on January 5, 1904,
regarding Standing Buffalo's statements that he had been given permission by Ottawa to dance: "Agent Graham has been upheld by the
Department . . . Patrol . . . and notify Indians that dancing is prohibited."[53]

By making dances test cases, the Treaty Four Indians had begun to
defend and entrench their dance gatherings as a cultural institution.
The Plains Indians knew that their persistence in dancing frustrated the
expensive government education policy. Now, through legal petitions to
Ottawa, they would try to entrench Indian civil rights to protect their
dancing "rites".

By 1906, an industrial school ex-pupil, Assiniboine Daniel Kennedy,
not only joined his elders in dances, but also assisted them in obtaining
legal help to draft petitions. Assiniboine Indians petitioned the Minister
of the Interior in March 1906, asking that July 18-20 be set aside as
"holidays whereupon the Indians may have feasts and sports and thanksgiving promenades; holidays exactly similar to those observed by White
people on Dominion Day." If permission were granted, the signators
believed "those Indians now in the habit of leaving the reserve in summer will not do so but will remain at their work on reserve here."
Barrister Levi Thompson of Wolseley, Saskatchewan, in his letter transmitting this petition to the Honourable Frank Oliver, remarked that "the
leaders of this movement seem to be among the best-educated and most
intelligent of them."[54]

J.D. McLean, an Ottawa Secretary of the Department of Indian
Affairs, granted the petitioners' request, since, "if confined to the amusements referred to in the petition," such permission "would appear to be

in line with the Department's policy in having the sun dances substituted by picnics or festivals at which games of various descriptions take the place of the objectionable features" of the dance gatherings. These "picnics" were thus held under the provisions of the Indian Act.[55] Telegraphic exchanges between the principal of the Qu'Appelle Industrial School, Inspector Graham, and the Department of Indian Affairs showed how much less sanguine were the field officers of the Indian administration about the harmless character of such Indian dancing. The Assiniboine Agent, W.S. Grant, wrote the Secretary of the Department of Indian Affairs that the thanksgiving promenade "really means some kind of a dance." Obviously, the Indians, by going to a lawyer, were trying to get away with something illegal. To Grant, all dancing was "demoralizing". He and Inspector Graham had worked to discourage dances. He thus remarked that it would help them in dealing with Indians "if the Department would take less notice of Indian letters, as many . . . are schemes and plots, talked over by the old people, who spend many nights advising those young boys who have returned from school."[56]

In 1907, the Assiniboine Indians petitioned agent Graham for permission "to hold similar 'sports' to those held in July, 1906." Again, the petition bore the signatures of over thirty Indians, including Daniel Kennedy.[57] The use of Daniel Kennedy, a Qu'Appelle Industrial School boy who had gone on to Saint Boniface College and had worked for the Indian Department as agency interpreter and assistant farmer,[58] demonstrated the incorporative capacities of the Assiniboine elders. In pre-reserve days, the Cree peoples had educated their young men by sending them to live with chiefs, care for chiefs' horses, and hunt for them while learning their skills in hunting and warfare. Ex-pupils who returned to the reserves able to read English newspapers, write letters, and obtain legal advice, lent considerable sophistication to the campaign to retain the dances. Indian Commissioner Laird grumbled to his superiors that Indians of Treaties Four and Six might read an article entitled "Bloods to Hold the Sun Dance" in the Manitoba *Free Press* as a concession made to the Bloods, and that they would "claim the same privilege."[59]

In his 1908 Annual Report, Deputy Superintendent General of Indian Affairs Frank Pedley remarked that "a certain recrudescence" of the sun dance was a "spasmodic and expiring effort" of the "older generation," an attempt of the "surviving medicine men to keep alive" superstitions and customs which were naturally "dying hard." He noted that "increasing contact with civilization has largely corrected the vagueness of the Indians' information as to their legal rights and the powers of the law" and lessened their dependence and diminished their meek obedience to the Department. Although he might have, he did not add that a degree of the Indians' independence may have come from literacy prompted by the industrial schools or from making trips and "outings" to "civilization".[60]

The missionaries had also inadvertently, and sometimes directly, promoted the retention of the dances. Occasionally the missionary directors of the school would not actually frown on the practice, and would be diplomatic towards parents visiting en route to sun dances, or would grant pupils leaves for "illness" in June and July. But one Methodist missionary intentionally aided the 1906-1907 "recrudescence" of the sun dance among Plains Indians. The Reverend John McDougall, by his own description "a lover of true liberty and fair play to all men, and also as a loyal British subject," admired the Blackfoot and Sioux desire to conserve "the harmless part of their ritual and service." McDougall's letters to his Methodist superiors and to Indian Department officials protested the government's prohibition of "Religious Liberty" for those Indians who kept up "the faith of their fathers" by denying them permission to dance. A Winnipeg *Free Press* article of November 22, 1907 about this verbal protest was headlined "SHOULD NOT BE SUPPRESSED: Reverend John McDougall Says Sun Dance Is a Religious Festival."[61]

Government and missionary efforts to transform western Indians into civilized Christians through the industrial-school policy had thus failed to halt native involvement in traditional social and religious institutions. Rather, it aided native persistence in these institutions and in the traditional education of the young. It had also promoted native resistance to white assimilative education policy; and, as anthropologists and historians might conclude, helped generate modern Indian-rights movements by providing trained personnel, political identity, and initiative. This conclusion seems to be in support of those of anthropologists like Vogt and Dozier regarding directed acculturation programs. If " 'forced' acculturation is not so extreme as to lead to early absorption of the subordinate group, it will result in a high degree of resistance to change in indigenous cultural patterns." Moreover, "despite all . . . pressures for change, there are still basically Indian systems of social structure and culture persisting with variable vigour within conservative nuclei of American Indian peoples."[62]

Studies of other late nineteenth-century directed acculturation situations in the United States and British Columbia involving industrial schools reveal a similar response pattern to that of Treaty Four Indian peoples. Sioux youngsters recruited by Capt. R.H. Pratt from Rosebud and Pine Ridge, South Dakota, were sent to the Indian School at Carlisle, Pennsylvania, and put through a classic set of "revolutionary" *rites de passage*. In an equally classic Indian response, returning pupils were inducted into dancing groups on their home reserves. Thus, "ironically one of the bulwarks of the acculturation policy – schools – had facilitated the spread of the Ghost Dance," a nativistic movement or revitalization cult of the 1890's, by training Indian youths to speak, read, and write English; by having them mix with and marry youths from other Indian groups; and by alienating them from the tribal culture to which they would return.[63] Plenty Horses said that he "murdered Lt. E.W. Casey" during the Ghost Dance "to wipe out the stain of Carlisle Indian School and win the favor of his people."

In southern British Columbia, the Salishan peoples of the Lower Fraser Valley and the Straits of Georgia responded to missionary- and government-directed acculturation in a manner similar to that of Canadian and American Plains Indians. There in the 1860's Bishop D'Herbomez, O.M.I., planned Industrial Schools as part of his "reduction scheme" for model village communities. In the 1880's and 1890's the federal government supported these plans with industrial schools, agency farming instructors for reserve communities, and even a model reserve community. Ex-pupils of these experiments as well as farmers in the Christian villages were, however, inducted into traditional spirit-dancing groups.[64] The Salishan peoples, like the Plains Indians, did not settle down to farming as the agents directed. Rather, the Coast Salish persisted in traditional economic and social patterns of the intervillage community, such as seasonal, semi-nomadic labour which did not interfere with ongoing spirit dancing.[65] In order to resist assimilative programs, the Salish exploited the opportunities behind the system offered for evasion. The non-compulsory character of the schools, the sporadic nature of official influence upon parents and ex-pupils, and especially the agents' toleration of Indians engaged in casual labour were but a few of the loopholes which invited social resistance.

Ironically, forced acculturation, whenever it was applied and however revolutionary its assimilative intent, assisted instead of displacing Indian aboriginal "rites". In every case, Indian society was sustained or even reinforced in its aboriginal economic and social patterns to the same if not to a greater degree than these were changed. There is little doubt that Indian resistance during the early decades of reserve life was bolstered by the relatively good economic position of natives in the West. In the absence of intensive immigration and settlement, there were few other people who would work seasonally and for low wages. Parallel weaknesses in the social systems imposed by the whites also offered considerable room for cultural escape. The non-compulsory character of school attendance, and institutional competition among the churches offered considerable opportunity for the Indian to divide, if not rule. Also, public opinion was often on their side and can be measured in the popularity of Indian festivals at town fairs, or the convivial wish that the chiefs and their braves be allowed their "social dances" or "canoe races". Faced by systems and ideologies which were often inconsistent and haphazard in their application of forced acculturation, the Plains Indians survived with their aboriginal rites intact.

Evidence of their short-run survival may be seen in the fact that by

1900 Indians in traditional regalia or performing pagan ceremonials were popular attractions for Western town fairs, notably the Calgary Stampede. In fact, the recrudescence of the sun dance and its accompanying defence by the fair boards brought angry letters from the Indian Department officials in Ottawa. But there were longer-term and subtler effects wrought by late nineteenth-century Indian education policy. The Cherokee anthropologist R.K. Thomas discusses the growth of the modern pan-Indian movement in the United States in terms of its links to the "boarding-school experience of nineteenth and twentieth-century Indians." That educational experience, in Canada as well as in the United States, increased the Indians' mobility and contacts with other groups, and resulted in "greater knowledge and concern about each other's character and interests, and a consequent common sense of identity."[66] Often, educated youths returning from industrial schools became, like Daniel Kennedy and Plenty Horses, leading members of nativistic movements and native rights movements. The residential schools which succeeded the industrial schools similarly produced trained and politicized personnel for modern Indian-rights movements. British Columbia's Indian leader Andrew Paull, and Alberta's Harold Cardinal were latter-day products of those same schools.

For an historian of Western Canada, other aspects of the preceding discussion are perhaps more pertinent than modern native-rights movements. Western Canadian native peoples expressed discontent with the Indian-education component of Macdonald and Laurier's "National Policy" for developing the Canadian West, at the same time as their white settler neighbours protested the railway, tariff, lands, or immigration aspects of that same policy. "National" history books tend to ignore both Western protests.

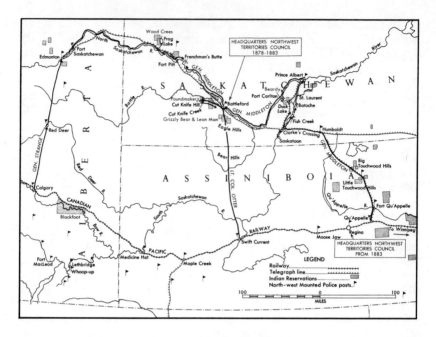

Map of the Northwest in 1885, from D.G.G. Kerr, ed., *A Historical Atlas of Canada*. (Thos. Nelson & Sons, Toronto).

Twelve

ON THE TRAIL OF BIG BEAR

Rudy Wiebe

For the story teller there is only one problem of historical reconstruction; A.M. Klein has described it exactly in his poem "Portrait of the Poet as Landscape":

Sometimes, depressed to nadir, he [the poet] *will*
think all lost,
will see himself as throwback, relict, freak,
his mother's miscarriage, his great-grandfather's ghost,
and he will curse his quintuplet senses, and their tutors
in whom he put, as he should not have put, his trust.

Trusting the "quintuplet senses", the story teller too has been tutoring them, to be his guide through the maze of life and imagination. Through the smoke and darkness and piled-up factuality of a hundred years to see a face; to hear, and comprehend, a voice whose verbal language he will never understand; and then to risk himself beyond such seeing, such hearing as he discovers possible, and venture into the finer labyrinths opened by those other senses: touch, to learn the texture of leather, of earth; smell, the tinct of sweetgrass and urine; taste, the golden poplar sap or the hot, raw buffalo liver dipped in gall.

This trust of the wayward though beloved senses: that is the problem of the story teller. The facts: all the facts he will ever need to know, and many more besides, they are very easily and often pleasantly found.

For, unless they are very carefully handled, facts are the invariable tyrants of story. They are as inhibiting as fences and railroads, whereas the story teller would prefer, like Big Bear, "to walk where his feet can walk." A hundred years ago Henry James said of story telling, "What is character but the determination of incident? What is incident but the illustration of character?" In terms of history I suppose that means that if we knew absolutely everything a person ever did, we could know his character absolutely. This theory has helped beget in literary circles the so-called "laundry-bag slip" school of biographers (as you might expect, its finest example is Leon Edel, biographer of Henry James), and it may have begotten similar historians, and, taken with temperance, such theory may even be useful. However, since not even laundry-bag receipts can reveal everything a person ever did, let alone thought, it is obviously silly to hope by the simple massing of facts to arrange for art. Daily life is choked with facts, and these facts mean mostly nothing; some incidents are more revealing of character than others. A profounder observation on story telling was made by Edith Wharton: "The possibilities of a given subject [i.e. the actions of a particular character] are whatever a given imagination can make of them."

Therefore, I decided to stick to historical incidents and characters in writing a novel about Big Bear – but it is impossible for me to speak of writing a novel that way. For I believe in "story" as a fact beyond and outside the entity of its maker. Michelangelo's beautiful (perhaps apocryphal but no matter) statement that he studied the rock for the shape that was inside it and then used his chisels not to create that shape out of the rock but rather to release the shape from all the encumbering rock around it – that has always seemed to me profoundly true of the story-maker's art also. At least of my own attempts. In the summer of 1968 I was working on one of the final versions of *The Blue Mountains of China*, but I was already probing about, wherever, for a large story beyond that novel. Somewhere during the winter of 1967-68 (having returned to Canada in the summer of '67 after four years I was feeling the goodness of the land where I belong) I had stumbled on William Fraser's fifteen-page monograph *Big Bear, Indian Patriot* (1966). This revived something begun in the later '50s when, while I was writing *Peace Shall Destroy Many*, I first read William Cameron's *The War Trail of Big Bear*. [It may be that I was again looking up Cameron's book and discovered Fraser's new publication in the card catalogue with it.] Anyway, it was from reading Cameron in the '50s that I first realized that the bush homestead where I was born in northern Saskatchewan probably was traversed in June, 1885, by Big Bear and his diminishing band as among the poplars they easily eluded the clumsy military columns of Strange and Middleton and Otter and Irvine pursuing them; that I first realized that the white sand beaches of Turtle Lake, where Speedwell School had its annual sportsday with Jackpine and Turtleview Schools, right there where that brown little girl had once beaten me in the grade four sprints, a race in which until then I was acknowledged as completely invincible: perhaps on that very beach Big Bear had once stood looking at the clouds trundle up from the north. Of course, thanks to our education system, I had been deprived of this knowledge when I was a child; we studied people with *history* – like Cromwell who removed a king's head, or Lincoln who freed slaves – but I can see now that this neglect contained an ambiguous good. For in forcing me to discover the past of my country on my own as an adult, my public school inadvertently roused an anger in me which has ever since given an impetus to my writing which I trust it will never lose. *All* people have history. The stories we tell of our past are by no means merely words: they are meaning and life to us as *people*, as *a particular people*; the stories are there, and if we do not know of them we are simply, like animals, memory ignorant, and the less are we people.

Anger, even anger at one's own ignorance, is hardly enough emotion to sustain years of work. One of the first things I noticed about the person of Big Bear was the contradictory feelings he aroused in people; this was true for whites as well as Indians. To William Cameron and Teresa Gowanlock, his prisoners for two months, he is an admirable old man, yet to Commissioner Irvine of the Mounted Police he is simply a trouble-maker, always demanding and never agreeing. Vankoughnet of Indian Affairs orders him either to take a reserve or starve, yet Edgar Dewdney gives him a character reference (albeit carefully unofficial) at his trial. He is spoken of as "the heart and soul of all the plains Indians" and has a personal following of over one thousand, an incredible number among the buffalo-hunting Crees; yet at Frog Lake this orator, this leader who has a power bundle given him by the Great Parent of Bear himself has no influence at all over a small group of his own Rattlers, led by his own son. He stands helpless, his great words falling into nothing as the white men he has personally pledged to protect are disarmed, sported with, and slaughtered before his eyes. Big Bear, I found, lived these contradictions, contained these extremes of greatness and of pathos. Beneath the giant slag heap left by the heroic white history of fur trader and police and homesteader and rancher and railroad builder (O, the heroism of that nineteenth-century computer Van Horne as sung by that twentieth-century computer Pierre Berton Incorporated!), somewhere, under there, is the story of this life. Can I dig it out? Will I dare to look at it once I have, if I dare, unearthed it?

When my mind is tumbling story possibilities about, a process which inevitably takes years sometimes even for short stories, I write down nothing except very occasional notes to myself. A note dated January 10, 1969 begins:

Themes for a novel / setting Edmonton, possibly Klondike days . . .

and ends:

People: modern business man? triangle? just fucking around?

Evidently that didn't hook very deep (I can still see why) because the next note is dated just over a month later (Feb. 28, 1969) and this one I'll give completely:

Big Bear. A novel of historical Big Bear, the greatest chief of the Plains Cree – defied whites and their treaties for the longest time – treated in tragic-farcical manner and tone – there is undoubtedly farce in it (especially re attack at Frog Lake)

But I find the next note dated a year and a half later, September, 1970, and after two summers working on the historical Big Bear it still begins

– novel: present day Indian . . . .

and ends

. . . just out of jail, as Big Bear is heading into jail – they live out each others lives [apparently some ninety years apart] in a kind of reverse?

Apparently I am still, in September 1970, struggling to get Big Bear's story unearthed so I can face it, so it will not disintegrate in our polluted modern atmosphere. But seven months later I seem to have reached some conclusions. The page is almost empty, just marked,

The Temptations of Big Bear

and underneath a line in brackets

title thought of on way home from U of A – passing Aberhart San March 8, 1971

To take the problems of following Big Bear's story to its final version, I can do no better than to quote here from an original introductory chapter, since dropped. It contained a sort of Henry Fielding narrator-type who hints at explanations in case his readers (whom I think he basically does not trust) don't catch on. This sometimes-coy narrator was one of the reasons the chapter did not survive, but there are a few things in it I very unwillingly let – well – here are the relevant passages:

"There are some stories into which the reader should be led gently, and I think this may be one of them."

I quote Hugh MacLennan's opening line, with thanks, because it says exactly what needs saying here. This story is another one of those that demands a gentle leading into. Factually, so that everyone is quite clear about some things, at the very beginning. Anyway.

To begin with, every individual who will appear in this story is an historic person. Not one name has been invented. Every person (and a fair number of the animals) who has a part was once, literally, a living

*being and there is documentary historic evidence available for each, if
you care to look for it. Of course, the evidence varies widely: books,
sometimes several, by or about a person; three to four feet of letters and
papers in archives; and 'X' at the bottom of a treaty or a courtroom
confession; a name mentioned in newspaper gossip; a smudged face on
a photograph with perhaps a pencilled name on its back followed by a
question mark that could refer to the spelling of the name or the identification itself – or, more likely, both. Usually, there are a great many,
but always there are at least two points of historic reference to help us
believe that these people actually breathed; that they were once born
and, after their allotted time, like us all, died.*

*The author – I hesitate to over-use the pronoun 'I' in the first short
chapter of what promises to be a lengthy novel; the reader will understand the gentle circumlocution – the author, I say, has never physically
met any of these people. (There is only one exception to that statement
and it will be noted in its place, which is not this story.) That is so
because this story's events all took place before January, 1888, and the
more it emerged out of the vacuum called history, which in Western
Canada is no vacuum at all but rather the great ocean of our ignorance
as horizonless as the prairies themselves, the more it became impossible
to invent a non-historic person to act as guide into and through it. For
if one is once willing to understand that he is beyond doubt thoughtlessly
treading water on his ancestral past, on the past of his place, and will
dare to plunge in, reckless of life and eyes wide open, he finds in that
ocean a teeming of wildlife and tamelife and every other kind of life
that takes his ordinary breath away anyway; he drowns in happiness,
into a new life altogether.*

I believe: Let that life itself be its own guide.

*That said, it remains clear that a certain minimum of historic 'facts'
are needed to make comprehension, recognition, possible.*

I then give paragraph summaries of the lives of the main persons
appearing in Section One: There is Wee-kas-koo-kes-pay-yin (translated, Sweetgrass), Alexander Morris, John Kerr, James McKay, Pakan,
and John McDougall, ending with:

"Mis-ta-ha-mus-kwa, translated Big Bear, *Plains Cree chief whose vital
statistics in the Admittance Record Book of Manitoba Penitentiary are
given as "Prisoner #103,* Received: *Sept. 29, 1885* Born: *Northwest Territories* Age: *60* Race: *Native Canadian* Religion: *None* Married: *Yes*
Height: *5 ft. 5¼* Complexion: *Dark* Eyes: *Black* Hair: *Black* Trade:
None Crime: *Treason-Felony." He may have been born near Fort Carlton. In the summer of 1875 he was warned in a letter by the Reverend
William Newton, first Anglican missionary ever to venture into the
Saskatchewan country and as soon as he arrived there: "To the Cree*

Chief, Big Bear: I am a priest of the Queen's religion. I have learned that thou art a turbulent and seditious fellow and I admonish thee to put aside such vain practises, etc."

So far my dropped introduction; I have concentrated on these imaginative problems in finding Big Bear's story, which is what being "on the trail of Big Bear" means to me, because that is the novelist's largest concern. The question for the novelist is not "Will I find the facts," it is rather, "Will I dare to fully contemplate with all my quintuplet senses the facts that I do find?

For the facts themselves I go to mostly the same places as historians:

PEOPLE   If there are any, matching one muddled memory against another; there was only Duncan Maclean left, 94 in Winnipeg when I met him, and now he too is dead;

BOOKS AND PAMPHLETS   Always trying to recognize the personal biases of writers, even those biased by their seemingly unbiased scholarliness. The list is long, and includes George Stanley, William Fraser, Joseph Kinsey Howard, John P. Turner, Wm. Bleasdell Cameron, Robert Jefferson, David Mandelbaum, Leonard Bloomfield, Alexander Morris, John Donkin, John McDougall, Charles Mulvaney in total, and many others in bits;

THE SESSIONAL PAPERS OF THE PARLIAMENT OF CANADA   Which include the annual Mounted Police and Indian Affairs reports, and the 1885 trials (but not, strangely enough, Big Bear's address to the court at his sentencing, although all the other major chiefs' responses are there. So, with the help of Cameron's summary, I have to write that one myself) ;

THE DIARIES, NOTES, SPEECHES, PERSONAL LETTERS, MEMOIRS, INTERVIEWS   All those miscellaneous treasures to be found in archives in Ottawa, Winnipeg, Regina, Saskatoon, Calgary, Edmonton – and even in Duck Lake or the cemetery at Ft. Qu'Appelle or Batoche or the marker at Frog Lake or the depressions in the soil on the Poundmaker Reserve, Battle River, Saskatchewan. And best of all, Big Bear's power bundle itself, intact in a canvas bag and tied with binder twine, in a place where one would expect it to be. Not anywhere in Canada of course, but in New York City. That's a complete story in itself which I canot tell here.

It is in these searches that I discover those details which make the past sing in my ear with sweet songs, and wild songs, and with the contradictions which all historians I am sure must, when they discover them, love. A small example: even at the Indian trials only four months after the fact not one of the witnesses who was at the sacking of Fort Pitt can agree on what day it took place. Four possible dates are suggested, I believe; yet men are hanged for their actions there.

But, in my idiosyncratic and certainly unscientific approach to historical research there are a few points I must emphasize:

THE NECESSITY OF CALENDAR   In writing this novel I found myself becoming almost psychotic about dates; I had to know whether something happened on Monday or Tuesday! In the 1970 Fraser Valley Telephone Directory I found "Calendars 1776-2000" which contained all fourteen possible calendars plus an index for any year from 1776 to 2000. Marvelous.

NEWSPAPERS   Often not too helpful with absolute facts but beyond peer in presenting contemporary opinion. The Saskatchewan *Herald*, 1879-88, with its outspoken editor Laurie, and the Regina *Leader*, beginning in 1883, are beyond price. One example will suffice. As I mentioned, the Sessional Papers do not record Big Bear's defence before his sentencing, and though I spent a week in Ottawa doing little else, I could find no trace of his defence in either the Archives or the Department of Justice. So there is nothing left but William Cameron's summary of what Big Bear said, and he concludes with Richardson's answer:

"Big Bear," said Justice Richardson, and his tone was not unkind, "you have been found guilty by an impartial jury. You cannot be excused from all responsibility for the misdoings of your band. The sentence of the court is that you be imprisoned in the penitentiary at Stony Mountain for three years."

That's recorded forty years after the fact; this is Nicholas Flood Davin's report in *The Leader*, October 1, 1885:

First came Big Bear, who made a long address to the Court, in the course of which he frequently used such language as, "when we owned the country" and he drew the Court's attention to the fact that he being in prison who was to protect his people.

Judge Richardson in sentencing him told him that they never owned the land [,] that it belonged to the Queen, who allowed them to use it, that when she wanted to make other use of it she called them together through her officers, and gave them the choicest portions of the country and that, as to his people, they would be looked after as though nothing had occurred. He was then sentenced to three years in the Penitentiary.

How time smears edges; how it liberalizes, softens our motivation!

PICTURES I don't really need to tell any researcher the value of pictures; how, far clearer than the sharpest observer, they give so much of certain kinds of information, as it were, quite incidentally. For a fiction-writer working on a convincing illusion of life, it is often their tiny details that make his story work.

MAPS AND PLACES Old maps, with the Indian names for topographical features, and what remains of those old places to this day. Strangely, considering the decades of industrious pioneering, some bits of the world crucial to Big Bear can still be seen, a few are not even greatly disturbed. One of the most enjoyable experiences of writing that novel for my whole family was visiting every place where it was recorded Big Bear had been. His life was lived approximately along what is now the Alberta-Saskatchewan border, from Cold Lake to the Missouri River, west and mostly east of that line several hundred miles. It is an immense world, especially when you think of walking and riding it.

As we travelled this world, we took such pictures of it as we could, and sometimes I would look at them again as I was writing: the North Saskatchewan near Carlton where Big Bear was born; the buffalo lands at Sounding Lake and Cypress Hills and Milk River; the Forks of the Red Deer and South Saskatchewan where the Great Spirit of Bear gave him his vision, his song, his power bundle; and then the sad sequence of Frog Lake and Fort Pitt and Frenchman's Butte and Loon Lake Crossing, and Regina and Stony Mountain Penitentiary; then to the bank of the Battle River, where we met Mary Peemee, Horsechild's wife now 89, and John Tootoosis showed us Big Bear's grave which seems more or less exactly on the site of his last thirst dance held that summer of 1884 when his power was still too strong to permit his young men to wipe out Crozier and his police, but no longer strong enough to unite his people. And finally, the Great Sand Hills. Simply seeing these few pictures, I think, you would recognize how necessary it was for me to see his world in order to find his story.

In the National Archives I discovered some cryptic notes in English of a Cree speech made by an unnamed chief in the summer of 1884. From the internal evidence I feel certain that the chief was Big Bear, and I found out later that George Stanley, who saw the notes long before I, had come to the same conclusions. Anyway, I used those sketchy notes to construct Big Bear's speech to the Carlton chiefs in Part III of the novel, and I would like to conclude with a paragraph of it here. He is speaking particularly of his People and the buffalo, but in a strange way it seems to me I have to understand what he is saying, understand it for myself, if I am to truly follow his trail, if I am to dare contemplate his story.

"My brothers!" Big Bear's deep voice lifted to a great shout that shivered the lodgeskins and rolled out into the afternoon heat, "the Whiteskins have brought all this evil on us, but we trust them. Who does not have a white friend? Who has not received good things from them? What Person was ever shot by police? The buffalo has been taken from us. On this earth he was our life, and how can he return except The One who took him from us return him again? I see his track in the deep paths he wore to sweet water, and at river crossings where wind moans through his wool hung on the low bushes, I see his shape in the wallows, the print of his tongue where salt gleams like frost in the Scattering Moon, I hear the thunder of his running under the Tramping Lakes, and at Sounding where the Giver of All runs the great herds still and they graze the soft spring grass and lick their little calves. Eiya-eiya-a-a, where have we gone, where, where.

Thirteen

BIBLICAL ARCHETYPE IN WESTERN CANADIAN FICTION

Sandra A. Djwa

As a Newfoundlander, I have always had a great fondness for the writings of Sinclair Ross. I do not quite understand the reason for this attraction, whether it is his concept of a prairie nature – hard, with overtones of fatalism – which corresponds to my own view of Newfoundland, or whether it is simply his wry observations of the circumlocutions of the Puritan way – a sensibility which also strikes a familiar note. In any event, whenever the term "Canadian novel" comes to mind, I find myself gravitating towards Ross and particularly towards his sometimes puzzling first novel, *As For Me and My House*, which was written in 1941.

Reviewing his short stories published in *Queen's Quarterly* in the late thirties and early forties and his three novels, *As For Me and My House* (1941), *The Well* (1958), and *A Whir of Gold* (1970), we find that character recedes into the emotional landscape. Throughout Ross's work, there is a sense of a bleak, hard nature – loneliness and isolation of the prairie winter, the indifferent sun which scorches the summer wheat. Against this nature, as we see in the following passage, man is insignificant.

In the clear, bitter light the long white miles of prairie landscape seemed a region alien to life. Even the distant farmsteads she could see, served only to intensify a sense of isolation. Scattered across the face of so vast and bleak a wilderness it was difficult to conceive them as a testimony of human hardihood and endurance. Rather they seemed futile, lost, to cower before the implacability of snow-swept earth and clear pale sun-chilled sky.[1]

Mrs. Bentley, in *As For Me and My House,* looking across the open prairies and towards the Alberta foothills, recognizes both man's insignificance and his need to project human meaning – perhaps even God – into the natural landscape. She says:

We've all lived in a little town too long. The wilderness here makes us uneasy. I felt it the first night I walked alone along the river bank – a queer sense of something cold and fearful, something inanimate, yet aware of us. A Main Street is such a self-sufficient little pocket of existence, so smug, compact, that here we feel abashed somehow before the hills, their passiveness, the unheeding way they sleep. We climb them, but they withstand us, remain as serene and unrevealed as ever. The river slips past, unperturbed by our coming and going, stealthily confident. We shrink from our insignificance. The stillness and solitude – we think a force or presence into it – even a hostile presence, deliberate, aligned against us – for we dare not admit an indifferent wilderness where we may have no meaning at all.[2]

This is a nature against which man must struggle – not just to become a man – but simply to exist, and perhaps, if he is particularly fortunate and determined, to exist in some meaningful way. Most of these stories are a legacy of the drought years of the thirties on the prairies – the Depression moving imperceptibly into the war years.

In Ross's more sober tales, character and environment can combine like a vise to grip a character and set up a course of direction that even repeated failure does not change. His characters appear to be driven, like those of Grove in *Settlers of the Marsh,* to act as they do until one or another of a partnership is destroyed. When Paul, in the short story "The Lamp at Noon" (1938), is finally willing to make some compromise with the land, he finds his wife mad and his child dead. Having betrayed her husband, Ann, the young wife of "The Painted Door" (1939), has a revelation of his intrinsic strength and determines to make it up. He, however, has already walked out into the blizzard where he freezes to death. Coulter, the inept recruit who has been repeatedly befriended by the soldier-narrator of "Jug and Bottle" (1939), is accidentally let down by his friend. Crushed by an overwhelming burden of guilt and despair, and with no one to turn to, Coulter kills himself, ". . . caught helpless in some primitive mechanism of conscience like a sheaf in the gear of a thresher, borne on inexorably by the chain of guilt to the blade of punishment."[3]

Many such scenes of human despair and futility suggest that Hardy's President of the Immortals also has his sport with the people of Ross's prairie. Mrs. Bentley comments on this when observing the work-torn country congregation which is still waiting and praying after five years without a crop: "And tonight again the sun went down through a clear, brassy sky. Surely it must be a very great faith that such indifference on the part of its deity cannot weaken – a very great faith, or a very foolish one."[4]

Despite suggestions of naturalism, particularly in the earlier threshing metaphor used to describe Coulter, Ross is not a naturalist in the sense of Frank Norris's *The Octopus* but rather in the modified sense of Robert Stead's *Grain* (1926). One of the first realistic novels of the Canadian prairies, *Grain* combines the tenets of naturalism with a kind of residual Christianity. In the final surprising scene of this book, Gander Stake, the naturalist hero, is allowed to step outside naturalism to make a moral choice: "There was only one way," he concludes. The "only way" here is the way of honour, an honour, in context, infused by Christianity. Similarly, Ross emphasizes a concept of moral choice described in terms of "the way" which must be taken – a way which can sometimes have overtones of the Puritan way. We find that "No Other Way" is the title of Ross's first story published in *Nash's Pall Mall Magazine*, (1934) and that variations on this phrase are often given to Ross's characters at moments of significant choice, as it is to Mrs. Bentley and to several of the young farm boys of the short stories.

As we have seen, there is a strong streak of determinism running through Ross's work, but it is most often kept firmly within a Christian context through a respectful address to "Providence", albeit with some irony as suggested by the title "Not By Rain Alone," a short story about crop failure.

The whole question of the ways of the Old Testament God to man is an important one for the characters of Ross's fictional world, particularly in relation to the first novel, *As For Me and My House*. Here this question carried with it that latter-day Puritanism of the psychological search for self, often expressed in terms of the "way" that must be taken. As in Rudy Wiebe's first prairie novel, *Peace Shall Destroy Many*, Harold Horwood's description of Newfoundland, *Tomorrow Will Be Sunday*, or Margaret Laurence's *A Jest of God*, the novels present a world in which some of the outward representations of Christianity are meaningless empty forms without spirit, and in which characters learn to reject the false gods before it is possible to find the true God within, and, as a sign of this, an authentic sense of direction.

Ostensibly, the "way" of *As For Me and My House* is the Christian way indicated by the title, and the Biblical myth underlying the novel is the account of the children of Israel described by Joshua:

And if it seems evil unto you to serve the Lord, choose you this day whom you will serve; whether the gods which your fathers served that were on the other side of the flood, or the gods of the Amorites, in whose land ye dwell: but as for me and my house, we will serve the Lord.

But this apparent religious structure is steadily and ironically reversed throughout the novel, until we come to see the Bentleys metaphorically as pagan priest and priestess serving an Old Testament world. The false-fronts of the novel – first introduced in relation to the false façades of the little Main Street stores – modulate into the psychological "false-front" or persona, the Jungian term used to describe the protective surface behind which the real self is hidden. In Ross's novel, this meta-phor is developed in relation to the social and religious conventions through which the Bentleys shield themselves from each other and from the townspeople. Mrs. Bentley says:

Three little false-fronted towns before this one have taught me to erect a false front of my own, live my own life, keep myself intact; yet tonight again, for all my indifference to what the people here may choose to think of me, it was an ordeal to walk out of the vestry. . . .[5]

Because the "well-bred Christianity" of the Bentleys is empty form with-out spirit, it emerges as a modern form of paganism in which the social conventions of a faith are perverted into a substitution for faith itself. This is explicit in the extended metaphor near the conclusion of Mrs. Bentley's first journal entry:

. . . the formal dinner of a Main Street hostess is invariably good. Good to an almost sacrificial degree. A kind of rite, at which we preside as priest and priestess – an offering, not for us, but through us, to the exacting small-town gods Propriety and Parity.[6]

In Ross's novel, as in the book of Joshua, idol worship and paganism are associated with the rejection of the true God, Jehovah, and the setting up of false gods in man's own "image". Philip's own strongest instincts are towards a kind of pagan Nemesis or fatalism. Mrs. Bentley, observing the country people of Philip's charge, senses this same primitive response in the "sober work-roughened congregation":

There was strength in their voices when they sang, like the strength and darkness of the soil. The last hymn was staidly orthodox, but through it there seemed to mount something primitive, something that was less a response of Philip's sermon and scripture reading than to the grim futility of their own lives. Five years in succession now they've been blown out, dried out, hailed out; and it was as if in the face of so blind and uncaring a universe they were trying to assert themselves, to insist upon their own meaning and importance.
"Which is the source of all religion," Paul discussed it with me after-wards. "Man can't bear to admit his insignificance. If you've ever seen a

hailstorm, or watched a crop dry up – his helplessness, the way he's ig-
nored – well, it was just such helplessness in the beginning that set him
discovering gods who could control the storms and seasons. Powerful,
friendly gods – on his side. . . . So he felt better – gratefully became a
reverent and religious creature. That was what you heard this morning –
pagans singing Christian hymns . . . pagan, you know, originally that's
exactly what it meant, country dweller."[7]

The primary Old Testament distinction between Israelites and pagans is
the monotheism of the chosen people. God's covenant given to Moses
states that the Ammonites and other pagans will be driven from the
Promised Land, but that the Israelites must guard themselves carefully
from the "images" of the pagans: "For thou shalt have no other gods
before me." This association of image or idol-worship with paganism
is also developed in Ross's novel. There are early references to Mrs.
Finley, the "small-town Philistine" who would like to model the town
"in her own image"; and to Philip, who attempts to impress his own
image upon the character of Steve, the young Roman Catholic orphan:
"There's a strange arrogance in his devotion to Steve, an unconscious
determination to mould him in his own image. . . ." When Steve is removed from the household, Mrs. Bentley's primary regret is that Philip
has never seen through to the real boy, who, as she astutely remarks, is
"fond of bed, his stomach, and his own way":

An idol turned clay can make even an earthly woman desirable . . . he's
one idol tarnish-proof. Philip will forget the real Steve before long, and
behind his cold locked lips mourn another of his own creating.[8]

The Bentley's have other false gods. Mrs. Bentley has built her life on her
initial vision of her husband as romantic artist. Philip is the product of
his own twisted "image" of his dead father; from a photograph he has
developed himself by emulation – as Mrs. Bentley comments: "Let a man
look long and devotedly enough at a statue and in time he will resemble
it." In Ross's novel, Philip, like his New Testament prototype who asks,
"Lord show us the Father and it sufficeth us," substitutes the image of an
earthly father (the photograph) for a spiritual father and so succumbs
to the worship of false gods.

Ross's whole mythological structure develops easily and naturally from
the cultural matrix of a small Canadian prairie town of forty years ago,
where the religious imagination was as much a part of existence as the
wind on the prairie, codified as it was in the patriarchal prairie family
and permeating the whole social structure of the community which
radiated out from church and family. As Mrs. Bentley confides to her
diary at one point: "This is a fundamentalist town. To the letter it be-

lieves the Old Testament stories that we, wisely or presumptuously, choose to accept only as tales and allegories."[9]

*   *   *   *   *

The second novelist whom I would like to discuss in detail, Margaret Laurence, also grew up in a small prairie town, and her novels chronicle the same world. In response to an inquiry of several years ago, she replied that she first read Ross's novel in her late teens and that "it was the first piece of fiction written out of a background very similar to mine which I could recognize as being true and genuine. I think perhaps it was only then that I really understood that writing could be done out of that background."[10]

In fact, a quick glance through Laurence's short stories and novels, particularly *A Jest of God*, leads us to wonder if she would have written the way she does, using Biblical allusion to provide a mythic framework for an essentially psychological study of character, if Sinclair Ross had not first written *As For Me and My House*. In particular, both share a literalist imagination and a common myth-making tendency which equates Biblical desert and prairie drought, Israelite and prairie farmer. Furthermore we regularly find slight echoes of Ross throughout Laurence's work: for example, the reference to the small-town gods of "Depression and Drought" in the short story "Horses of the Night" (1967), suggest Ross's small-town gods of "Propriety and Parity". Most important, Laurence and Ross share a central vision – a sense of the ironic discrepancy between the spirit and the letter of the religious dispensation.

The characters of Margaret Laurence, like those of Sinclair Ross, all live in the same little "fundamentalist town" characterized by Mrs. Bentley, and they all live their lives in stifling relation to the old gods of their fathers. Ruled by these gods, each character – Nathaniel Amegbe of *This Side of Jordan* (1960), Hagar of *The Stone Angel* (1964) and Rachel of *A Jest of God* (1966) – lives a child-like or unauthentic existence dominated by the dead parental voices of the past. The significance of this experience is clear: if an individual is not able to break away from the ancestral voices of the past, he dies, either psychologically, as is the threat for Rachel in *A Jest of God* and for Philip Bentley in *As For Me and My House*; or quite literally, as is the fate of the young man Adamo, in Laurence's short story "The Voices of Adamo".

Many of the characters of Ross and Laurence are given explicitly Biblical names – Philip, Paul, Judith, Stephen, Nathaniel, Moses, Joshua,

Rachel, Hagar, John, Jacob, Esau – and often they are specifically identified with the central concerns of their Biblical archetypes: Ross's Steve
undergoes a social martyrdom, Laurence's Hagar is exiled to an emotional
wilderness, and Rachel is without child. Laurence, in particular, appears
to favour Biblical myth because it invokes a sense of archetypal human
nature. Stacey of *The Fire-Dwellers* watching her two sons fighting, remarks: "Cain and his brother began that way."

Like Ross in *As For Me and My House*, Laurence is particularly concerned with the myths of the Israelites. The mythic background of *The
Stone Angel* is basically the Genesis account of Abram and Hagar which
also makes reference to God's covenants with Jacob and with Hagar;
A Jest of God refers ironically to the Rachel-Jacob relationship and also,
although not at all ironically, to God's promise to Rachel and to the
Jonah story; *This Side of Jordan* explicitly parallels Nathaniel Amegbe's
struggle out of the old Africa with Joshua's attempt to cross Jordan into
the Promised Land; *The Fire-Dwellers* (1969) fuses contemporary fear
of nuclear holocaust with Dante's hell and the Day of Judgement from
Revelations, although the parallel is slightly less explicit than in preceding novels.

Laurence's interest in the growth of the human spirit into self-knowl-
edge and freedom is suggested by her first collection of African short
stories, *The Tomorrow-Tamer and Other Stories* (1963). There is a
sense in which all of these tales are parables of salvation or the failure
to attain it, a failure which is always linked to personal bondage.

Similarly, the graveyard stone angel of her second novel – "doubly
blind, not only stone, but unendowed with even a pretense of sight" –
is a metaphor for the spiritual condition of the protagonist of the novel,
Hagar Shipley. Reminiscences of her times past by the now ninety-year-
old Hagar chart for us a process of emotional petrification; she recalls
that as a child she was too proud to comfort a dying brother and that
both pride and stubborness kept Hagar, the young wife, from admitting
that she responded to her husband, Bram:

*My bed is cold as winter, and now it seems to me that I am lying as the
children used to do, on fields of snow. . . . The icy whiteness covers me,
drifts over me, and I could drift to sleep in it, like someone caught in a
blizzard, and freeze.*[11]

When her beloved son John dies, Hagar's emotional metamorphosis is
complete: "I found my tears had been locked too long and wouldn't
come now at my bidding. The night my son died I was transformed to
stone and never wept at all."

Hagar's release from her own nature, and, in another sense, the
release of incipient death, are not to come until after her encounter in
the deserted fish cannery with the salesman Murray Lees and the visit to

the hospital by the clergyman Mr. Troy. Each in his own way helps Hagar to recognize her real feelings and with them her real self:

I must always, always, have wanted that – simply to rejoice. . . . Every good joy I might have held, in my man or any child of mine or even the plain light of morning, of walking the earth, all were forced to a standstill by some brake of proper appearances – Oh, proper to whom? When did I ever speak the heart's truth?

Pride was my wilderness, and the demon that led me there was fear. I was alone, never anything else, and never free, for I carried my chains within me and they spread out from me and shackled all I touched.[12]

In this last reference, Laurence's African experiences of nomadic Arabs and Somalis implicitly fuse with prairie background and Biblical myth. The book continually alludes to Hagar as "the Egyptian" and her wandering in the desert is transformed into psychological bondage on the Canadian prairie. Hagar's references to her son John, whom she ultimately recognizes to be without inheritance, an Ishmael figure (traditionally regarded as the forefather of the Arabs); and her allusions to her tolerated son, Marvin, whom she finally sees as the inheritor, a Jacob figure, move through the Genesis account of Abram (Bram) and Hagar into the New Testament allegory of the covenant of grace as opposed to the covenant of the law.

Rachel, the central figure of *A Jest of God*, is also associated with the covenant of grace and the new Jerusalem. Rachel Cameron, spinster school teacher, like the Rachel of the Old and New Testaments, weeps for the children she does not have. In Genesis this is a lament by a barren wife; in the allegory of Rachel in Jeremiah it is a lament by the Israelites who have fallen away from the fruits of the spirit into the worship of false gods; both concepts are contained in Laurence's presentation of Rachel's character.

Just as Rachel is associated with Jerusalem and the golden city, so her lover Nick is identified with the prince of romance and with the Israelites. Rejecting his Ukrainian family, he states explicitly: "I have forsaken my house – I have left mine heritage – mine heritage is unto me as a lion in the forest – it crieth out against me – therefore have I hated it."[13] Because a Jacob-Esau relationship is implied to exist between Nick and his dead brother and because Rachel's speech, "If I had a child, I would like it to be yours," is immediately followed by the words of Rachel of Genesis: *"Give me my children,"* Nick is identified as a Jacob figure. Ironically, however, the character of Nick is dual in aspect: he is both the bringer of gifts that his name implies (St. Nicholas) but is also one of the devil's party.

When Rachel asks Nick for a child, he answers, "I'm not God," (the reply which we find in Genesis of the Biblical Jacob to Rachel) and produces the photograph of a young boy. This particular detail, together with Nick's reference to his father "It's this fantastic way he has of creating the world in his own image," followed by Rachel's concurrent realization "Have I finished with facades?", all strongly suggest the thematic concerns of Sinclair Ross's *As For Me and My House*. Like the Bentleys, Rachel does not finish with her false self to go on as an authentic person, but Nick (whose past almost exactly parallels Rachel's) is still tied to his own false god, his image of himself as child in relation to the photograph of his dead brother. Ironically, Nick as Jacob rejects his birthright, and the novel ends, as does *As For Me and My House*, with the journey to the city and Rachel's sense of a new dispensation: "Make me to hear joy and gladness. . . . Create in me a clean heart, O God; and renew a right spirit within me."

Although both Ross and Laurence use Biblical myth in the development of their major novels, their techniques are somewhat different. Ross's major novel is thematically connected to the myth of the Israelites, but individual characters, although related to their Biblical prototypes, are not always related on the mythic level.

Laurence, on the other hand, consistently invokes Biblical myth as archetypes of psychological man. Her characters are related mythically as are Abram and Hagar, Jacob and Ishmael of *The Stone Angel*, and are often part of a controlling myth which verges on psychological allegory, because Laurence does not set up rigid levels of interpretation. Nonetheless, because Hagar refers to herself as "the Egyptian" and describes Marvin explicitly as "Jacob", it is impossible to read *The Stone Angel* without recognizing that Laurence presents the human situation in terms of Biblical allegory.

Furthermore, the characters of both Ross and Laurence verge on the moral universal: it is not just that Ross's Philip is representative artist, and Laurence's Stacey everyday housewife, but that both authors have a tendency to set up characters as types within a distinctly moral framework. The bitterness of Ross's description of the town busybody, Mrs. Finley, stems from the fact that she is legion and her malice uncontrollable; the irony in his caricature of Mrs. Bird emerges from her situation as every small-town doctor's wife attempting to preserve her individuality.

"Satire," as W.L. Morton notes, "feeds on the gap between profession and performance, and the puritan both displays the gap more and sees it in other men's performances more readily than those of less rigid standards."[14] This angle of vision often gives form to the work discussed, as in the case of Ross's false front or Laurence's stone angel, both of which emerge through an ironic awareness of the discrepancy between performance and profession. Both authors have a lingering moralistic streak, common, I suspect, to much Canadian writing, which in the largest and most affirmative sense can add to the human stature; but which, in its more narrow manifestations, can result in such occurrences as the death of the girl Judith as a kind of punishment by the Old Testament God of judgement in Ross's *As For Me and My House*, or in the threatened death of a child by this same God as a judgment upon its mother in Laurence's *The Fire-Dwellers*.

Laurence, like Ross, seems to write from a two-tiered world, ostensibly with God above and man below; a world in which there is always the ironic possibility of a reversal of man's plans by God. For Laurence's characters, the old gods of the fathers are dead, or, if they still exist, they no longer manifest themselves in the old ways and must be redefined by each person according to his own experience, as does Rachel of *A Jest of God*:

My God, I know how suspect You are. I know how suspect I am. If You have spoken, I am not aware of having heard. If you have a voice, it is not comprehensible to me. No omens. No burning bush, no pillar of sand by day or pillar of flame by night.[15]

Similarly, Ross's characters receive no explicitly supernatural guidance, although there is some suggestion that when Philip in *As For Me and My House* pushes aside propriety to act in accordance with his inner self, he is in fact being guided by the spirit within, albeit with ironic consequences. Mrs. Bentley, in her time of greatest suffering, admits she is guided by a conviction expressed as the Old Testament "pointing finger."

What is more interesting about the use of Biblical allusion by both Ross and Laurence is the ironic equipoise of their characters between faith and disbelief. Although both employ Biblical myth for psychological investigation, neither relegates God to the status of a childish illusion as does Freud in his references to the gods of the fathers in *Civilization and Its Discontents*. Despite authorial irony and despite qualifications of belief by individual characters ("God knows why I chat to you, God — it's not that I believe in you. Or I do and I don't like echoes in my head," says Stacey in *The Fire-Dwellers*), this sensibility does seem to emerge as a kind of latter-day psychological puritanism in which salvation is redefined in relation to the discovery of the self and true grace is manifested by a new sense of life's direction. In the largest sense, Ross and Laurence are humanists, concerned with the process through which human potential becomes actualized. Both work out contemporary problems in terms of their own ancestral roots of received religion.

*   *   *   *   *

I have attempted to give a close reading of the Biblical myth, plot, and characters presented by Ross and Laurence, to introduce the more interesting problem of why this archetype has persisted in Canadian prairie fiction from 1920 to 1970, a period when religious myth had passed out of contemporary literary consciousness. Furthermore, a dominantly moral strain – sometimes specifically Christian – has infused Canadian writing in general, as is demonstrated by the following titles: Grove's *Our Daily Bread*, and *Fruits of the Earth*; much of Callaghan, including *Such is My Beloved, They Shall Inherit the Earth, More Joy in Heaven* and *The Loved and the Lost*; Mitchell's *Who Has Seen the Wind*; Klein's *The Second Scroll*; MacLennan's *Each Man's Son* and *The Watch that Ends the Night*; Buckler's *The Mountain and The Valley* with its David Canaan; Wiseman's *The Sacrifice*; Watson's *The Double Hook*; and Horwood's *Tomorrow Will Be Sunday*. When reading the four novels of Rudy Wiebe, *Peace Shall Destroy Many* (1962), *First and Vital Candle* (1966), *The Blue Mountains of China* (1970) and *The Temptations of Big Bear* (1973), we recognize that the first three novels in particular are explicitly concerned with the problems of the interpretation of Christianity in the modern world.[16]

REFERENCE NOTES

1. Characterological, Strategic, and Institutional Interpretations of Prairie Settlement
John W. Bennett and Seena B. Kohl

1 John W. Bennett, *Northern Plainsmen: Adaptive Strategy and Agrarian Life* (Chicago: Aldine Publishing Co., 1969); John W. Bennet, "Adaptive Strategy and Processes in the Canadian Plains", in Richard Allen, ed., *A Region of the Mind* (University of Saskatchewan, Regina; Canadian Plains Study Centre, Canadian Plains Studies, no. 1, 1973).

2 Mody C. Boatright, "The Myth of Frontier Individualism", in R. Hofstadter & S.M. Lipset, ed., *Turner and the Sociology of the Frontier* (N.Y.: Basic Books, 1968), p. 62.

3 George F.G. Stanley, "The Western Canadian Mystique", in David P. Gagan, ed., *Prairie Perspectives* (Toronto: Holt, Rinehart and Winston, 1970), p. 23.

4 M.L. Lautt, "Sociology and the Canadian Plains", in Richard Allen, ed., *A Region of the Mind*, pp. 125-51.

5 See also David Smith, "Interpreting Prairie Politics", in Richard Allen, ed., *op. cit.*, pp. 103-23.

6 For a fine literary-biographical account of such people, see Wallace Stegner, *Wolf Willow* (N.Y.: Viking Press, 1962). This is a memoir of the Eastend, Saskatchewan area, adjacent to the region we studied.

7 For an analysis of the succession process see Seena Kohl & John W. Bennett, "Kinship, Succession, and the Migration of Young People in a Canadian Agricultural Community", *International Journal of Comparative Sociology*, 6:96-115. Reprinted with revisions and additions, in Ishwaran, *The Canadian Family* (Toronto: Holt, Rinehart and Winston, 1971).

8 For a study of migration of Saskatchewan ruralites to urban areas and employment, see, Jane A. Abramson, *Adjustments Associated with Migration from Farm Operator to Urban Wage Earner* (Saskatoon: The Canadian Centre for Community Studies, 1966).

9 For additional discussion of family and continuity of enterprise, see Seena Kohl, "The Family in a Post-Frontier Society", in K. Ishwaran, ed., *The Canadian Family, A Book of Readings* (Toronto: Holt, Rinehart and Winston, 1971).

10 See among others, Vernon C. Fowke, *An Introduction to Canadian Agricultural History* (Toronto: University of Toronto Press, 1947); W.A. Mackintosh, *Prairie Settlement: The Geographic Background*, vol. 1 of *Canadian Frontiers of Settlement* (Toronto: Macmillan, 1934).

11 For an appreciation of the district history as source material, see Hugh A. Dempsey, "Local Histories as Source Materials for Western Canadian Studies", in Anthony W. Rasporich & Henry C. Klassen, *Prairie Perspectives 2* (Toronto: Holt, Rinehart and Winston, 1973), pp. 171-80.

12 Royal Commission on Agriculture and Rural Life. Report No. 10: *The Home and Family in Rural Saskatchewan* (Regina: Government of Saskatchewan, 1956), p. 41.

13 For a study of this phenomenon among the Saskatchewan settlers, see John W. Bennett, "Microcosm-Macrocosm Relationships in North American Agrarian Society", *American Anthropologist*, 69: 441-454, 1968. Revised version published in M. Micklin, ed., *Current Issues in Human Ecology* (Hinsdale: The Dryden Press, 1973).

14 For a discussion of the essentially populist character of the CCF, and the significant role of the co-operative movement under Liberalism, see John W. Bennett & Cynthia Krueger, "Agrarian Pragmatism and Radical Politics", supplementary chapter in Doubleday Anchor edition of S.M. Lipset, *Agrarian Socialism* (Garden City, N.Y., 1968), pp. 347-363.

2. The Formal Organizations of Saskatchewan Farmers *Donald E. Willmott*

1 S.M. Lipset, *Agrarian Socialism* (New York: Anchor Books edition, 1968), 244-245.

2 *Ibid.*, 245.

3 J.W. Bennett, *Northern Plainsmen* (Chicago: Aldine Publishing Co., 1969), 259.

4 Mary Pattison, *Cory in Recall*, published by R.M. of Cory No. 344, 1967.

5 Jean Burnet, *Next-Year Country: A Study of Rural Social Organization in Alberta* (Toronto: University of Toronto Press, 1951), 123.

6 A.N. Reid, "Local Government in the Northwest Territories: I. The Beginnings of Rural Local Government, 1883-1905", *Saskatchewan History*, II, no. 1 (Jan. 1949), p. 71.

7 James N. McCrorie, *In Union is Strength* (Saskatoon Centre for Community Studies, University of Saskatchewan, 1964).

8 M. Pattison, *Cory in Recall*, p. 107. Burnet gives a similar account of the U.F.A. locals in the Hanna area, *Next-Year Country*, 124-125.

9 S.M. Lipset, *Agrarian Socialism*, 251-252.

10 J.F.C. Wright, *Prairie Progress: Consumer Co-operation in Saskatchewan* (Saskatoon: Modern Press, 1956), ix.

11 *Ibid.*, 36-37.

12 J. Burnet, *Next-Year Country*, 22-23.

13 J.W. Bennett, *Northern Plainsmen*, 74.

14 Paul Santha, *Three Generations: The Hungarian Colony, 1901-1957* (Stockholm, Saskatchewan, 1958), 21-27.

15 J. Burnet, *Next-Year Country*, 54, 78-83, 154-156; J. Burnet, "Town-

Country Relations and the Problem of Rural Leadership", *Canadian Journal of Economics and Political Science*, v. 13, no. 3 (August, 1947), 395-409; D. Willmott, *Organizations and Social Life of Farm Families in a Prairie Municipality* (Saskatoon: Center for Community Studies, University of Saskatchewan, 1964).

16 J. Burnet, *Next-Year Country*, 122.

17 J.W. Bennett, *Northern Plainsmen*, 207-208.

18 D.E. Willmott, *Organizations and Social Life of Farm Families in a Prairie Municipality*, 22.

19 J.H. Kolb and A.F. Wiledon, *Special Interest Groups in Rural Society*, Bulletin 84, Agricultural Experiment Station, University of Wisconsin, 1927, 1-2.

20 D.E. Willmott, *Organizations and Social Life of Farm Families*, 56-58; J. Burnet, *Next-Year Country*, 89-95.

3.   Life in Frontier Calgary   *Henry C. Klassen*

1 For studies on Calgary see Grant MacEwan, *Calgary Cavalcade: From Fort to Fortune* (Edmonton, 1958); L.G. Thomas, "The Rancher and the City: Calgary and the Cattlemen, 1883-1914", *Transactions of the Royal Society of Canada*, VI, Series IV, Section II (June, 1968), pp. 203-215; M.L. Foran, "The Calgary Town Council, 1884-1895: A Study of Local Government on a Frontier Environment", unpublished M.A. thesis, University of Calgary, 1969; M.L. Foran," Urban Calgary 1884-1895", *Social History*, Vol. 5, No. 9 (April, 1972), pp. 61-76; J.M.S. Careless, "Aspects of Urban Life in the West, 1870-1914," in Anthony W. Rasporich and Henry C. Klassen, eds., *Prairie Perspectives II* (Toronto, 1973); P.J. Smith, "Change in a Youthful City: The Case of Calgary, Alberta", *Geography, LVI* (January, 1971), pp. 1-14; Richard P. Baine, *Calgary: An Urban Study* (Toronto, 1973).

2 Glenbow-Alberta Institute Archives, John C. Bown Letterbook, 1887-1891, Calgary, January 6, 1888, John C. Bown to E. Clements.

3 Glenbow-Alberta Institute Archives, *Picturesque Calgary*, 1900 (Calgary, 1900).

4 Calgary *Herald*, April 6, 1899.

5 Calgary *Tribune*, February 1, 1888.

6 Glenbow-Alberta Institute Archives, Wesley F. Orr Letterbook, IV, Calgary, June 23, 1895, Wesley F. Orr to Thomas L. Orr.

7 Calgary *Tribune*, June 8, 1892.

8 *Ibid.*, January 9, 1886.

9 *Ibid.*, March 20, 1886.

10 Calgary *Herald*, February 13, 20, 1889.

11 Calgary *Tribune*, April 9, December 17, 1890.

12 Calgary *Herald*, November 18, December 28, 1892; Calgary *Tribune*, December 28, 1892; Calgary *Herald*, February 13, 25, 29, 1896; March 24, 1896; Alberta *Tribune*, February 29, 1896; May 2, 1896.

13 Calgary *Herald*, April 17, 1886; Calgary *Tribune*, August 15, 1888; October 16, 1889; November 18, 1891; Alberta *Tribune*, July 2, 1895.

14 Calgary *Tribune*, March 19, 1893.
15 Calgary *Herald*, February 14, 1896.
16 Calgary *Herald*, March 21, 1888.
17 Calgary *Tribune*, April 15, 29,
1887; January 11, 1893.
18 Calgary *Herald*, April 10, 1898.
19 *Ibid.*, January 16, 1900.

4. Inter-Urban Rivalry in Port Arthur and Fort William   *Elizabeth Arthur*

1 Neil B. Thompson, "A Half Century of Capital Conflict: How St. Paul Kept the Seat of Government", *Minnesota History*, v. XLIII, no. 7 (Fall, 1973), p. 247.

2 Alan F.J. Artibise, "An Urban Environment: The Process of Growth in Winnipeg, 1874-1914", paper presented at annual meeting of Canadian Historical Association, 1972, p. 41.

3 F.H. Armstrong and D.J. Brock, "The Rise of London: A Study in Urban Evolution in Nineteenth Century Southwestern Ontario", in F.H. Armstrong, H.A. Stevenson and J.D. Wilson (eds.), *Aspects of Nineteenth Century Ontario* (Toronto, 1974), pp. 83-84.

4 Michael Cross, "The Lumber Community of Upper Canada, 1815-1867", Ontario History, v. LII, no. 4 (December, 1960), p. 221.

5 Peter McKellar, "How Nepigon Bay Lost the CPR Shipping Port on the Great Lakes," Thunder Bay Historical Society *Papers*, 1911-12, p. 27; *The Question of the Terminus of the Branch of the Pacific Railway North Shore of Lake Superior* (Ottawa, 1874).

6 Elizabeth Arthur, "The Landing and the Plot," *Lakehead University Review*, v. I, no. 1 (Spring, 1968), pp. 6-12.

7 *Census of Canada*, 1901, v. I, p. 54.

8 *Ibid.*, v. IV, p. 432; it is apparently this figure which the Lakehead planners accepted as accurate six decades later, see *Lakehead Renewal Study*, 1964, p. 8.

9 *Census of Canada*, 1891, v. I, pp. 146-147.

10 *Ibid.*, 1881, v. I, pp. 90-91.

11 *Port Arthur Illustrated* (Winnipeg, 1889), n.p.

12 *Summer Tours by the Canadian Pacific Railway* (Montreal, 1887), p. 68.

13 *Census of Canada*, 1891, v. I, pp. 146-7.

14 *Fort William Journal*, March 16, 1892.

15 Public Archives of Canada (PAC) MG 28 III-20, Van Horne Letter Books, Van Horne to CPR Board of Directors, March 2, 1883.

16 Canada, *Sessional Papers*, 1883, No. 27, Memorandum on Thunder Bay and the River Kaministiquia by Henry F. Perley, C.E., Feb. 24, 1883.

17 PAC, Van Horne Letter Books, Van Horne to J.H. Egan, Feb. 23, 1884.

18 Corporation of the City of Thunder Bay (CTB) Port Arthur Council Minutes, v. II, pp. 397-399, W.H. Langworthy (town clerk) to William Whyte, Feb. 21, 1887.

19 J.P. Bertrand, *Highway of Destiny* (New York, 1959), p. 265.

20 Peter McKellar, "Incident in the History of the Canadian Pacific Railway," Thunder Bay Historical Society *Papers*, 1925, pp. 10-11.

21 Port Arthur *Weekly Herald*, Dec. 14, 1889.

22 Thunder Bay *Sentinel*, Dec. 13, 1889.

23 *Ibid.*, May 15, 1891.

24 PAC RG 12 A-1, Port Arthur Shipping Register. Records began in 1886; by far the largest vessel registered at Port Arthur in these years was the *Algonquin* in 1892, the property of Thomas Marks, who had been the town's first mayor.

25 Ontario Archives (OA) Lands and Forests Department Papers, Applications for Timber Licenses, *passim*, Woods and Forests Report Book, v. II, p. 197, Recommendation of October 1892, that pulpwood licenses be granted; p. 235, the plan submitted Apr. 24, 1895 by George Clavet and James Whalen of Port Arthur.

26 CTB By-Laws, Town of Port Arthur, June 28, 1897, no. 485 and 486, exempt various companies from taxation on grounds that they have invested heavily in the town and employed many workers; no. 482, May 15, 1897, offered tax concessions to the Ontario and Rainy River Railway Company, provided its terminus was Port Arthur and continued to be there for 21 years; no. 592, August 15, 1901, included the agreement with the Pigeon River Lumber Company.

27 *Ibid.*, Port Arthur Council Minutes, v. III, p. 392, May 13, 1889.

28 G.R. Stevens, *The Canadian National Railways*, (2 vols. Toronto, 1960-62), v. II, pp. 30-31.

29 Bertrand, pp. 277-279 gives a complete account of the banquet.

30 *Fort William – the Gateway to the Gold Fields*, (Fort William, 1898), n.p.

31 Thunder Bay *Sentinel*, August 3, 1889; Fort William *Journal*, Jan. 9, 1892, March 16, 1892.

32 CTB Fort William Council Minutes, v. II, pp. 192, 213, Feb. 13 and May 15, 1900.

33 Ontario *Statutes*, 1891, p. 339, An Act to Incorporate the Port Arthur and Fort William Railway Company (54 Vic: ch. 93).

34 *Ibid.*, 1893, p. 342, Schedule A, a copy of the Order-in-Council approved by the Lieutenant-Governor, Dec. 31, 1892, and appended to 56 Vic: ch. 78, An Act Respecting the Town of Port Arthur.

35 John F. Due, *The Intercity Electric Railway Industry in Canada* (Toronto, 1966), p. 12.

36 Thunder Bay *Sentinel*, Sept. 18, 1891.

37 Ontario *Statutes*, 1892, p. 698, An Act to Incorporate the Town of Fort William (55 Vic: ch. 70).

38 *Ibid.*, 1893, pp. 338-345, Schedule A.

39 CTB, Fort William Council Minutes; enforcement of Schedule A was a continuing theme; the following references from January 1893 to July 1897 are typical – v. I, pp. 73, 77, 91, 227, 319, 330, 345, 369.

40 Ontario *Statutes*, 1889, p. 340, An Act respecting the Town of Port Arthur (62 Vic: ch. 73, sect. 2).

41 CTB, Fort William Council Minutes, v. I, pp. 430, 438, Sept. 21 and Nov. 16, 1897; v. II, p. 254, Nov. 20, 1900, etc.

42 Fort William *Journal*, July 6, 1889.

43 Thompson, "A Half Century of Capital Conflict . . . ," p. 239.

44 CTB, Port Arthur Board of Health Minutes, 1892, pp. 198-199, July 18, 1892.

45 CTB, Sanitary Investigation *Report* by T.A. Starkey, March 21, 1906.

46 Ontario, Department of Health *Report*, 1894, p. 41.

47 *Ibid.*, p. 40.

48 CTB, Port Arthur Board of Health Minutes, 1892, p. 199, July 21, 1892.

49 PAC, Van Horne Letter Books, Van Horne to Sir Hector Langevin, March 5, 1886.

50 *Ibid.*, Van Horne to Major J.M. Walsh, Jan. 15, 1884.

51 OA, Lands and Forests Department Papers, Minutes of Association of Ontario Lumbermen, Copy of brief of western lumbermen to Laurier, March 21, 1898.

52 Thunder Bay *Sentinel*, Feb. 20, 1891.

53 CTB, Fort William Council Minutes, ∀. II, pp. 252, 368, Nov. 15, 1900, Jan. 21, 1902, etc.

54 *Ibid.*, pp. 214-215, May 22, 1900, motion urging public ownership of telephone company; Port Arthur Council Minutes, v. VI, p. 132, July 11, 1899, response to demands of the Bell Telephone Company.

55 OA, Ontario, Legislative Assembly Debates [newspaper Hansard], March 18, March 30, April 13, 1904 (microfilm); CTB, Port Arthur Council Minutes, v. VI, pp. 145, 252, 286 for 1899 debates over Jenison power project; Fort William Council Minutes, v. II, pp. 36, 39, 41 for discussion of same topic.

56 Anthony W. Rasporich, "A Boston Yankee in Prince Arthur's Landing: C.D. Howe and His Constituency," *Canada, A Historical Magazine*, v. I, no. 2 (Winter, 1973), p. 25.

57 Lakehead University Library, D.F. Burk papers, clipping from the *Winnipeg Tribune* enclosed in F.E. Trautman (editor, Fort William *Times-Journal*) to Burk, March 7, 1901; Thunder Bay *Sentinel*, April 1 and April 23, 1892.

58 Jean Morrison, "Community in Conflict: A Study of the Working Class in the Canadian Lakehead, 1903-1913" (unpublished MA thesis, Lakehead University, 1974).

59 J.M.S. Careless, "Aspects of Urban Life in the West, 1870-1914," in A.W. Rasporich and H.C. Klassen (eds.), *Prairie Perspectives* II (Toronto, 1973), p. 31.

5.   William Mackenzie, Donald Mann, and the "Larger Canada"   *T. D. Regehr*

1 R.M. Hamilton, ed., *Canadian Quotations and Phrases, Literary and Historical* (Toronto: McClelland and Stewart, 1965), p. 178. CANADA. *House of Common Debates, 1905*, p. 1422.

2 Public Archives of Canada (PAC), *Board of Arbitration, Canadian Northern Railway, Transcript of Hearings, (Arbitration)*, p. 2703.

3 D.B. Hanna, *Trains of Recollection, drawn from fifty years of Railway Service in Scotland and Canada* (Toronto: Macmillan, 1924) (Hanna), p. 143.

4 Two editions of the Canadian Northern Railway Encyclopedia are available at the Canadian National Railways Headquarters Library (CNHQ) in Montreal.

5 The James Bay Railway was expected to link up with another still-born scheme, the Trans-Canada Railway. J.G. Scott, *Paper on the Trans-Canada Railway, read before the Literary and Historical Society of Quebec* (Quebec: Chronicle Printing Company, 1903), p. 13.

6 Hanna, p. 229.

7 Arbitration, p. 2771. *Majority Report of the Royal Commission on Railways and Transportation.* (Drayton-Acworth Report). O.D. Skelton, *The Railway Builders* (Toronto: Oxford, 1916), p. 189.

8 PAC. *W. Thomas White Papers*, Files 50 and 51 contain extensive and convincing evidence in this regard.

9 It was this fact that led critics to argue that Mackenzie and Mann were not entitled to any compensation for the common stock when the Canadian Northern Railway was nationalized. Arbitration, p. 2703.

10 Arbitration, p. 2771.

11 *Surrogate Court of the County of York*, File no. 49474, Probate of Will and Passing of Accounts, Estate of Sir William Mackenzie; *Ibid.*, File 76027, Probate of Will and Passing of Accounts, Estate of Sir Donald Mann; *Ibid.*, File 48898, Probate of Will, Estate of Roderick Mackenzie.

12 W.T. Easterbrook and Hugh G. Aitken, *Canadian Economic History* (Toronto: Macmillan, 1956), see particularly the Introduction.

13 PAC. *Laurier Papers, Vol. 353*, pp. 94248-49; Laurier to Lighthall, 2 Feb. 1905.

14 Arbitration, pp. 40-41.

15 MANITOBA. *Sessional Paper No. 9, 1902.* Report of the Department of the Railway Commissioner for the year ending 31 Dec., 1901.

16 Public Archives, British Columbia (PABC) *McBride Papers*, R.P. Roblin to McBride, 26 Oct., 1909.

17 T.D. Regehr, "The Canadian Northern Railway: The West's Own Product," *Canadian Historical Review*, LI (June, 1970), pp. 177-187.

18 Angus MacMurchy and Shirley Denison, *Canadian Railway Cases, Vol. 17* (Toronto: Canada Law Book Co.) p. 215. CANADA. Board of Railway Commissioners, Transcript of Hearings in the Western Tolls Case, (Western Tolls Case). R.A.C. Henry and Associates, *Railway Freight Rates in Canada, A Study Prepared for the Royal Commission on Dominion-Provincial Relations*, Ottawa, 1939.

19 PAC. *Hays Papers*, pp. 109-111; Hays to Wilson, 27 March, 1903.

20 T.D. Regehr, "The Canadian Northern Railway: Agent of National Growth, 1896-1911" (Unpublished Ph.D. Thesis, University of Alberta, 1967) pp. 96-142.

21 T.D. Regehr, ed., *The Possibilities of Canada are Truly Great: Memoirs, 1906-1924, by Martin Nordegg* (Nordegg) (Toronto: Macmillan, 1971) p. 136. University of Toronto Archives, (UTA) *Walker Papers*, Plummer to Walker, 4 Oct., 1902.

22 Nordegg, pp. 122-148.

23 G.R. Stevens, *Canadian National Railways, Vol. 2, Towards the Inevitable, 1896-1922* (Stevens) (Toronto: Clarke, Irwin, 1962), pp. 169-170.

24 PAC. *Department of Marine and Fisheries*, File 4572.

25 Stevens, p. 125.

26 PAC. *Laurier Papers, Vol. 409*, p. 109053; Laurier to Cameron, 7 April, 1906.

27 For a concise statement of Sifton's opinions regarding some of his col-

leagues and their reluctance to support strongly Canadian Northern projects see: Public Archives, Saskatchewan (PAS), Scott Papers, pp. 37873-76, Sifton to Scott, 9 Nov., 1905.

28 One well documented and controversial campaign contribution involved $25,000, given to British Columbia Attorney-General M.A. Macdonald in 1916. A Royal Commission, headed by John Sedgwick Cowper, investigated the details of this transaction. A copy of the Cowper Commission evidence is available in PABC, Premier's Papers.

29 CNHQ. Transcript of an interview by Col. G.R. Stevens with O.D. Prosser. UTA. *Walker Papers*, Plummer to Walker, 4 Oct., 1902.

30 Hanna, pp. 254-256.

31 *Western Tolls Case*, pp. 9883-9896.

32 PAC. *Sifton Papers, Vol. 57*, p. 40597; Burrows to Sifton, 23 Nov., 1899; *Ibid., Vol. 462*, p. 45128; Hanna to Sifton; 10 Dec., 1899. *Ibid., Vol. 57*, p. 40525; Burrows to Sifton, 10 Dec., 1899. *Ibid.*, pp. 40527-40528; Burrows to Sifton, 20 Dec., 1899.

33 PAC. *Sifton Papers*, Numerous letters between Davis and Sifton discussing the former's political activities and problems.

34 PAS. *Scott Papers*, pp. 53719-53720; Scott to W.H. Church, 14 July, 1909.

35 Victoria *Daily Times*, 20 Oct., 1909.

36 Stevens, p. 50.

37 PAC. *Sifton Papers, Vol. 166*, pp. 133935-133936; Mann to Sifton, 22 March, 1904.

38 Hanna, pp. 132-147.

39 *Western Tolls Case*, pp. 9872, 9909.

40 Manitoba *Free Press*, 1 July, 1902 and 27 Jan., 1903.

41 PAC. *Borden Papers*, File OC 294, pp. 33120-33123, Chairmen of Canadian Northern employee groups to Borden, 18 May, 1917.

42 Edmund Bradwin, *The Bunkhouse Man* (Toronto: University of Toronto Press, 1972, reprint).

43 Manitoba *Free Press*, 31 Dec., 1901 and 2 Jan., 1902.

44 CNHQ. Transcript of interview by Col. G.R. Stevens with Osborne Scott.

45 PAC. Unpublished autobiography by H.W.D. Armstrong.

46 PAC. Department of the Interior, Superintendent of Immigration Files 594511 and 39501.

47 Osborne Scott interview.

48 PAC. *Borden Papers*, File OCA 201A, Janet Tupper to Borden, 27 Sept., 1911. This letter is typical of many written by sub-contractors and their friends and associates.

49 *Canadian Railway and Marine World* (CRMW) Dec., 1934, p. 523. Arbitration, pp. 2663-68.

50 PAC. Shaughnessy Letterbook No. 21, p. 336; Shaughnessy to Mann, 20 March, 1890; p. 343; Shaughnessy to Mackenzie, 22 March, 1890.

51 PAC. *Borden Papers*, File OC 153, Application by William Mackenzie on behalf of the Canadian Northern Railway for government aid, 4 Jan., 1913.

52 *Western Tolls Case*, p. 9891.

53 PAC. *Canadian National Railways Records, Vol. 10210*, Black Book, Secretary's Office.

54 G.R. Stevens, *History of the Canadian National Railways* (New York: Collier-Macmillan, 1973) p. 242.

55 Pierre Berton, *The Last Spike: The Great Railway, 1881-1885*, (Toronto: McClelland and Stewart, 1971), pp. 328-381.

56 Arbitration, p. 540.

57 Canadian Railway Cases, Vol. 17, pp. 123-230; Western Rates Case,

evidence given by Isaac Pitblado.

58 CRMW, Oct., 1919, p. 528.

6.   Railways and Alberta's Coal Problem
A. A. den Otter

1 Alfred R. C. Selwyn, "Observations in the North West Territory on a Journey Across the Plains, From Fort Garry to Rocky Mountain House," Geological Survey, Report of Progress, 1873 (Montreal: Dawson Brothers, 1874), pp. 17-62; R.W. Ellis, "Report on the Boring Operations in the North West Territory, Summer of 1875," Geological Survey, Report of Progress, 1875-1876 (Montreal: Dawson Brothers, 1877), pp. 281-291; R.C. Dawson, "Report on the Explorations from Fort Simpson on the Pacific Coast to Edmonton on the Saskatchewan, Embracing a Portion of the Northern Part of British Columbia and the Peace River Country, 1879," Geological Survey, Report of Progress, 1879-1880 (Montreal: Dawson Brothers, 1881); and Sandford Fleming, Report on Surveys and Preliminary Operations on the Canadian Pacific Railway up to January, 1877 (Ottawa: Maclean, Roger and Company, 1877), pp. 43, 203, 228-234, 252.

2 George M. Dawson, Preliminary Notes on the Geology of the Bow and Belly River Districts, North West Territory, With Special Reference to the Coal Deposits, Geological Survey of Canada (Montreal: Dawson Brothers, 1882).

3 Cited in The Lethbridge News, Oct. 26, 1887.

4 C.A. Magrath, The Galts, Father and Son: Pioneers in the Development of Southern Alberta: and How Alberta Grew Up: Brief Outline of the Development in the Lethbridge District (Lethbridge: The Lethbridge Herald, n.d.), p. 37.

5 Even though the Galt railways were narrow-gauge, they received the full 6,400 acres per mile subsidy. For a fuller discussion of Galt's relationship with the federal government and his activities in the Lethbridge area see my "Sir Alexander Tilloch Galt, the Canadian Government and Alberta's Coal," Canadian Historical Association, Historical Papers, 1973.

6 Canada, Department of the Interior, Annual Report, 1881 (Ottawa: Maclean, Rogers and Company, 1882), p. ix; Canada, House of Commons, Debates, March 27, 1882, p. 562; and Public Archives of Canada, Macdonald Papers, Macdonald to Galt, Oct. 17, 1889, 93938-93941.

7 Canada, Department of the Interior, Annual Reports, 1890-1896.

8 Ibid., 1890-1896; see also Sally Anne Hamilton, "An Historical Geography of the Coal Mining Industry of the City of Edmonton" (Unpublished M.A. dissertation, University of Alberta, 1971), pp. 48-60.

9 The Fort Macleod Gazette, Oct. 24, 1887.

10 *The Lethbridge News*, July 24, 1889.

11 William James Cousins, "A History of the Crow's Nest Pass" (Unpublished M.A. dissertation, University of Alberta, 1952), pp. 36-60; and H.A. Innis, *Settlement and the Mining Frontier*, Canadian Frontiers of Settlement, edited by W.A. Mackintosh and W.L.E. Joerg (Toronto: The Macmillan Company of Canada Limited, 1936), p. 282.

12 Alberta, Mines Division, File 48, inspector's annual reports, 1900 and 1910; File 87, Dec., 1903; File 88, Nov. 5, 1905; File 40, Nov. 3, 1905; File 204, June 30, 1909. Unless otherwise indicated all statistics quoted in this paper are taken from the annual reports of Alberta, Department of Public Works, 1911-1912; Mines Branch, 1918-1948; or Mines Division, 1949-1973.

13 D.B. Dowling, "Coal Fields South of the Grand Trunk Pacific Railway, in the Foothills of the Rocky Mountains," *Summary Report, Geological Survey, Sessional Paper, No. 26*, 1910.

14 *Edson-Jasper Signal*, Oct. 18, 1928; and *Canadian Mining Journal*, Nov. 1, 1910, p. 66.

15 A.A. den Otter, "A Social History of the Alberta Coal Branch" (Unpublished M.A. dissertation, University of Alberta, 1967), pp. 17-22.

16 Alberta, Mines Division, File 282, inspector's report, Feb. 5, 1914.

17 Martin Nordegg, *The Possibilities of Canada are Truly Great; Memoirs, 1906-1924*, edited and with an introduction by T.D. Regehr (Toronto: Macmillan of Canada, 1971).

18 The C.P.R. leased Galt's Dunmore line in 1893 and in 1897 purchased the road and collieries. See H.A. Innis, *A History of the Canadian Pacific Railway* (Toronto: McClelland & Stewart, 1923), p. 139.

19 Until the early 1920's, the Grand Trunk Pacific (or C.N.R.) could purchase coal at the large collieries at Pocahantas and Brulé.

20 Theodore David Regehr, "The Canadian Northern Railway: Agent of National Growth, 1896-1911" (Unpublished Ph.D. dissertation, University of Alberta, 1967), pp. 202-203.

21 On the Canadian Northern's capitalization, see Nordegg, *Possibilities of Canada*, pp. 142-148, 155; T.D. Regehr, "Canadian Northern," pp. 199-202. The Canadian Northern also built the Alberta Midland Railway to exploit the Drumheller reserves but found the coal too soft for economical use. The Drumheller area became a very large producer of domestic fuel and as such became a shipping customer of the railway.

22 Alberta, Mines Division, File 256, inspector's report, May 26, 1915.

23 A multitude of small coal mines were scattered throughout the bituminous fields. In addition Alberta had large domestic, or lignite, developments at Pembina, Edmonton, Ardley, Drumheller, Lethbridge and Taber.

24 R.G. Seale, "Some Geographical Aspects of the Coal Industry in Alberta" (Unpublished M.A. dissertation, University of Alberta, 1966), p. 52.

25 Alberta, *Report of Coal Mining Industry Commission, 1919* (Edmonton: King's Printer, 1920).

26 Alberta, Report of the Alberta Coal Commission, 1925 (Edmonton: King's Printer, 1926), p. 83.

27 *Ibid.*, pp. 326, 328-333.

28 Canada in 1927 consumed 35.6 millions of tons of coal of which it

imported 19.3 millions of tons. Canada, Dominion Fuel Board, *Second Progress Report of the Dominion Fuel Board, 1923-1928* (Ottawa: King's Printer, 1928), p. 12.

29 Seale, "Aspects of the Coal Industry," pp. 251, 254-256.

30 Canada, House of Commons, *Debates*, 1923, p. 1267.

31 *Ibid.*, p. 1284.

32 Canada, Dominion Fuel Board, *Second Progress Report of the Dominion Fuel Board, 1923-1928* (Ottawa: King's Printer, 1928), p. 9. The Board was not created to formulate a national fuel policy but to gather data to enable the House of Commons to do so. In 1921 and 1923 special parliamentary committees looked into the matter and in March, 1923 a Special Committee of the Senate stated, "The fact that we imported for consumption last year 13,017,025 tons of coal at an approximate cost of $61,112,428 from the United States and other countries should impress everybody with the necessity of utilizing our own fuel resources to the fullest extent." Cited, p. 46.

33 *Alberta*, Coal Commission, 1925, p. 150.

34 Alberta, Report of the Royal Commission Respecting the Coal Industry of Alberta, 1935 (Edmonton: King's Printer, 1936), p. 38. The subvention policy was actually aimed at bringing Maritime coal to the Ontario-Quebec market. The cabinet set a ceiling of $200,-000 for subventions for the 1924-1925 season. See Order-in-Council, P.C. 1537, Sept. 3, 1924. Cited in Canada, *Dominion Fuel Board*, p. 37.

35 Canada, Board of Transport Commissioners, Judgments and Orders, Vol. XVII, Sept. 22, 1927, p. 467. Cited in Alberta, *Submission on Coal Resources and the Coal Industry in Alberta to the Royal Commission on Coal* (Edmonton: King's Printer, 1945), p. H-5.

36 Alberta, *Submission on Coal Resources*, p. H-5.

37 William Alexander Sloan, "The Crowsnest Pass During the Depression: A Socio-economic History of Southeastern British Columbia, 1918-1939" (Unpublished M.A. dissertation, University of Victoria, 1968).

38 Alberta, *Royal Commission Respecting Coal*, 1935, p. 21.

39 William Nordegg, *The Fuel Problem of Canada* (Toronto: Macmillan, 1930).

40 Alberta, *Submission on Coal Resources*, p. H-5.

41 Canada, Report of the Royal Commission on Coal, 1946 (Ottawa: King's Printer, 1947), pp. 532-556; and Stuart Jamieson, *Times of Trouble: Labour Unrest and Industrial Conflict in Canada, 1900-1966*, Task Force on Labour Relations, No. 22 (Ottawa: Information Canada, 1968), pp. 288-291. The federal government spent a total of 44.3 million dollars in subsidies to coal mines, grants, wage equalization payments, cost of living bonuses and administration during the war time. Canada, *Report of Royal Commission on Coal, August, 1960* (Ottawa: Queen's Printer, 1960), pp. 94-95.

42 Citations from Alberta, *Submission on Coal Resources*, pp. A-1, E-8.

43 Canada, *Commission on Coal*, 1946, p. 582. The latest Royal Commission simply pointed out that further assistance was extravagant and not good business policy. Canada, *Commission on Coal, 1960*, p. 19.

44 See Alberta, *Submission on Coal*

Resources, pp. K-1, 2 and 3. Chris Pattinson, "Freight Rates and the Coal Mining Industry," *Western Miner*, XXVI (March, 1951), p. 45.

45 Seale, "Coal Industry in Alberta," pp. 56-58.

46 H.D. Trace, "An Examination of Some Factors Associated with the Decline of the Coal Industry in Alberta" (Unpublished M.A. dissertation, University of Alberta, 1958), p. 67.

47 Alberta, *Submission on Coal Resources*, p. G-8.

48 Canada, *Commission on Coal, 1960*, pp. 81-95.

7.   The Instability of the Community of Goods in the Social History of the Hutterites   *Karl Peter*

1 A.J.F. Zieglschmid, *Das Klein-Geschichtsbuch der Hutterischen Brüder*, The Carl Schurz Memorial Foundation Inc. (Philadelphia, Pennsylvania, 1947), p. 629.

2 *Ibid.*, p. 632.

3 *Ibid.*, p. 634.

4 A. Klaus, *Unsere Kolonien* (Odessa: Verlag der Odessaer Zeitung 1887), p. 65.

5 *Ibid.*, p. 67.

9.   Hutterite Education in Alberta   *Robert J. MacDonald*

1 J.E. Rea, "The Roots of Prairie Society," in David P. Gagan, ed., *Prairie Perspectives* (Toronto: Holt, Rinehart and Winston of Canada, Ltd., 1970), pp. 48-51.

2 *Report to the Honourable the Legislative Assembly of Manitoba of the Select Committee appointed to obtain information regarding colonies or societies of Hutterites or Hutterian Brethren and to report and make recommendations upon the same*, 1947-1948, p. 14.

3 *Brief of the United Farmers of Alberta*, 1947, p. 2.

4 *Submission by the New Dayton Branch Farmers' Union of Alberta to the Hutterite Investigations Committee*, 1958, p. 6.

5 Paul Gross, *The Hutterite Way* (Saskatoon: Freeman Press, 1965), p. xvii.

6 *The Lethbridge Herald*, 26 Feb., 1960.

7 Paul Gross, *op. cit.*, p. 50.

8 *Brief of Alberta's Hutterian Brethren to the Cabinet*, 25 Jan., 1967, p. 1.

9 Author's conversations with Rev. J. Kleinsasser, 23 Aug., 1971.

10 Paul Gross, *The Hutterite Way*, p. 53.

11 *Ibid.*, p. 55.

12 Edwin L. Pitt, *The Hutterite Brethren in Alberta* (Unpublished M.A. thesis, University of Alberta, 1949), p. 74.

13 John K. Wurz, *The Hutterite Brethren of Alberta* (Lethbridge, 1964), p. 16.

14 U.F.F. Zieglschmid, *Das Klein-Geschichtsbuch der Hutterischen Brüder* (Philadelphia, 1947), p. 631.

15 Alberta, *Department of Education Annual Report 1919*, p. 14.

16 Alberta, *Department of Education Annual Report 1920*, p. 93.

17 Alberta, *Department of Education Annual Report 1920*, p. 93.

18 Glenbow Archives, *Earl Cook Correspondence*, 15 Feb., 1927, 28 Feb., 1927.

19 *The Lethbridge Herald*, 7 Dec., 1928.

20 *The Lethbridge Herald*, 10 Dec., 1928.

21 Glenbow Archives, *Earl Cook Correspondence, U.F.A. Minutes and Resolutions.*

22 Alberta, *Department of Education Annual Report 1930*, p. 67; Alberta, *Department of Education Annual Report 1935*, p. 74.

23 Alberta, *Department of Education Annual Report 1932*, p. 52.

24 Alberta, *Department of Education Annual Report 1935*, p. 75.

25 Edwin Pitt, *The Hutterite Brethren in Alberta*, pp. i-iv.

26 Members of the Legislative Committee were Ivan Casey of High River, L.C. Halmrast of Lucky Strike, H.G. Hammell of Carstairs, H.B. Macdonald and F.C. Colbourne of Calgary.

27 Report of the Legislative Committee regarding *The Land Sales Prohibition Act* 1944 as amended, 1947, p. 4.

28 *Ibid.*, p. 6.

29 *Report of the Hutterite Investigation Committee*, Sept. 1959.

30 *The Lethbridge Herald*, 2 Dec., 1958.

31 *The Albertan*, 11 Dec., 1958.

32 *The Lethbridge Herald*, 4 Dec., 1958.

33 *Report of the Hutterite Investigation Committee*, p. 36.

34 *Ibid.*, pp. 42-43.

35 *Ibid.*, p. 46.

36 *Submission to the Executive Council*, 13 Jan., 1960, p. 18.

37 *Submission to the Agricultural Committee*, 29 March, 1960, p. 19.

38 *A.T.A. Magazine*, March 1961, May 1961.

39 *The Calgary Herald*, 18 March, 1960; *The Lethbridge Herald*, 18 Jan., 1960.

40 *The Edmonton Journal*, 18 May, 1962; *The Calgary Herald*, 3 April, 1962.

41 *The Calgary Herald*, 19 Aug., 1967; *The Albertan*, 19 Aug., 1967.

42 *The Lethbridge Herald*, 21 Sept., 1967.

43 *The Lethbridge Herald*, 7 Sept., 1967.

44 *The Calgary Herald*, 16 Oct., 1967.

45 Alberta Federation of Home and School Associations, *Resolution Booklet*, 1969, p. 19.

46 AFHSA, *Minutes*, 1969, pp. 57-58.

47 AFHSA, *Minutes*, 1970, p. 9.

48 *Nanton News*, 19 March, 1970.

49 *The Calgary Herald*, 27 June, 1970.

50 Alberta, *Department of Education Annual Report 1969*, p. 33.

51 *The Albertan*, 26 March, 1969.

52 *Regina vs. Stahl*, pp. 52, 53, 54, 56, 58, 60, 73.

53 Author's Correspondence with Superintendent of Foothills School Division, 15 Sept., 1971.

10.   The Ojibwa, the Cree, and the Hudson's Bay Company in Northern Ontario
Charles A. Bishop

I wish to thank the Governor and Committee of the Hudson's Bay Company for permission to quote from their Archival materials. Research for this paper was supported by grants from the National Museum of Canada and from the State University of New York.

1 Written records, however, are not synonymous with history. Nor does their absence imply an absence of history. (M.G. Smith, "History and Social Anthropology," *Man*, 62: p. 73.) Anthropologists and historians alike have used oral records with considerable success to reconstruct history. J. Vansina, *Oral Tradition* (Chicago: Aldine, 1965); J. Vansina, "Cultures Through Time," in R. Narroll and R. Cohen, *A Handbook of Method in Cultural Anthropology* (New York: The Natural History Press, 1970).

2 M.G. Smith, "History and Social Anthropology," p. 77.

3 R.G. Thwaites, *The Jesuit Relations and Allied Documents: Travels and Explorations of the Jesuit Missionaries of New France* (Cleveland: Burrows Bros., 1896-1901), v. 44, p. 249; E.H. Blair, *The Indian Tribes of the Upper Mississippi Valley, and the Region of the Great Lakes* (Cleveland: A.H. Clark, 1911), vol. 1, 37, 281-282 footnote.

4 H. Hickerson, *The Southwestern Chippewa: An Ethnohistorical Study*, American Anthropological Association Memoir 92, 1962; H. Hickerson, *The Chippewa and Their Neighbors: A Study in Ethnohistory* (New York: Holt Rinehart and Winston, 1970).

5 Thwaites' *Jesuit Relations* of 1956-58 (v. 44:249) lists four "nations" of Kilistinons which he has attempted to locate:

Those of the first are called Alimibegouek Kilistinons [Lake Nipigon Cree]; of the second, the Kilistinons of Ataouabouscatouek Bay [Cree residing west of James Bay]; of the third, the Kilistinons of the Nipisiriniens [Nipissings], because the Nipisiriniens discovered their country [between the Moose River and Lake Nipigon], whither they resort to trade or barter goods.

The fourth mentioned group resided on the east side of James Bay.

6 J.B. Tyrell, *Documents Relating to the Early History of Hudson Bay*, (Toronto: The Champlain Society, 1931), 263-264. Father Gabriel Marest, also writing from Port Nelson in 1695 remarked that of the Indians who traded there, the "most distant, the most numerous, and the most important are the Assiniboines and the Crees, as they are otherwise known, the Kiristinnons." Father Antoine Silvy made a similar distinction between these Inland Cree and those nearer coastal Hudson Bay and added that it took the former from fifteen to twenty days to reach Port Nelson. J.B. Tyrell, *Documents*, 123-124; 68-69.

7 E.H. Blair, *Indian Tribes,* I, 107-108; R.G. Thwaites, Jesuit Relations, v. 51; 57.

8 J.B. Tyrell, *Documents,* 124-125.

9 *Ibid.,* 265-266. Pierre Radisson in 1661 also reported a gathering of over 1,000 Cree somewhere northwest of Lake Superior (R.G. Thwaites, *Jesuit Relations,* 1888: 90-92), while Duluth's brother met 1,500 Indians on Lake Nipigon in 1687 (A. Henry, *Travels and Adventures in Canada and the Indian Territories Between the Years 1760 and 1776,* Edmonton: M.G. Hurtig, 1969, 233 footnote).

10 J. Helm, "Bilaterality in the socioterritorial organization of the Arctic Drainage Dene," *Ethnology,* 4: 361-385.

11 Lewis Henry Morgan in his travels to Pembina and Fort Garry in the Upper Red River in 1861 stated with regard to the issue of Cree clans:

> The subject I have had up again with several persons and cannot find the least trace of a present division into tribes. Neither can I learn that they have any tradition or recollection of a former division into tribes, but deny having of the kind themselves. They mark their tents with certain devices of animals, but that is the extent.

L.A. White, ed., *Lewis Henry Morgan: The Indian Journals:* 1859-1862 (Ann Arbor: University of Michigan Press, 1959), p. 115, 120.

12 J.B. Tyrell, *Documents,* p. 262; J. Oldmixon, *The British Empire in America,* London: 1741), p. 553, Jesuit Relations, v. 56, 203.

13 J. Oldmixon, *The British Empire in America,* 548.

14 J.B. Tyrell, *Documents,* 229-230. The data does not support the hypothesis that Northern Algon-

kian bands were patrilocal as Service has argued (E.R. Service, *Primitive Social Organization: An Evolutionary Perspective,* New York: Random House, 1971, 1973-1975). Nor is matrilocality incongruent with a hunting economy. If in face leaders settled the disposition of winter group boundaries, this would make meaningless the argument concerning the hunters' knowledge of an area, since winter groups would occupy different areas from year to year. J.R. Honigmann, on the basis of field data from Attawapiskat on James Bay has also speculated that the Cree had a Hawaiian kinship system which preceded the present-day Neo Yuman system. The Hawaiian system, however, may trace "more remotely to some matrilocal structure whose survivals persisted in matripatrilocal residence and sororal polygyny." (J.J. Honigmann, "Social Organization of the Attawapiskat Cree," *Anthropos,* 48, 809-816. The Ojibwa, nevertheless, appear to have practiced patrilocal residence obligations.

15 A.L. Kroeber, *Cultural and Natural Areas of North America* (University of California Press, 1963), pp. 139-141, J.R. Swanton, *The Indian Tribes of North America* (Smithsonian Institute Bureau of American Ethnology, Bulletin no. 45, 1952), pp. 263-556.

16 A.T. Adams, *The Explorations of Pierre Esprit Radisson* (Minneapolis: Ross and Haines, 1961) p. 144; E.H. Blair, *Indian Tribes . . .,* I, 173-174.

17 J. Delanglez, *Life and Voyages of Louis Jolliet (1645-1700)* (Chicago: Institute of Jesuit History Publications, 1948), p. 175.

18 The forts established included: Fort Caministogoyan, present-day

Thunder Bay (1678), Fort La Maune on Lake Nipigon (1684), and Fort de Francis (1685) near the forks of the Kenogami and Albany Rivers (Voorhis 1930:128; Innis 1962:49). E. Voorhis, *Historic Forts and Trading Posts of the French Regime and of the English Fur Trading Companies* (Ottawa: Department of the Interior, National Resources Intelligence Branch, 1930), p. 128; H.A. Innis, *The Fur Trade in Canada* (New Haven: Yale University Press, 1962).

19 *Hudson's Bay Company Archives* (hereafter referred to as HBC Arch.) Ottawa and London, B3/a/1 and B3/a/2.

20 Successive references to HBC Arch. B3/a/9; B3/a/14; A/11/2 (quot.); B3/a/22.

21 During the 1730's there were about 100 Cree and Monsoni warriors on Rainy Lake while along the Nipigon River were 200 Monsoni warriors, 150 Sturgeon warriors, 140 Swampy Cree and 40 Oskemanettigons (either Ojibwa or Nipissing), along with a few Abitibis and Têtes de Boule. On Lake Nipigon itself were 60 Christinaux and 150 Assiniboine warriors, and at the Kaministiquia River were 60 Ouace (Ojibwa of the Catfish Clan) (*Documents Relating to the Colonial History of New York* 1853-1887, vol. 9:1054).

22 HBC Arch. B3/a/23; L.J. Burpee, ed., *Journals and Letters of Pierre Gaultier de Varennes de la Verendrye and his Sons* (Toronto: The Champlain Society, 1927), pp. 233-234, 238.

23 HBC Arch. B3/a/30.

24 J. Carver, *Travels Through the Interior Parts of North America in the Years 1766, 1767, and 1768* (Minneapolis: Ross and Haines Inc., 1956), pp. 108-113; A. Henry, *Travels and Adventures . . . ,* pp. 246-249.

25 HBC Arch., B 198/a/4; B 198/a/12. The "made beaver" became the standard currency after the 1690's. Both trade goods and fur bearers were evaluated in terms of the made beaver, originally worth one beaver pelt but later modified to conform with price and demand mechanisms and in accordance with the quality and size of different pelts.

26 The names of some of these early eighteenth century bands include the *Salkemys, Shoshoogamies* and *Papanashes* from near Moose River, *Metawosenes* and *Rabbit* Indians from the northward and *Tibitiby* (Abitibi from Lake Abitibi).

27 HBC Arch. B3/a/9.

28 HBC Arch. A/11/2.

29 *Ibid.*

30 E.E. Rich, ed., *Isham's Observation and Notes: 1743-1749* (Toronto: The Champlain Society, 1949), pp. 118-119.

31 HBC Arch. B 198/a/18.

32 HBC Arch. B 3/e/15.

33 *Documents Relating to the Colonial History of New York, 1853-1887*, vol. 9, 1054. John Long, *Voyages and Travels of an Indian Interpreter and Trader* (London, 1791), pp. 51, 85, 86.

34 G. Williams, ed., *Andrew Graham's Observations on Hudson Bay: 1767-1791* (London: The Hudson's Bay Record Society, 1969), p. 204; *Ibid.*, p. 191.

35 L.R. Masson, ed., *Les Bourgeois de la Compagnie du Nord Ouest, Récits de Voyages, Lettres et Rapports Inédit Relatifs au Nord-Ouest Canadien* (Québec: A Côté, 1960), vol. 2, 241-242.

11. White "Rites" and Native "Rites": Indian Education Policy and Native Responses
Jacqueline Gresko

1 J.M.S. Careless, *Canada: A Story of Challenge* (Toronto: Macmillan, 1970), p. 22.

2 J.W. Walker, "The Indian in Canadian Historical Writing," *C.H.A. Historical Papers*, 1971, p. 31.

3 E.P. Patterson II, *The Canadian Indian: A History Since 1500* (Don Mills: Collier-Macmillan Canada Ltd., 1972), pp. 130-131.

4 *Ibid.*, p. 171.

5 M. Herskovits, *Acculturation: The Study of Culture Contact* (Gloucester, Mass.: Peter Smith, 1958, copyright 1938), p. 10.

6 R. Linton, *Acculturation in Seven American Indian Tribes* (New York: Appleton Century, 1940), p. 501.

7 J. McLean, *The Indians of Canada* (London: Charles N. Kelly, 1892), p. 329. Reverend McLean, a Protestant missionary to the Blood Indians often wrote for N.W.T. papers under the pseudonym of Robin Rustler.

8 A. van Gennep, *The Rites of Passage* ("Les rites de passage"), trans. by M.B. Vizedom and G.L. Caffee (Chicago: University of Chicago Press, 1966, copyright 1908), pp. 2-3.

9 *Ibid.*, pp. 10, 189, 191-192.

10 A. Morris, *The Treaties of Canada with the Indians of Manitoba and the North West Territories* (Toronto: Belfords, 1880), pp. 95-96.

11 John Collier's Introduction to E. Adams, *American Indian Education* (New York: King's Crown Press, 1946), p. xi.

12 D. Mandelbaum, *The Plains Cree*, Anthropological Papers of the American Museum of Natural History, 1940, p. 167.

13 D. Mandelbaum, *The Plains Cree*, pp. 203-204. L. O'Brodovich, "Plains Cree Sun Dance – 1968," *The Western Canadian Journal of Anthropology*, Vol. 1, No. 1 (November, 1969), p. 72 says that "the term 'Sun Dance' is a recent incorporation into their culture." O'Brodovich quotes V. Dusenberry's (*The Montana Cree*, Stockholm: Amqvist and Wiksell, 1962, p. 186) literal translation of the Cree equivalent for the English term "Sun Dance," or ni•pa'kee•simo• win," as beseeching-for-water-to-allay-the-thirst dance."

14 *Missions de la Congrégation des Missionnaires Oblats de Marie Immaculée* (Paris: A. Hennuyer, 1862-1900; Rome: Maison Générale, 1900-1929), 1890, p. 206 (Hereafter cited as *Missions*).

15 See G. Carrière, o.m.i., "Oblates of Mary Immaculate," *New Catholic Encyclopedia*, 1967, X, pp. 611-612 for a discussion of the order's history; and G. Carrière, o.m.i, *L'Apôtre des Prairies: Joseph Hugonnard, o.m.i., 1848-1917* (Montréal: Rayonnement, 1967), p. 35 for a description of Hugonnard's first school.

16 See Canada: Report of the Superintendent General of Indian Affairs 1874, p. 9 in *Canada: Sessional Papers* 1875, Vol. VIII, No. 8. Since the title of the Indian Affairs Branch of the Public Service of Canada has varied (Indian Branch of the Department of the Secretary of State 1871-1872; of

the Department of the Interior 1873-1879; and Department of Indian Affairs 1880-1936), during the period focused on in this essay, I have thought it best to refer hereinafter to its *Annual Reports* as *Indian Affairs Report* or IAR.

17 Macdonald to Lorne, n.d. in *Canada: Sessional Papers 1880*, Vol. III, No. 4 cited in G.F. Stanley, *The Birth of Western Canada* (Toronto: University of Toronto Press, 1960, copyright 1936), p. 228.

18 *Canada: Sessional Papers 1885* No. 116f. "Papers and Correspondence in Connection with Half-Breed Claims and Other Matters Relating to the North West Territories," pp. 93-96, (Hereafter cited as CSP 1885 No. 116f).

19 J.E. Hodgetts, *Pioneer Public Service: An Administrative History of the United Canadas, 1841-1867* (Toronto: University of Toronto Press, 1965), p. 207.

20 N.F. Davin, *Report on Industrial Schools for Indians and Half-Breeds, To the Right Honourable the Minister of the Interior* (Ottawa, 14th March, 1879), Printed Copy in Public Archives of Canada, pp. 1-2, 5-7.

21 See J.J. Kennedy, "Qu'Appelle Industrial School: White 'Rites' for the Indians of the Old North West" (Unpublished M.A. Thesis Carleton University, 1970), pp. 43-47. (Hereafter cited as Kennedy, "Qu'Appelle Industrial School").

22 Report of E. Dewdney. Indian Commissioner, N.W.T., 13 April, 1883 to the Superintendent General of Indian Affairs in Public Archives of Canada: Record Group 10 Black Series 11, 422 (Hereafter cited as RG 10 Black).

23 Deputy Superintendent General of Indian Affairs L. Vankoughnet to Archbishop Taché of Saint Boniface, February 16, 1884, RG 10 Black 11, 422-2.

24 Although English language instruction was an important part of the government Industrial School policy, Roman Catholic missionary Father Hugonnard taught a daily catechism class in Cree as well as in English to encourage education for Indian youth by winning parental approval, and to prepare "des auxiliaires pour le missionnaire" for the reserves. *Missions* 1889, p. 150.

25 Superintendent General of Indian Affairs Edgar Dewdney in IAR 1888, p. 25; L. Vankoughnet, Deputy Superintendent General of Indian Affairs in IAR 1892, p. xvii.

26 *Missions* 1885, p. 246, 1890, p. 203.

27 See R.H. Pratt, *Battlefield and Classroom*, edited by R.M. Utley (New Haven: Yale University Press, 1964), p. 335. Pratt summarized his educational philosophy in an 1883 speech: "In Indian civilization I am a Baptist, because I believe in immersing the Indians in our civilization and when we get them there holding them there until they are thoroughly soaked."

28 See Qu'Appelle *Vidette* August 5, 1886; Winnipeg *Free Press* July 23, 1891.

29 IAR 1889, p. xi; Regina *Leader* June 3, 1890.

30 See J.A. Macrae to Indian Commissioner, Regina, 18 December, 1886, RG 10 Black, 8128; IAR 1884, pp. 25-26; IAR 1888, pp. 20-23; IAR 1889, pp. 22-23. Also Kennedy, "Qu'Appelle Industrial School," pp. 111-114 regarding the parallel programs of the other Industrial Schools.

31 IAR 1885, p. 138; IAR 1893, p. 178; IAR 1897, pp. 265-268. IAR

on Qu'Appelle Industrial School e.g., IAR 1891, p. 149 and IAR 1893, p. 76 and p. 88.

32 IAR 1895, p. xxiv and IAR 1890, pp. 138-139.

33 Indian Commissioner Forget had directed Father Hugonnard to arrange marriages between ex-pupils so as not to allow them to retrogress. Forget to Hugonnard, "Marriage of Ex-pupils," 17 January, 1893, circular letter in OHAO Carrière's Notes. Hugonnard had arranged betrothals and marriages of ex-pupils for a decade or more. IAR 1890, p. 124.

34 IAR 1897, p. 268; IAR 1891, p. 201; *Missions* 1883, pp. 128-129; *Missions* 1889, pp. 149-155.

35 IAR 1904, p. 177. For a description of the File Hills colony, see E. Brass, "The File Hills Ex-Pupil Colony," *Saskatchewan History*, Vol. 6, No. 2 (Spring, 1953), pp. 66-69.

36 See *Les Cloches de Saint-Boniface* (8) 1909, p. 8; Regina *Leader*, December 18, 1902; IAR 1904, pp. 345-346; and F. H. Abbott, *The Administration of Indian Affairs in Canada* (Washington, D.C., 1915), pp. 51-52.

37 Hugonnard à Provincial 22 fevrier, 1909 (Archives Provinciales Manitoba) in OHAO Carrière's Notes with reference to the "discrimination" of the government against Roman Catholic schools, specifically the government giving the Anglican Battleford school larger grants.

38 IAR 1903, p. xxi: P.H. Bryce M.A., M.D., Chief Medical Officer, Department of Indian Affairs, *Report on the Indian Schools of Manitoba and the North-West Territories* (Ottawa: Government Printing Bureau, 1907) provides much detail on this long, terrible story.

39 IAR 1897, p. xvii.

40 Hugonnard à Taché, 17 fevrier, 1884, Manitoba 38 (Archives Provinciales, o.m.i., Winnipeg, dossier Lebret Ecole), in OHAO Carrière's Notes.

41 IAR 1896, p. 180; IAR 1899, p. xxxi.

42 IAR 1886, p. 140; IAR 1888, p. 70.

43 *Missions* 1890, p. 206; H. Reed to the Supt. Gen. Ind. Aff., 10 February, 1895, RG 10 Black 45905. IAR 1898, pp. 280-281; IAR 1899, pp. 152-153. Regina *Leader*, June 14, 1904.

44 A. Fisher in "White Rites versus Indian Rites," *Transaction* Vol. 7, No. 1 (November, 1969), pp. 30-38, considers "all formal education from kindergarten to grade twelve . . . as a rite of passage" and the school as a set of "ideological rituals."

45 IAR 1900, p. xvii contrasts with Father Hugonnard in IAR 1897, p. 265.

46 IAR 1900, p. 224 and IAR 1896, p. 180; E. Brass, "The File Hills Ex-Pupil Colony," *Saskatchewan History* Vol. 6 No. 2 (Spring, 1953), p. 67.

47 For example the *Vidette* of July 5, 1888 reported that during "Dominion Day Celebrations, (the) pony races brought together quite a large sprinkling of half-breeds and Indians." The Qu'Appelle *Progress* of June 16, 1887 told how "THE SUN DANCE THRILLING SCENES AMONG THE INDIANS OF THE ASSINIBOINE RESERVE," the gathering of Pasqua's, Piapot's and Chief Jack's bands under teepees, streamers and flags, "seemed to pass off like a grand picnic."

48 See Asst. Indian Commissioner, N.W.T. J.A. McKenna to the Secretary of the Department of In-

dian Affairs, 15 June, 1903, RG 10 Black 60, 511-1 and Codex of the Qu'Appelle Industrial School August 31, 1903.

49 IAR 1896, p. 347; IAR 1903, p. 398; IAR 1904, p. 380.

50 J. Hugonnard to N.W.T. Indian Commissioner D. Laird, Winnipeg, March 31, 1903, RG 10 Black 60, 511-1.

51 D. Laird to SGIA C. Sifton, 17 December 1903, RG 10 Black 60, 511-1 transmitting relevant correspondence on this matter.

52 Archbishop Langevin of Saint-Boniface to Clifford Sifton, SGIA, 26 December, 1903, RG 10 Black, 60, 511-1.

53 C. Sifton to Archbishop of Saint-Boniface, 31 December, 1903, RG 10 Black, 60, 511-1. DSGIA F. Pedley to Corporal Dubuque in RG 10 Black 60, 511-2.

54 L. Thompson to the Hon. F. Oliver, Minister of the Interior, Ottawa, 19 March, 1903, enclosing a petition from Assiniboine Indians. RG 10 Black 60, 511-2.

55 J.D. McLean to Levi Thompson, Barrister, Wolseley, Sask., 5 April, 1906, RG 10 Black 60, 511-2.

56 See RG 10 Black, 60, 511-2. Grant to the Secretary of the Department of Indian Affairs, July 2, 1906, RG 10 Black 60, 511-2.

57 W.S. Grant to the Secretary of the Department of Indian Affairs, 19 January, 1907, RG 10 Black 60, 511-2.

58 IAR 1892, p. 88; IAR 1889, p. 196.

59 Laird to the Secretary of the Department of Indian Affairs, Ottawa, 12 July, 1902, with clipping attached. RG 10 Black 60, 511-2.

60 IAR 1908, pp. xxi-xxii, and xxxi.

61 See clippings in RG 10 Black 60, 511-2.

62 E.Z. Vogt, "The Acculturation of American Indians," *The Annals of the American Academy of Political and Social Science*, Vol. 311 (May, 1957), pp. 138, 143.

63 R.M. Utley, *The Last Days of the Sioux Nation* (New Haven: Yale University Press, 1963), p. 266. Also see W. Hagan, *American Indians* (Chicago: University of Chicago Press, 1961), pp. 133-134; and A.F.C. Wallace, "Revitalization Movements," *American Anthropologist* Vol. 58 (April, 1956), pp. 264-281.

64 J.J. Kennedy, "Roman Catholic Missionary Effort and Indian Acculturation in the Fraser Valley, B.C. 1860-1900" (Unpublished B.A. Honours Essay, U.B.C., 1969), pp. 76-86 and IAR 1889, p. xi on the extension of the Industrial School policy from the N.W.T. to B.C.

65 See W. Suttles, "The Persistence of Intervillage Ties Among the Coast Salish," *Ethnology*, Vol. 2 (1963), pp. 513-523.

66 Cited in E.P. Patterson, *The Canadian Indian*, p. 8.

13. The Biblical Archetype in Western Canadian Fiction *Sandra Djwa*

1 Sinclair Ross, "The Painted Door," *The Lamp at Noon and Other Stories* (Toronto: McClelland, 1968), p. 100.

2 Ross, *As For Me and My House* (Toronto: McClelland and Stewart, 1941), pp. 99-100.

3 Ross, "Jug and Bottle," *Queen's Quarterly*, 56 (Winter 1949-50), 500-521.

4 Ross, *As For Me and My House*, p. 84.

5 *Ibid.*, p. 9.

6 *Ibid.*, p. 6.

7 *Ibid.*, p. 19.

8 *Ibid.*, p. 119.

9 *Ibid.*, p. 111.

10 Laurence to Djwa, Nov. 2, 1971.

11 Margaret Laurence, *The Stone Angel* (Toronto: McClelland and Stewart, 1968), p. 81.

12 *Ibid.*, p. 292.

13 Laurence, *A Jest of God* (Toronto: McClelland and Stewart, 1966), p. 110.

14 W.L. Morton, "The Relevance of Canadian History," *Contexts of Canadian Criticism*, ed. Eli Mandel (Chicago: University of Chicago Press, 1971), p. 67.

15 Laurence, *A Jest of God*, p. 117.

16 Much of the material in this paper was developed in the preparation of two articles: "No Other Way: Sinclair Ross' Stories and Novels," *Canadian Literature*, 47 (Winter 1971), 49-66; and "False Gods and the True Covenant: Thematic Continuity between Margaret Laurence and Sinclair Ross," *Journal of Canadian Fiction*, 1, no. 4 (Fall 1972), 43-50.